ARMENIAN AMERICAN ALMANAC

Armenian American Almanac

A guide to organizations, churches, newspapers and periodicals, foundations, television and radio programs, library collections, schools and colleges, bookstores and book publishers, bibliographies, scholarships, Armenian studies programs, and special collections in the U.S.A.

Hamo B. Vassilian, Editor

First Edition

1985-86

ARMENIAN REFERENCE BOOKS CO.
P.O. BOX 7106   GLENDALE, CALIFORNIA 91205   (818) 507-1525

i

Armenian American Almanac
Published by
Armenian Reference Books Co.
P.O. Box 7106
Glendale, California 91205
(818) 507-1525

First Edition

Cover design by Vardges Zohrabian

Library of Congress Catalog Card Number: 84-72326

No payment is either solicited or accepted for the inclusion of entries in this publication. Every possible precaution has been made to avoid errors. However, the publisher does not assume and hereby disclaims any liability to any party for any loss or damage caused by errors or omissions in the Armenian American Almanac, whether such errors or omissions result from negligence, accident, or any cause.

Library of Congress Cataloging in Publication Data

Main entry under title:

Armenian American Almanac.

    Bibliography: P.
    Includes indexes.

    1. Armenian Americans — Societies, etc. — Directories.
I. Vassilian, Hamo B.

E184.A7A76   1985   973'0491992'0025   84-72326

ISBN 0-931539-14-5 (soft)

Manufactured in the United States of America

This book is dedicated with deep affection to my parents and sisters.

HELP WANTED

Armenian American Almanac is a package of hundreds of answered questionnaires sent to us by Armenian organizations in this country. To expand the second edition, we ask that you help us prepare a more comprehensive almanac in the future.

Please, complete the **Questionnaire Request and the appropriate forms** at the end of this book. Your response to these forms is vital. It will help us up-to-date the information on hand and serve you better in the future.

PREFACE

Hereby, I am proud to present the Armenian American Almanac as the first comprehensive guide to Armenian institutions and organizations, which is designed to help you find the most current information on Armenian American communities in the U.S.A. It is also hoped that this guide will serve as a useful reference book to those who are interested in learning about the Armenian culture in this country.

The Armenian American Almanac is a guide to Armenian organizations, churches, newspapers and periodicals, foundations, television and radio programs, library collections, schools and colleges, booksellers and book publishers, scholarships, bibliographies, Armenian studies programs, and special collections in the U.S.A.

All the information in this guide is obtained through responses to questionnaires sent out to Armenian organizations in the course of preparation. Due to incomplete information supplied by some institutions or organizations, it was not possible to include all the requested data. I encourage interested individuals to contact the organizations personally, for further information.

This guide has been arranged in twelve different sections, each being broken down into more specific categories. For example, in the Library Collections section, libraries are specified as public libraries, university libraries, organization and research libraries, etc. Entries contain specific information about the institutions. Each category is arranged in terms of its geographical area. The entries are alphabetized by state and name of the institutions. Each organization has been assigned an access number which precedes its primary entry. These numbers substitute the page numbers in the three different indexes provided at the end of the text unless specified.

Since it is planned that the Armenian American Almanac will be revised in the future, I encourage those organizations that are not included, to fill out the **Questionnaire(s) Request Form** at the end of this book, and send it back to me, to be included in the second edition. Any errors and/or omissions will be handled through sending of the Correction/Addition Form.

I wish to thank all of those who responded to the questionnaires, without which this guide would have never been completed. Also, special thanks to Gia Aivazian, Armenian Bibliographer at the U.C.L.A. Research Library, and Osheen Keshishian, Editor and Publisher of the Armenian Observer, whose assistance made this book a challenge but a possible experience for me.

To improve this almanac and to insure that all information is current, I welcome your comments and suggestions. For your convenience, an **Opinion Form** has been provided. Please send your correspondence to: Armenian Reference Books Co., P.O. Box 7106, Glendale, California 91205. (818) 507-1525

Hamo B. Vassilian
Editor/Publisher

Contents

Section One
Organizations

Section Two
Churches & Religious Schools

Section Three
Newspapers & Periodicals

Section Four
Schools

Indexes

Forms

Questionnaire Request Form
Your Opinion Form
Correction/Addition Form
Book Order Form

Section One

ORGANIZATIONS

Cultural and Educational

Charitable and Social Service

Political and Public Affairs

Athletic

Religious

Nursing Homes and Hospitals

Armenian Studies and Research

Professional

Cultural and Educational Organizations
California

(1)
A.A.I.C. ALUMNI ASSOCIATION
AMERICAN ARMENIAN INTERNATIONAL COLLEGE
1950 THIRD STREET
LA VERNE, CALIFORNIA 91750   (714) 593-0432 (714) 593-2594

ACRONYM: A.A.I.C.-AA. **DATE FOUNDED:** 1978. **DIRECTORS & OFFI-CERS:** Raffi Zinzalian, President; Hovsep Kanimian, Vice President; Khosrov Temrekjian, Treasurer; Sylva Katchiguian, Recording Secretary; other: Vartan Reihanabad, Arda Krochian and Maggie Ghanimian. **PURPOSE & ACTIVITIES OF ORGANIZATION:** The association is a non-profit, independent organization, and its purposes include the following: to assist the American Armenian International College in all possible ways toward enhancing its educational and cultural environment, improving and advancing the college itself, and recognizing the basic obligations of all alumni to the college; to render services to its members and, in its discretion, to others, in strengthening the ties and contacts between the college and its alumni; to preserve and strengthen the association formed among its members while they were students at the college; to inspire, develop, maintain, and promote higher education among Armenian students; to engage in any lawful purposes which do not contemplate the distribution of gains, profits, or dividends to the members thereof, including, but not restricted to charitable, social, cultural, educational, and recreational purposes. **SCHOLARSHIPS, GRANTS, LOANS:** Available. **CONTACT PERSON:** Hovsep Kanimian, Vice President.

(2)
ARMENIAN ALLIED ARTS ASSOCIATION
552 WOODLAND CT.
DUARTE, CALIFORNIA 91010   (818) 303-2023

ACRONYM: A.A.A.A. **DATE FOUNDED:** 1934 **DIRECTORS & OFFI-CERS:** Victoria Parian, Chairman & President; Leon Partamian, Vice Chairman & Vice President; Steven Samerjian, Treasurer; Alice Bogosian, Recording Secretary; Lillian Erickson, Corresponding Secretary. **PURPOSE & ACTIVITIES OF ORGANIZATION:** A non-profit organization, the purpose of which is to promote the interest of its members in various arts. To encourage and aid the creative efforts of Armenian artists; to give awards and scholarships to the deserving and needy students of arts; to sponsor and introduce to the public the works of art of professional artists; to arrange for auditions of talented Armenian singers and musicians, and to hold art exhibitions. **SCHOLARSHIPS, GRANTS, LOANS:** Available.

(3)
ARMENIAN ALUMNI ASSOCIATION
P.O. BOX 27280
LOS ANGELES, CALIFORNIA 90027   **(818) 507-7686**

(4)
ARMENIAN AMERICAN ASSOCIATION
4175 FAIRMOUNT AVE.
SAN DIEGO, CALIFORNIA 92105   **(619) 280-1105**

(5)
ARMENIAN AMERICAN CITIZENS' LEAGUE
6720 EAST KINGS CANYON ROAD
FRESNO, CALIFORNIA 93727   **(209) 251-9995**

(6)
ARMENIAN AMERICAN CITIZENS' LEAGUE
4121 WEST 60TH STREET
LOS ANGELES, CALIFORNIA 90043

(7)
ARMENIAN AMERICAN MIDDLE EAST CLUB
P.O. BOX 15175
NORTH HOLLYWOOD, CALIFORNIA 91615
CONTACT PERSON: Yervant Nahabedian.   **(818) 248-8399**

(8)
ARMENIAN ART SOCIETY OF AMERICA
2445 WEST WHITTIER BLVD. #202
MONTEBELLO, CALIFORNIA 90640   **(213) 722-0238**
ACRONYM: A.A.C.A. **DATE FOUNDED:** 1973. **DIRECTORS & OFFI-CERS:** G. Tumanjan, President; J. Andikian, Treasurer; A. Keosian, Recording Secretary; M. Minasian, Corresponding Secretary. **PURPOSE & ACTIVITIES OF ORGANIZATION:** Invites, sponsors and promotes concerts for the Armenian artists and poets or writers from Armenia in the U.S.A. and Canada.

(9)
ARMENIAN CULTURAL ASSOCIATION HAMAZKAYIN
108¹/₂ N. BRAND BLVD.
GLENDALE, CALIFORNIA 91203   **(818) 244-4477**

(10)
ARMENIAN CULTURAL FOUNDATION
419 WEST COLORADO STREET
GLENDALE, CALIFORNIA 91204   **(818) 243-0197 (818) 243-9219**

(11)
ARMENIAN FILM FOUNDATION
580 EAST THOUSAND OAKS BLVD. SUITE 101
THOUSAND OAKS, CALIFORNIA 91360   **(805) 495-0717**

ACRONYM: A.F.F. **DATE FOUNDED:** 1979. **DIRECTORS & OFFICERS:** Dr. V. Michael Hagopian, Chairman; Walter Karabian, Vice Chairman; Leo Garapedian, Treasurer; Levon Marashlian, Recording Secretary; Armik Safarian, Administrative Assistant. **PURPOSE & ACTIVITIES OF ORGANIZATION:** To produce and distribute motion pictures and other visual aids on Armenian subjects, or of interest to Armenians; to thereby enhance the positive image of the Armenians; to encourage Armenian youth to enter the film and T.V. profession, through granting of scholarships and internships, and by conducting film festivals, film screenings and related activities. **SCHOLARSHIPS, GRANTS, LOANS:** Available. **CONTACT PERSON:** Dr. J. Michael Hagopian.

(12)
ARMENIAN GENERAL BENEVOLENT UNION
589 NORTH LARCHMONT BLVD.
LOS ANGELES, CALIFORNIA 90004   **(213) 467-2428**

(13)
ARMENIAN NUMISMATIC SOCIETY
8511 BEVERLY PARK PLACE
PICO RIVERA, CALIFORNIA 90660   **(213) 695-0380**

DATE FOUNDED: 1971. **DIRECTORS & OFFICERS:** Luther Eskijian, President; Wartan Gewenian, Treasurer; Y. T. Nercessian, Executive Director & Corresponding Secretary. **PURPOSE & ACTIVITIES OF ORGANIZATION:** To study Armenian coins, bank notes, medals, and publish literature relating to these items. **PUBLICATION:** Armenian Numismatic Journal. **BOOK SELLING SERVICE:** Available. **CONTACT PERSON:** Y. T. Nercessian, Secretary.

(14)
ARMENIAN SOCIETY OF LOS ANGELES
221 SOUTH BRAND BLVD.
GLENDALE, CALIFORNIA 91204   **(818) 241-1073**
ACRONYM: A.S.L.A. **DATE FOUNDED:** 1956. **DIRECTORS & OFFI-CERS:** Varoujan Lalaian, President; Alice Ghotanian, Vice President; Rosa Markarian, Treasurer; Alice Avanessian, Corresponding Secretary. **PURPOSE & ACTIVITIES OF ORGANIZATION:** The purpose is to promote cultural, educational and community activities. The society has an Armenian Language Saturday School; a chorus which has its yearly concerts; a theatre group; dance groups for youth and children and women's community activities. The Arts Chapter organizes seminars, lectures and debates. The Senior Chapter organizes outdoor activities, such as picnics, as well as fund raising. The Youth Chapter organizes camping, games, discos, seminars and debates. **LIBRARY:** Yes: **SATURDAY SCHOOL:** Yes. **CONTACT PERSON:** Alice Avanessian, Executive Secretary.

(15)
HAI-EM ASSOCIATION
P.O. BOX 67E66
LOS ANGELES, CALIFORNIA 90067   **(213) 467-5606**

(16)
HAIGAZIAN COLLEGE ALUMNI ASSOCIATION — LOS ANGELES
421 SOUTH OGDEN DRIVE
LOS ANGELES, CALIFORNIA 90036   **(213) 939-2435**
ACRONYM: H.C.A.A. — LA. **DATE FOUNDED:** 1977. **DIRECTORS & OFFICERS:** Gregory W. Kubler, President; Vicken O. Berjikian, Vice President; Samir Saliba, Treasurer; Vera Haitayan, Recording Secretary; Anie Najarian, Corresponding Secretary. **PURPOSE & ACTIVITIES OF ORGANIZATION:** The association is a non-profit, independent organization with cooperative relationships with the Haigazian College Alumni Association, the Administration of the College in Beirut, Lebanon, and the Board of Trustees of the College in Los Angeles, California. The purpose of the association is to promote the interest and welfare of Haigazian College, and to inspire, develop and maintain the interest of the alumni in the College. **SCHOLARSHIPS, GRANTS, LOANS:** Available. **CONTACT PERSON:** Gregory W. Kubler, President.

(17)
KESSAB EDUCATIONAL ASSOCIATION OF LOS ANGELES
P.O. BOX 29490
LOS ANGELES, CALIFORNIA 90029   **(213) 794-5150**

(18)
MESROBIAN ALUMNI ASSOCIATION
600 NORTH 21ST STREET
MONTEBELLO, CALIFORNIA 90640   **(213) 721-6230**

DATE FOUNDED: 1975. DIRECTORS & OFFICERS: Anush Magdesian, Chairperson & President; Sevag Pakradouni, Vice President; Bedig Araradian, Treasurer; Armen Hairapetian, Corresponding Secretary. AFFILIATION TO OTHER ORGANIZATIONS: Mesrobian Armenian School. PURPOSE & ACTIVITIES OF ORGANIZATION: The organization helps the Mesrobian School through fundraising, community activities, and dues. Also, provides counseling services to Mesrobian students entering college and uses its resources to improve the educational facilities of Mesrobian's School. PUBLICATION: Bugle. SCHOLARSHIPS, GRANTS, LOANS: Available. LIBRARY. Yes. CONTACT PERSON: Shahen Hairapetian, General Council.

(19)
RAFFI NON-PROFIT ORGANIZATION
P.O. BOX 29039
LOS ANGELES, CALIFORNIA 90029   **(213) 665-2537**

(20)
TEKEYAN CULTURAL ASSOCIATION
7466 BEVERLY BLVD.
LOS ANGELES, CALIFORNIA 90036 (213) 933-8248 (213) 932-8756

(21)
U.C.L.A. ARMENIAN STUDENTS ASSOCIATION
308 WESTWOOD PLAZA — BOX 533
LOS ANGELES, CALIFORNIA 90024

ACRONYM: U.C.L.A. ASA. DIRECTORS & OFFICERS: Raffi Kuredjian, Chairman & President; Emil Baktar, Vice President; Ani Boyadjian, Recording Secretary; Alice Funoukian, Corresponding Secretary; Jim Amirkhan, Narbik Manoukian, Ara Barmaksezian and Barlow Der Mugrdechian. PURPOSE & ACTIVITIES OF ORGANIZATION: The U.C.L.A. ASA represents Armenian students and staff at U.C.L.A. It is involved in cultural, social, and educational activities at the U.C.L.A. campus with the purpose of educating the campus community about Armenians. The Armenian Students Association represents the views of Armenian students to the Armenian community in general. PUBLICATION: Armenian Horizon. CONTACT PERSON: Contact through U.C.L.A. ASA, c/o President.

(22)
U.S.C. FRIENDS OF ARMENIAN MUSIC
UNIVERSITY PARK
LOS ANGELES, CALIFORNIA 90089 (213) 743-6935 (213) 743-8901
ACRONYM: F.A.M. **DATE FOUNDED:** 1979. **DIRECTORS & OFFI-CERS:** Audrey Gregor, President; Fred Mickaelian, Vice President; Martin Eskijian, Treasurer; Any Yacoub, Recording Secretary; Anne Mills Corresponding Secretary. **PURPOSE & ACTIVITIES OF ORGANIZA-TION:** The U.S.C. Friends of Armenian Music is an organization devoted to the well-being of the Program for Armenian Musical Studies at U.S.C. The "Friends" generous financial support underwrites much of the program's public and specialized activities and its operational expenses. **SCHOLARSHIPS, GRANTS, LOANS:** Available. **LIBRARY:** Yes. **CONTACT PERSON:** Audrey Gregor, President.

District of Columbia
Washington, D.C.

(23)
AMERICAN ARMENIAN FRIENDSHIP FOUNDATION, INC.
5347 28th STREET N.W.
WASHINGTON, D.C. 20015   (202) 363-2704 (202) 244-2361
ACRONYM: A.A.F.F. **DATE FOUNDED:** 1972. **DIRECTORS & OFFI-CERS:** Dicran Jamgochian, Chairman; Jean Boatman, Vice Chairman; Board Members; Ara Berberian, Lili Chookasian, Hrair Hovnanian, Michael Kermoyan, Elizabeth Kirkpatrick. Dicran Jamgochian, Executive Director. **PURPOSE & ACTIVITIES OF ORGANIZATION:** Create friendship and understanding through presentation around the U.S.A. and elsewhere of art shows and cultural activities (concerts, programs, record publication, contests for young children in Armenian composition, etc.) **SCHOLARSHIPS, GRANTS, LOANS:** Available. **CONTACT PERSON:** Prof. Dicran Jamgochian, Director.

(24)
ARMENIAN ASSEMBLY OF AMERICA, INC.
122 C STREET, N.W., Suite 350
WASHINGTON, D.C. 20001   (202) 393-3434 (800) 368-5895
DATE FOUNDED: 1972. **DIRECTORS & OFFICERS:** Dr. Mihran Agbabian, Chairman; Robert Kaloosdian, Vice Chairman; Vartkess Balian, Treasurer; Barry Zorthian, Secretary; Ross Vartian, Executive Director. Members of Executive Committee: James Renjilian and Adrienne Berenson; Officers of the Assembly's Board of Trustees: Hirair Hovnanian, Chairman; Edward Mardigian, Vice Chairman; Joyce Stein, Secretary.

NO. OF CHAPTERS IN THE U.S.A.: One chapter in Los Angeles. **PURPOSE & ACTIVITIES OF ORGANIZATION:** The Armenian Assembly of America was founded in 1972 as a charitable educational trust. It is a national organization predicated on the belief that Armenians in the United States need a broad-based voice to speak effectively on Armenian issues at the seat of the American government. The Assembly's programs include government relations, public affairs and anti-defamation, student affairs, grants, academic and educational affairs and human rights. **PUBLICATION:** Armenian Assembly Journal. **LIBRARY:** Yes. **CONTACT PERSON:** Ross Vartian, Executive Director.

(25)
FEDERATION OF ARMENIAN STUDENT CLUBS OF AMERICA
122 C STREET, N.W., Suite 350
WASHiNGTON, D.C. 20001   **(202) 393-3434 (800) 368-5895**

ACRONYM: FASCA. **DATE FOUNDED:** 1980. **DIRECTORS & OFFICERS:** Laurens Ayvazian, Director. **AFFILIATIONS TO OTHER ORGANIZATIONS:** A program of the Armenian Assembly of America. **NO. OF CHAPTERS IN THE U.S.A.:** Sixty chapters. **PURPOSE & ACTIVITIES OF ORGANIZATION:** To provide services to the Armenian-American college student club community; to provide information & guidance to existing clubs, and to assist in establishing new clubs; to enhance the participation of Armenian-American students in campus activities; to encourage communication & cooperation between clubs on a regional and national level through frequent meetings and a national newsletter. **PUBLICATION:** FASCA Newsletter. **CONTACT PERSON:** Laurens Ayvazian, Director.

(26)
GEORGETOWN ARMENIAN LAW STUDENT ASSOCIATION
GEORGETOWN UNIVERSITY LAW CENTER
600 NEW JERSEY AVE., N.W.
WASHINGTON, D.C. 20001   **(202) 332-9314**

ACRONYM: G.A.L.S.A. **DATE FOUNDED:** 1982. **DIRECTORS & OFFICERS:** Raffi K. Hovannisian, President; Van Krikorian, Treasurer; Meline Haratunian, Recording Secretary; Jane Minasian, Public Relation. **PURPOSE & ACTIVITIES OF ORGANIZATION:** To serve Armenian interests at the Law Center; to increase awareness of Armenian culture and history among fellow students; to serve as an avenue of communication between the law center community and Armenian communities throughout the country; to study Armenian issues from both international and domestic law perspectives. **CONTACT PERSON:** Raffi K. Hovannisian.

Maryland

(27)
ARMENIAN RUGS SOCIETY
C/O 6930 WISCONSIN AVE.
CHEVYCHASE, MARYLAND 20815   **(301) 654-4044**
DATE FOUNDED: 1980. **DIRECTORS & OFFICERS:** A. T. Gregorian, Chairman; Arthur T. Gregorian, President; Harold Bedoukian, Vice President; James M. Keshishian, Treasurer; Loretta Boxdorfer, Recording & Corresponding Secretary. **PURPOSE & ACTIVITIES OF ORGANIZATION:** The A.R.S. is a non-profit association devoted to the study and diffusion of the arts, crafts and sciences related to Armenian rugs, carpets and textiles. One specific goal of the A.R.S. is to seek rugs and textiles with Armenian inscritpions, to create a data bank of these rugs and make them available by reproductions to scholars and collectors. **PUBLICATION:** Armenian Rugs Society Newsletter. **BOOK SELLING SERVICE:** Available. **CONTACT PERSON:** James M. Keshishian, Treasurer and A. T. Gregorian, Chairman.

(28)
MAMIGONIAN FOUNDATION
14513 WOODCREST DRIVE
ROCKVILLE, MARYLAND 20853   **(301) 460-0353**
DATE FOUNDED: 1982. **DIRECTORS & OFFICERS:** John L. Gueriguian, M.D. Executive Director; Charles Kumkumian, Ph.D. Chairman of the Board. Board Members: George Derderian and Dean Shahinian, Esq. **PURPOSE & ACTIVITIES OF ORGANIZATION:** The foundation and its affiliates work towards the cultural survival of the diaspora by creating; 1) A reference collection open to all interested parties, 2) self-instructional materials in Armenian and English to teach Armenian language and Armenian civilization, 3) computer-based administrative services and public relation consultantships available to all Armenian cultural organizaitons, 4) centers where Armenian academicians and professionals may be offered a chance to serve their communities. **BOOK SELLING SERVICE:** Available. **LIBRARY:** Yes. **CONTACT PERSON:** John L. Gueriguian, M.D., Executive Director.

Massachusetts

(29)
ARMENIAN ARTISTS ASSOCIATION OF AMERICA
59 BIGELOW AVE. BOX 140
WATERTOWN, MASSACHUSETTS 02172   **(617) 923-9174**

ACRONYM: A.A.A.A. **DATE FOUNDED:** 1983. **DIRECTORS & OFFI-CERS:** John Terzian, Chairman & President; Richard H. Tashjian, Vice Chairman & Vice President; John Dasho, Treasurer; Zoya Ormatian, Recording & Corresponding Secretary; George Ormatian, Executive Director. **PURPOSE & ACTIVITIES OF ORGANIZATION:** To bring together artists of Armenian descent in the various arts media; to foster and promote artists of Armenian descent in America and abroad; to plan and execute art exhibits by the active members; to promote interest in and knowledge of artistic fields through lectures and other functions; to exchange information with Armenian artists abroad as well as to exchange artists; to establish scholarships. **SCHOLARSHIPS, GRANTS, LOANS:** Available. **CONTACT PERSON:** Richard H. Tashjian, Vice Chairman.

(30)
ARMENIAN CATHOLIC COMMUNITY
100 MOUNT AUBURN STREET
CAMBRIDGE, MASSACHUSETTS 02138   **(617) 547-2122**

(31)
ARMENIAN CULTURAL AND EDUCATIONAL CENTER
47 NICHOLS AVENUE
WATERTOWN, MASSACHUSETTS 02172   **(617) 926-6067**

ACRONYM: A.C.E.C. **DATE FOUNDED:** 1980. **DIRECTORS & OFFI-CERS:** Richard V. Sanasarian, President; Kenneth Bedrosian, Vice President; Ashod Jelalian, Treasurer; Rosine Paterson, Recording & Corresponding Secretary; Enoch Lachinian, Executive Director; Helen Sookikian, Assistant Director. **PURPOSE & ACTIVITIES OF ORGANI-ZATION:** To promote the Armenian culture. **LIBRARY:** Yes. **ONE-DAY/ SATURDAY AND SUNDAY-SCHOOL:** Yes. **CONTACT PERSON:** Enoch Lachinian, Director.

(31-A)
ARMENIAN CULTURAL ASSOCIATION
OF AMERICA, INC.
P.O. BOX 31
NEEDHAM, MASSACHUSETTS 02192

(31-B)
ARMENIAN GENERAL BENEVOLENT UNION
247 MOUNT AUBURN
WATERTOWN, MASSACHUSETTS 02172   **(617) 926-1373**

(32)
ARMENIAN RENAISSANCE ASSOCIATION, INC.
67 LEONARD STREET
BELMONT, MASSACHUSETTS 02178   **(617) 489-1365**
ACRONYM: ARA. **DATE FOUNDED:** 1979. **DIRECTORS & OFFICERS:**
Seta Terzian, President; Lorig Hamasdegh, Vice President; Dorothy
Piligian, Treasurer; Eva Guzelian, Recording Secretary; Grace Siroo-
nian, Corresponding Secretary; Martha Hananian, Secretary. **NO. OF
CHAPTERS IN THE U.S.A.:** Six chapters. **PURPOSE & ACTIVITIES OF
ORGANIZATION:** The Armenian Renaissance Association is a non-
profit, charitable organization formulated with the ideals of democracy
and free thought, to promote Armenian culture including language, his-
tory, arts, music, literature, social services for the elderly, and to ensure
the well being of the Armenian people. **PUBLICATION:** Armenian
Renaissance Association Newsletter. **SCHOLARSHIPS, GRANTS,
LOANS:** Available. **CONTACT PERSON:** Martha Hananian, Secretary.

(33)
ARMENIAN YOUTH FEDERATION OF AMERICA
76 BIGELOW AVENUE
WATERTOWN, MASSACHUSETTS 02172   **(617) 923-1933**

(34)
THE BAIKAR ASSOCIATION
468 MOUNT AUBURN STREET
WATERTOWN, MASSACHUSETTS 02172   **(617) 923-1933**

(35)
HAIRENIK ASSOCIATION
80 BIGELOW AVENUE
WATERTOWN, MASSACHUSETTS 02172   **(617) 926-3974**

(36)
HAMAZKAYIN ARMENIAN CULTURAL ASSOCIATION
47 NICHOLS AVENUE
WATERTOWN, MASSACHUSETTS 02172   **(617) 926-4977**

(37)
HYE TAVLOO ASSOCIATION
3 ASHLAND STREET   **(617) 926-8006**
WATERTOWN, MASSACHUSETTS 02172   **(617) 523-5565**
DATE FOUNDED: 1974. **DIRECTORS & OFFICERS:** John Kebadjian,
President; Russell Nahigian, Vice President; John Kebadjian, Treasurer;
Abraham Bazarian, Recording Secretary; Peter Alemian, Corresponding

Secretary. **PURPOSE & ACTIVITIES OF ORGANIZATION:** Meets once a month for the purpose of getting together and having a social evening, to play as well as teach the game of Tavloo (not backgammon) to interested individuals. **CONTACT PERSON:** John Kebadjian.

(38)
TEKEYAN CULTURAL ASSOCIATION
4 WINSOR AVENUE
WATERTOWN, MASSACHUSETTS 02172   (617) 926-2323

Michigan

(39)
PATRIOTIC UNION OF KGHI KHOOPS VILLAGE
20901 CRESTMONT LANE
DEARBORN HEIGHTS, MICHIGAN 48127   (313) 271-3594

DATE FOUNDED: 1900. **DIRECTORS & OFFICERS:** Edward Arvanigian, President; Mitchell Kehetian, Vice President; Ichran Kochyan, Treasurer; Helen Derderian, Recording Secretary. **PURPOSE & ACTIVITIES OF ORGANIZATION:** To preserve the identity of Armenian men and women of Khoops descent through a group perpetuating fraternity and friendship, and to observe August 1, annually, as Khoops Memorial Day, to pay homage to all deceased Khoopsetzees. **SCHOLARSHIPS, GRANTS, LOANS:** Available. **CONTACT PERSON:** Ichran Kochyan, Treasurer.

Minnesota

(40)
ARMENIAN CULTURAL ORGANIZATION OF MINNESOTA
1015 IVES LANE
PLYMOUTH, MINNESOTA 55441   (612) 545-5894

ACRONYM: A.C.O.M. **DATE FOUNDED:** 1980. **DIRECTORS & OFFICERS:** Arek Tathevossian, President; Garo Soghomonian, Cultural Director; Sue Davidian, Treasurer; Pauline Vandergraft, Recording Secretary; Vega Soghomonian, Social Director; Francis Bulbulian, Past President; George Yaghsegian, Administrative Director; Hanriette Tathevossian, Editor. **PURPOSE & ACTIVITIES OF ORGANIZATION:** To provide programs and events which encourage members to learn Armenian culture, language, history and heritage for the general Minnesota area. **PUBLICATION:** Armenian Cultural Organization of Minnesota Newsletter. **CONTACT PERSON:** Arek Tathevossian, President.

New Jersey

(41)
ARMENIAN GENERAL BENEVOLENT UNION OF AMERICA
585 SADDLE RIVER ROAD
SADDLE BROOK, NEW JERSEY 07662   **(201) 797-7600**

(42)
EVEREG-FENESSE MESROBIAN ROUPINIAN EDUCATIONAL SOCIETY
3 MOLLER STREET
TENAFLY, NEW JERSEY 07670
DATE FOUNDED: 1955. **DIRECTORS & OFFICERS:** Frank Avakian Stoneson, President; Edward G. Bashian, Vice President; Haig Dadourian, Treasurer; Zabelle Ambariantz, English Secretary; Rose Hachadourian, Armenian Secretary; Charles Kouzoujian, Assistant Treasurer. **NO. OF CHAPTERS IN THE U.S.A.:** Three chapters in New York, Detroit and Los Angeles. **PURPOSE & ACTIVITIES OF ORGANIZATION:** To Perpetuate ethnic identity and heritage; to assist in the education of students with preference given to those of Evereg-Fenesse background; to provide limited grants and loans for Armenian day school, and junior and senior year college students of Evereg-Fenesse background; to participate in Armenian philanthropic activities free of partisan and political coloring. **SCHOLARSHIPS, GRANTS, LOANS:** Available.

New York

(43)
ARMENIAN CHURCH YOUTH ORGANIZATION OF AMERICA
THE ARMENIAN CHURCH OF NORTH AMERICA — EASTERN DIOCESE
630 SECOND AVE.
NEW YORK, NEW YORK 10016   **(212) 686-0710**
ACRONYM: A.C.Y.O.A. **DATE FOUNDED:** 1946. **DIRECTORS & OFFICERS:** Arda Nazerian, Chairman; Melanie Barsamian, Vice Chairman; Archbishop Torkom Manoogian, President; Vaughan Totovian, Treasurer; George Jevarjian, Recording Secretary; Sona Palvetzian, Corresponding Secretary; James K. Magarian, Executive Director. **AFFILIATION TO OTHER ORGANIZATIONS:** Under the auspices of the Diocese of the Armenian Church of North America. **NO. OF CHAPTERS IN THE U.S.A.:** Twenty-nine chapters. **PURPOSE & ACTIVITIES OF ORGANIZATION:** To encourage its members to learn, practice,

uphold, and propagate the principles and teachings of Christian faith according to the doctrine, sacraments and canons of the Armenian Apostolic Church; to support and work for the strengthening of the Armenian Church and to promote the study and appreciation of Armenian culture and heritage; to strengthen spiritual and social bonds and to contribute towards the development of a healthy community life among Armenians; to enhance and strengthen among its members the spirit of human freedom, universal justice and brotherhood of men. **SCHOLARSHIPS, GRANTS, LOANS:** Available. **CONTACT PERSON:** James Magarian, Youth Director (617) 256-7234.

(44)
THE ARMENIAN CLUB OF HUNTER COLLEGE
695 PARK AVENUE
NEW YORK, NEW YORK 10021   (212) 786-8320 (212) 565-6546
ACRONYM: A.C.H.C. **DATE FOUNDED:** 1982. **DIRECTORS & OFFICERS:** Robert Haroutunian, President; Anna Djirdjirian, Treasurer. **PURPOSE & ACTIVITIES OF ORGANIZATION:** To create a friendly atmosphere for members, and to introduce the Armenian people and their culture to the people. Activities: Armenian history presentations, musical programs, Armenian genocide commemoration, Christmas dances, trips, donation of Armenian books to the Hunter Library, etc. **CONTACT PERSON:** Robert Haroutunian, President; and Anna Djirdjirian, Treasurer.

(45)
ARMENIAN EDUCATIONAL COUNCIL, INC.
BRUNSWICK HILLS, EAST ROAD
TROY, NEW YORK 12180   (518) 274-4526
ACRONYM: A.E.C., INC. **DATE FOUNDED:** 1966. **DIRECTORS & OFFICERS:** V. L. Parsegian, President; Philip Natcharian, Treasurer; Paul Der Ohanessian, Recording Secretary. **AFFILIATIONS TO OTHER ORGANIZATIONS:** Architectural project in cooperation with Rensselaer Polytechnic Institute, Troy, New York. **PURPOSE & ACTIVITIES OF ORGANIZATION:** To support and to undertake academic projects involving research in Armenian Art, Architecture, Archaeology, History, language, and the advancement of these academic interests among universities and Armenian communities. **SCHOLARSHIPS, GRANTS, LOANS:** Available. **BOOK SELLING SERVICE:** Available. **CONTACT PERSON:** V. L. Parsegian, Chairman & President.

(45-A)
ARMENIAN LANGUAGE LAB & RESOURCE CENTER
MESROB MASHDOTS INSTITUTE
630 SECOND AVENUE
NEW YORK, NEW YORK 10016   (212) 686-0710
CONTACT PERSON: Sylva Der Stepanian.

(46)
ARMENIAN LITERARY SOCIETY, INC.
114 FIRST STREET
YONKERS, NEW YORK 10704   (914) 237-5751 (914) 761-2127

DATE FOUNDED: 1965. **DIRECTORS & OFFICERS:** Vartkes Gregorian, President; Arthur Hamparian, Treasurer; K. Magarian, Executive Director & Secretary. **PURPOSE & ACTIVITIES OF ORGANIZATION:** Educational and charitable association for the advancement of Armenian culture. Gives assistance to Armenian authors, by helping them in the distribution of their books to the general public. Also collects books and other publications for distribution to Armenian schools, libraries and students. Makes available to the public social and literary programs, lectures, and literary contests. **PUBLICATION:** Kiroukirk. **BOOK SELLING SERVICE:** Available. **LIBRARY:** Yes. **CONTACT PERSON:** Kachatur Magarian, Executive Secretary.

(47)
The ARMENIAN NATIONAL EDUCATION COMMITTEE
138 EAST 39th STREET
NEW YORK, NEW YORK 10016   (212) 689-7231 (212) 689-7810

ACRONYM: A.N.E.C. **DATE FOUNDED:** 1959. **DIRECTORS & OFFICERS:** Albert Bagian, Chairman; Vahe Amirian, Vice Chairman; His Eminence Archbishop Mesrob Ashjian, President; Osky Cascone, Treasurer; Hourig Papazian-Sahagian, Executive Director & Corresponding Secretary. **AFFILATION TO OTHER ORGANIZATIONS:** Co-sponsored by the Eastern Prelacy of Armenian Apostolic Church of America and the Armenian Relief Society of North America, Regional Executive. **PURPOSE & ACTIVITIES OF ORGANIZATION:** A.N.E.C. seeks to instill an unquenchable Armenian spirit in each student, based on knowledge of the Armenian language and culture. A.N.E.C. is committed to improve the effectiveness and quality of Armenian one-day and day schools under its jurisdiction, in the eastern and mid-western U.S.A. and Canada. A.N.E.C. is composed of an all-volunteer board of professionals who have demonstrated deep concern for Armenian education in their respective communities. A.N.E.C. commissions, produces, recommends and disseminates educational materials and textbooks to network schools, conducts teacher-training seminars, organizes students festivals and other regional activities and sponsors experimental schools, academies and educational programs. **BOOK SELLING SERVICE:** Available: **LIBRARY:** Yes. **ONE-DAY/SATURDAY SCHOOL:** Yes. **CONTACT**

PERSON: Hourig Papazian-Sahagian, Executive Director.

(48)
ARMENIAN NETWORK OF AMERICA, INC.
211 EAST 53rd STREET SUITE 2A
NEW YORK, NEW YORK 10022   **(212) 838-0860**
ACRONYM: A.N.A. **DATE FOUNDED:** 1983. **DIRECTORS & OFFICERS:**
Levon Boyajian, President; Michael Kasparian, Vice President; Edele
Hovnanian, Treasurer; Alice Amirian, Recording Secretary. **PURPOSE &**
ACTIVITIES OF ORGANIZATION: Emphasizes the connection between
career pursuits and Armenian identity, by creating a network of college
youth professionals and established career people to promote community leadership and enhance participation of Armenians in the American
society. Program includes: a computerized clearinghouse of information
on Armenians in professions and businesses and formation of a network
of Armenian professional societies. **SCHOLARSHIPS, GRANTS,**
LOANS: Available. **CONTACT PERSON:** Levon Boyajian, President.

(49)
ARMENIAN PROGRESSIVE LEAGUE OF AMERICA
42 GREENWAY CIRCLE SOUTH
SYOSSET, NEW YORK 11791   **(516) 921-6425**

(50)
ARMENIAN STUDENTS' ASSOCIATION OF AMERICA, INC.
P.O. BOX 1557
NEW YORK, NEW YORK 10116   **(617) 965-2350**
ACRONYM: A.S.A. **DATE FOUNDED:** 1910. **DIRECTORS & OFFICERS:**
Jeffrey Boghossian, President; Margie Kalajian, Vice President; Diane
Mathesian, Corresponding Secretary; Dianne Sahagian, Recording Sec-
retary; Beatrice Babgouni, Treasurer; Anita Aginian, Advisor; Carol
Najarian, Scholarship Chairperson; Board of Trustees: R. Carol Norigian, Secretary; Dr. Michael G. Mensoian, Jr., Chairperson; Edward
Eranosian, Treasurer. **NO. OF CHAPTERS IN THE U.S.A.:** Ten Chapters. **PURPOSE & ACTIVITIES OF ORGANIZATION:** Purposes are of
educational and charitable origins to encourage educational pursuits, to
provide financial assistance through scholarships, grants and interest-
free loans to qualified Armenian students, develop fellowships, to culti-
vate the spirit of service and acquaint members and the American
community to the Armenian culture. The association is strictly non-
political, non-partisan and non-sectarian. **PUBLICATION:** A.S.A. NEWS.
SCHOLARSHIPS, GRANTS, LOANS: Available. **CONTACT PERSON:**
Dr. Michael G. Mensoian, Jr., Chairman of Board of Trustees and C.
Carol Norigian, Secretary of Board of Trustees.

(51)
HAMAZKAYIN ARMENIAN CULTURAL AND EDUCATIONAL
ASSOCIATION OF NEW YORK
P.O. BOX 804
WOODSIDE, NEW YORK 11377   (914) 268-2521
CONTACT PERSON: Hrand Markarian.

(52)
TEKEYAN CULTURAL ASSOCATION, NEW YORK
114 EAST 27th STREET
NEW YORK, NEW YORK 10016

Pennsylvania

(53)
KNIGHTS OF VARTAN, INC.
844 ORMOND AVENUE
DREXEL HILL, PENNSYLVANIA 19029

(54)
NOAH WILSON ARMENIAN FOUNDATION
38 LINWOOD AVENUE
ARDMORE, PENNSYLVANIA 19003   (215) 642-9882
ACRONYM: N.W.A.F. DATE FOUNDED: 1972. DIRECTORS & OFFI-
CERS: Charles N. Mahjoubian, Chairman; Diran Karageusian, Trea-
surer. PURPOSE & ACTIVITIES OF ORGANIZATION: The foundation
was founded after the naming of Armenia Mountain of Pennsylvania in
1802 by Noah Wilson, a veteran of the American Revolutionary War.
Sponsors trips to Armenia Township in Bradford County, Pennsylvania;
and holds lectures, tours and publications to enhance and preserve
Armenian ethnic identity.

Charitable and Social Service Organizations
California

(55)
AMERICAN NATIONAL COMMITTEE TO AID HOMELESS ARME-
NIANS
c/o S. M. SAROYAN
160 SANSOME STREET SUITE 900   (415) 433-0440
SAN FRANCISCO, CALIFORNIA 94104   (415) 564-8877

ACRONYM: ANCHA. **DATE FOUNDED:** 1947. **DIRECTORS & OFFI-CERS:** Arpi Papazian, Chairman; S. M. Saroyan, President and Trea-surer; Mendouhi Mardirossian, Executive Director; Ray and Mary Koobatian, Directors. **AFFILIATIONS TO OTHER ORGANIZATIONS:** Cooperative agencies: World Council of Churches in Geneva, Switzer-land, and Tolstoy Foundation in New York. **NO. OF CHAPTERS IN THE U.S.A.:** Three. **PURPOSE & ACTIVITIES OF ORGANIZATION:** This charitable corporation was organized in 1947 and recognized by the United States State Department as an organization to aid and assist displaced people or refugees of Armenian descent who have or are escapees from communist countries such as Soviet Armenia, Bulgaria, Romania and Near Eastern countries such as Iran, Iraq and previously in certain cases from Egypt. It renders documentation and paper service and submits required assurances to the U.S. government. These incom-ing Armenians are given required processing in refugee ports such as Athens, and Beirut by the cooperative agencies, the World Council of Churches in Geneva and the Church World Service. In reference to ports such as Athens and Beirut and upon arrival at port of New York the volunteers of this organization along with the president, greet the refu-gees and put them through an orientation and Americanization program and then make arrangements for transportation to their final resettlement destination.

(56)
ARMENIAN EVANGELICAL SOCIAL SERVICE CENTER
5250 SANTA MONICA BLVD. SUITE 201
LOS ANGELES, CALIFORNIA 90029   **(213) 664-1137**

(57)
ARMENIAN GENERAL BENEVOLENT UNION
589 NORTH LARCHMONT BLVD.
LOS ANGELES, CALIFORNIA 90004   **(213) 467-2428**

(58)
ARMENIAN RELIEF SOCIETY
108-A NORTH BRAND BLVD.
GLENDALE, CALIFORNIA 91203   **(818) 241-7533**

(59)
GENERAL SOCIETY OF VASBOURAGAN
C/O LILYAN CHOOLJIAN
6071 EAST BUTLER AVENUE
FRESNO, CALIFORNIA 93727   **(209) 251-7272**

ACRONYM: G.S.V. **DATE FOUNDED** 1931. **DIRECTORS & OFFICERS:** Jack H. Gahvejian, National President; George Sarkisian, National Treasurer; Lilyan Chooljian, National Secretary; Lillian A. Lewis, Scholarship Coordinator; Vanouhi Muradian, Eastern Regional Representative; Michael Barian, Western Regional Representative; Seda der Garabedian-Barnes, National Officer. **NO. OF CHAPTERS IN THE U.S.A.** Nine chapters. **PURPOSE & ACTIVITIES OF ORGANIZATION:** To render assistance to all needy Vasbouragantzies (i.e. Armenians from the former Armenian province of Vasbouragan and their descendents, otherwise known as "Vanetzies"); to preserve the historic and cultural heritage of the Armenian people, as well as the national tradition; to keep alive in the hearts of the new generation of "Vanetzies" the love of their heritage, and to extol the memory of the illustrious scenes of Vasbouragan by observing every year the anniversary of the Epic of Vasbouragan. **PUBLICATION:** Varak. **SCHOLARSHIPS, GRANTS, LOANS:** Available. **CONTACT PERSON:** Lilyan Chooljian, National Secretary.

Massachusetts

(60)
ARMENIAN CULTURAL AND EDUCATIONAL CENTER
47 NICHOLS AVENUE
WATERTOWN, MASSACHUSETTS 02172   **(617) 926-6067**

ACRONYM: A.C.E.C. **DATE FOUNDED:** 1980. **DIRECTORS & OFFICERS:** Richard V. Sanasarian, President; Kenneth Bedrosian, Vice President; Ashod Jelalian, Treasurer; Rosine Patterson, Recording & Corresponding Secretary; Enoch Lachinian, Executive Director; Helen Sookikian, Assistant Director. **PURPOSE & ACTIVITIES OF ORGANIZATION:** To promote the Armenian culture. **LIBRARY:** Yes. **SATURDAY & SUNDAY-SCHOOL:** Yes. **CONTACT PERSON:** Enoch Lachinian, Director.

(60-A)
ARMENIAN GENERAL BENEVOLENT UNION
247 MOUNT AUBURN
WATERTOWN, MASSACHUSETTS 02172   **(617) 926-1373**

(61)
ARMENIAN RELIEF SOCIETY OF NORTH AMERICA, INC.
38 ELTON STREET
WATERTOWN, MASSACHUSETTS 02172   **(617) 926-5892**

(62)
ARMENIAN RENAISSANCE ASSOCIATION, INC.
67 LEONARD STREET
BELMONT, MASSACHUSETTS 02178 **(617) 489-1365**
ACRONYM: ARA. **DATE FOUNDED:** 1979. **DIRECTORS & OFFICERS:**
Seta Terzian, President; Lorig Hamasdeg, Vice President; Dorothy Pili-
gian, Treasurer; Eva Guzelian, Recording Secretary; Grace Siroonian,
Corresponding Secretary; Martha Hananian, Secretary. **NO. OF CHAP-
TERS IN THE U.S.A.:** Six chapters. **PURPOSE & ACTIVITIES OF
ORGANIZATION:** The Armenian Renaissance Association is a non-
profit, charitable organization, formulated with the ideals of democracy
and free thought to promote Armenian culture, including language, history, arts, music, literature, social services for the elderly and to ensure
the well being of the Armenian people. **PUBLICATION:** A.R.A. Newsletter. **SCHOLARSHIPS, GRANTS, LOANS:** Available. **CONTACT PER-
SON:** Martha Hananian, Secretary.

Michigan

(62-A)
ARMENIAN GENERAL BENEVOLENT UNION
22001 NORTHWESTERN HWY.
SOUTHFIED, MICHIGAN 48075 **(313) 569-3401**

(63)
PATRIOTIC UNION OF KGHI KHOOPS VILLAGE
20901 CRESTMONT LANE
DEARBORN HEIGHTS, MICHIGAN 48127 **(313) 271-3594**

DATE FOUNDED: 1900. **DIRECTORS & OFFICERS:** Edward Arvani-
gian, President; Mitchell Kehetian, Vice President; Ichran Kochyan,
Treasurer; Helen Derderian, Recording Secretary. **PURPOSE & ACTIVI-
TIES OF ORGANIZATION:** To preserve the identity of the Armenian men
and women of Khoops descent through a group perpetuating fraternity
and friendship, and to observe August 1, annually, as Khoops Memorial
Day to pay homage to all deceased Khoopsetzees. **SCHOLARSHIPS,
GRANTS, LOANS:** Available. **CONTACT PERSON:** Ichran Kochyan,
Treasurer.

New Jersey

(64)
ARMENIAN GENERAL BENEVOLENT UNION OF AMERICA
585 SADDLE RIVER ROAD
SADDLE BROOK, NEW JERSEY 07662   **(201) 797-7600**

New York

(65)
CONSTANTINOPLE ARMENIAN RELIEF SOCIETY INC.
P.O. BOX 769
TIMES SQUARE STATION
NEW YORK, NEW YORK 10108   **(201) 549-8963**

ACRONYM: C.A.R.S. **DATE FOUNDED:** 1926. **DIRECTORS & OFFI-CERS:** Boghos K. Horasanu; Berc Araz, President; Ashod N. Krikoryan, M.D. First Vice President; Frank Kabarajian, Second Vice President; Angele Cubukuyan, Treasurer; Hacatur Ermarkaryan, Treasurer; Avedis Gazal, Recording Secretary; Jirayr Tezel, M.D., Corresponding Secretary; Hirant Gulian, Publicity; Louise H. Tezel, Publicity; Toros Celiksu, Publicity. **AFFILIATION TO OTHER ORGANIZATIONS:** Mekhitarist Alumni Association. **PURPOSE & ACTIVITIES OF ORGANIZATION:** To give financial and moral support to Armenian institutions in Istanbul and in the U.S.A. for example Surp Pirgic Armenian National Hospital, Kalfayan Orphanage in Istanbul and Holy Martyrs Armenian Day School in Bayside, New York, and Hovnanian Amenian School in New Milford, New Jersey. **CONTACT PERSON:** Berc Araz, President.

(66)
HOWARD KARAGHEUSIAN COMMEMORATIVE CORPORATION
79 MADISON AVE. ROOM # 904
NEW YORK, NEW YORK 10016   **(212) 725-0973**

PURPOSE & ACTIVITIES OF ORGANIZATION: An operating foundation as opposed to a grant making one and, consequently, does not have funds available to individuals or organizations. The foundation expands its own specific purposes, which include providing health, medical and social services to children in Greece, Lebanon and Syria. **CONTACT PERSON:** Walter Bandazian, Executive Director.

(67)
PAN-SEBASTIA REHABILITATION UNION
P.O. BOX 198 MADISON SQUARE STATION
NEW YORK, NEW YORK 10159   **(212) 679-1728**

DATE FOUNDED: 1926. **DIRECTORS & OFFICERS:** Zareh K. Kapikian,

Chairman; Vahan Derdiarian, Vice Chairman; Harry Assarian, Treasurer; Krikor Vosganian, Recording & Corresponding Secretary. **NO. OF CHAPTERS IN THE U.S.A.:** Seven chapters. **PURPOSES & ACTIVITIES OF ORGANIZATION:** To diffuse news and information about Sebastatzee compatriots; to preserve the compatriotic spirit alive and active; to promote cordial and faithful relationship with Armenians and extend financial assistance to Daniel Varoujan School, Sebastia Kindergarten, and Biochemistry Institute in Erevan, Armenia. **PUBLICATION:** Nor Sebastia. **SCHOLARSHIPS, GRANTS, LOANS:** Available. **LIBRARY:** Yes. **ONE-DAY/SATURDAY-SCHOOL:** Yes. **CONTACT PERSON:** Zareh K. Kapikian, President.

Political and Public Affairs Organizations
California

(68)
ARMENIAN ASSEMBLY OF AMERICA, INC.
4250 WILSHIRE BLVD. SUITE 211
LOS ANGELES, CALIFORNIA 90010   **(213) 933-5238**
CONTACT PERSON: Sylva Mokhtarian, Director.

(69)
ARMENIAN DEMOCRATIC LIBERAL ORGANIZATION
7466 BEVERLY BLVD.
LOS ANGELES, CALIFORNIA 90036   **(818) 933-3298**

(70)
ARMENIAN NATIONAL COMMITTEE, WESTERN REGION
419-A WEST COLORADO STREET
GLENDALE, CALIFORNIA 91204   **(818) 243-0197**
ACRONYM: A.N.C. **DATE FOUNDED:** 1890. **DIRECTORS & OFFICERS:** Serge L. Samoniantz, Executive Director. **AFFILIATION TO OTHER ORGANIZATIONS:** Armenian Revolutionary Federation. **NO. OF CHAPTERS IN THE U.S.A.:** Eighty-two chapters. **PURPOSE & ACTIVITIES OF ORGANIZATON:** Political arm of A.R.F.; lobbies elect officials in favor of Armenian community for successful solution of the Armenian case; achieves national sovereignty on Armenian homeland; promotes and secures U.S. support for the establishment of a free, united and independent Armenia; develops Armenian American political power in the United States. **PUBLICATION:** Armenian National Committee Newsletter. **CONTACT PERSON:** Serge L. Samoniantz, Executive Director.

(71)
ARMENIAN REVOLUTIONARY FEDERATION
419 WEST COLORADO STREET
GLENDALE, CALIFORNIA 91204   (818) 243-9219

(71-A)
ARMENIAN RIGHTS COUNCIL OF AMERICA, WESTERN DISTRICT
7466 BEVERLY BLVD.
LOS ANGELES, CALIFORNIA 90036   (213) 933-8248

(72)
SOCIAL DEMOCRATIC HUNCHAKIAN PARTY, WESTERN DISTRICT
1060 NORTH ALLEN AVENUE
PASADENA, CALIFORNIA 91104   (818) 797-2727

District of Columbia
Washington D.C.

(73)
ARMENIAN ASSEMBLY OF AMERICA, INC.
122 C STREET, N.W. # 350
WASHINGTON, D.C. 20001   (202) 393-3434 (800) 368-5895

DATE FOUNDED: 1972. DIRECTORS & OFFICERS: Dr. Mihran Agba-
bian, Chairman; Robert Kaloosdian, Vice Chairman; Vartkess Balian,
Treasurer; Barry Zorthian, Secretary; Ross Vartian, Executive Director.
Members of Executive Committee: James Renjilian and Adrienne Beren-
son. Officers of the Assembly's Board of Trustees: Hirair Hovnanian.
Chairman; Edward Mardigian, Vice Chairman; Joyce Stein, Secretary.
NO. OF CHAPTERS IN THE U.S.A.: One chapter in Los Angeles.
PURPOSE & ACTIVITIES OF ORGANIZATION: The Armenian Assembly of America was founded in 1972 as a charitable, educational trust. It
is a national organization predicated on the belief that Armenians in the
United States need a broad-based voice to speak effectively on Armenian issues at the seat of the American government. The Assembly's
programs include government relations, public affairs and anti-defamation, student affairs, grants, academic and educational affairs, and
human rights. PUBLICATION: Armenian Assembly Journal. LIBRARY:
Yes. CONTACT PERSON: Ross Vartian, Executive Director.

Massachusetts

(74)
ARMENIAN DEMOCRATIC LIBERAL ORGANIZATION
468 MOUNT AUBURN STREET
WATERTOWN, MASSACHUSETTS 02172   (617) 924-4420

(75)
ARMENIAN NATIONAL COMMITTEE, EASTERN REGION
76 BIGELOW AVENUE
WATERTOWN, MASSACHUSETTS 02172   (617) 923-1918

(76)
ARMENIAN REVOLUTIONARY FEDERATION OF AMERICA
76 BIGELOW AVENUE
WATERTOWN, MASSACHUSETTS 02172   (617) 926-3685

(77)
ARMENIAN RIGHTS COUNCIL OF AMERICA
468 MOUNT AUBURN STREET
P.O. BOX 302
WATERTOWN, MASSACHUSETTS 02172   (617) 923-9759

New Jersey

(79)
SOCIAL DEMOCRATIC HUNCHAKIAN PARTY OF EASTERN U.S.A.
353 FOREST AVENUE
P.O. BOX 742
PARAMUS, NEW JERSEY 07652   (201) 262-5363
DATE FOUNDED: 1890. **DIRECTORS & OFFICERS:** Arsen V. Jerejian, President; D. Ishlemejian, Treasurer; Mosushegh Derderian, Recording and Corresponding Secretary. **AFFILIATION TO OTHER ORGANIZA-TIONS:** Social Democratic Hunchakian Party of Western U.S.A. **NO. OF CHAPTERS IN THE U.S.A.:** Six chapters. **PURPOSE & ACTIVITIES OF ORGANIZATION:** The Hunchakian Party was founded in 1887 in Geneva. Turkey was its field of action. Its plan has been to free the Armenian people from the yoke of the Ottoman Empire and the establish-ment of a socialist Armenian state. At the present, the principal aims of S.D.H. Party are: a) preservation of the Armenian race, b) pursuit of the Armenian rights, c) development of cultural relations with the mother-land. **PUBLICATION:** Eritassart Hayastan.

Athletic Organizations
California

(80)
HOMENMEN ARMENIAN ATHLETIC ASSOCIATION
1060 NORTH ALLEN AVENUE
PASADENA, CALIFORNIA 91104   (818) 797-2727

(81)
HOMENTMEN ARMENIAN GENERAL ATHLETIC UNION, WESTERN U.S.A.
108 1/2 BRAND BLVD.
GLENDALE, CALIFORNIA 91203   **(818) 244-3868**

(82)
WESTERN ARMENIAN ATHLETIC ASSOCIATION
1055 SEMINARY AVENUE
OAKLAND, CALIFORNIA 94621   **(415) 531-9434 (415) 569-6566**
ACRONYM: W.A.A.A. **DATE FOUNDED** 1969. **DIRECTORS & OFFI-CERS:** James K. Taylor, III, President; Robert Pinomaki, Vice President; James Boghosian, Treasurer; Becky Pennington, Recording Secretary. **PURPOSE & ACTIVITIES OF ORGANIZATION:** Sponsors annual "Armenian Games" commonly known as "The Armenian Olympics", usually held in late June or early July in the San Francisco Bay Area. Events include Men's Basketball, Women's Volleyball, and Track and Field Competitions. The only requirement for eligibility is that participants must be of Armenian descent. **SCHOLARSHIPS, GRANTS, LOANS:** Available. **CONTACT PERSON:** James K. Taylor, III, President.

Massachusetts

(82-A)
HOMENTMEN ARMENIAN GENERAL ATHLETIC UNION
47 NICHOLS AVENUE
WATERTOWN, MASSACHUSETTS 02172   **(617) 924-6992**

New Jersey

(83)
ARMENIAN GENERAL ATHLETIC UNION
116 38th STREET
UNION CITY, NEW JERSEY 07087   **(201) 865-0057**

Religious Organizations
California

(84)
ARMENIAN APOSTOLIC CHURCH OF NORTH AMERICA WESTERN DIOCESE
1201 NORTH VINE STREET
HOLLYWOOD, CALIFORNIA 90038   **(213) 466-5265**
Primate: Archbishop Vatche Hovsepian.

(85)
ARMENIAN APOSTOLIC CHURCH OF AMERICA WESTERN PRE-LACY
4401 RUSSELL AVENUE
LOS ANGELES, CALIFORNIA 90027   **(213) 663-8273**
Prelate: The Most Rev. Archbishop Datev Sarkissian.

(86)
ARMENIAN EVANGELICAL UNION OF NORTH AMERICA
1743 WEST VARTIKIAN AVENUE
FRESNO, CALIFORNIA 37111   **(209) 431-7718 (209) 435-0500**
CONTACT PERSON: Rev. Harry M. Missirlian, Minister to the Union.

Massachusetts

(87)
HOLY CROSS ARMENIAN CATHOLIC CHURCH
ARMENIAN CATHOLIC COMMUNITY CENTER
100 MOUNT AUBURN STREET
CAMBRIDGE, MASSACHUSETTS 02138   **(617) 547-2122**
CONTACT PERSON: Father Luke Arakelian.

New Jersey

(88)
ARMENIAN MISSIONARY ASSOCIATION OF AMERICA
140 FOREST AVENUE
PARAMUS, NEW JERSETY 07652   **(201) 265-2607**

New York

(89)
ARMENIAN APOSTOLIC CHURCH OF NORTH AMERICA EASTERN DIOCESE
630 SECOND AVENUE
NEW YORK, NEW YORK 10016   **(212) 686-0710**
Primate: Archbishop Torkom Manoogian.

(90)
ARMENIAN APOSTOLIC CHURCH OF AMERICA EASTERN PRELACY
138 EAST 39th STREET
NEW YORK, NEW YORK 10016   **(212) 689-7810**
Prelate: Bishop Mesrob Ashjian.

(91)
ARMENIAN RELIGIOUS EDUCATION COUNCIL
138 EAST 39th STREET
NEW YORK, NEW YORK 10016   **(212) 689-4481**
CONTACT PERSON: Denis Arakelian.

(91-A)
ASSOCIATION OF ARMENIAN CHURCH CHOIRS OF AMERICA
HEADQUARTERS
630 SECOND AVENUE
NEW YORK, NEW YORK 10016

(Mailing Address)
3211 SYNOTT ROAD
HOUSTON, TEXAS 77082   **(713) 558-2722**
ACRONYM: A.A.C.C.A. **DATE FOUNDED:** 1947. **DIRECTORS & OFFICERS:** Fr. Nersess Jebejian, Chairman; Diane Chevian, Vice Chairman; Archbishop Torkom Manoogian, President; Norman Noorjanian, Treasurer; Christine Sarkissian, Recording Secretary; Patricia Buttero, Corresponding Secretary. **AFFILIATION TO OTHER ORGANIZATIONS:** A department of the Diocese of the Armenian Church of America, Eastern Diocese. **NO. OF CHAPTERS IN THE U.S.A.:** 50 chapters. **PURPOSE & ACTIVITIES OF ORGANIZATION:** To bring coordination among the choirs of the Diocesan Churches; publish liturgical books; supply choirs with robes, veils and stoles; organize training programs and seminars; distribute scholarships, etc. **SCHOLARSHIPS, GRANTS, LOANS:** Available. **CONTACT PERSON:** Fr. Nersess Jebejian, Chairman of the Central Council of the Association.

Nursing Homes and Hospitals
California

(92)
ARARAT CONVALESCENT HOSPITAL
2372 COLORADO BLVD.
LOS ANGELES, CALIFORNIA 90041   **(213) 256-8012**
DATE FOUNDED: 1979. **DIRECTORS & OFFICERS:** Lorraine Thomas, Administrator. **PURPOSE & ACTIVITIES OF ORGANIZATION:** To provide health care and welfare to the Armenian elderly.

(93)
THE ARARAT HOME OF LOS ANGELES
3730 WEST 27th STREET
LOS ANGELES, CALIFORNIA 90018   **(213) 733-5502**
DATE FOUNDED: 1949. **DIRECTORS & OFFICERS:** Herb Tertzag, Chairman; Armina Davitian, First Vice Chairman; Bill Kludjian, Second Vice Chairman; Helen Abajian, Treasurer; Popkin Simonian, Secretary; Rev. Hagop Janbazian, Administrator; Lorraine Thomas, Administrator of the hospital. **PURPOSE & ACTIVITIES OF ORGANIZATION:** To provide health care and welfare to the Armenian elderly. **PUBLICATION:** Ararat Hyelight. **CONTACT PERSON:** Rosine De Cervantes, Editor, and Diane Ansoorian, Editor.

(94)
CALIFORNIA HOME FOR THE AGED, INC.
CALIFORNIA ARMENIAN HOME
6720 EAST KINGS CANYON ROAD
FRESNO, CALIFORNIA 93727   **(209) 251-8414**
DATE FOUNDED: 1950. **DIRECTORS & OFFICERS:** M. J. Papazian, M.D., President; Kay Cloud, Vice President; Ralph Saroyan, Treasurer; Joe Garabedian, Recording Secretary. **PURPOSE & ACTIVITIES OF ORGANIZATION:** A non-profit organization providing quality care, treating each patient and resident as an individual. Encourages the support of the family and friends to assist in providing the best services. Provides three levels of care: skilled nursing, intermediate, and community care. **CONTACT PERSON:** Louise Emerzian, MSW, Administrator.

(95)
NORCAL ARMENIAN HOME
P.O. BOX 1785
LAFAYETTE, CALIFORNIA 94549
DATE FOUNDED: 1982. **DIRECTORS & OFFICERS:** George Rustigian,

President; Shavarsh Hazarabedian, Vice President; Edward Minasian, Treasurer; Florence Kashian, Recording Secretary; Roxana Giragossiantz, Corresponding Secretary; Edward Minasian, Executive Director. **PURPOSE & ACTIVITIES OF ORGANIZATION:** To raise funds toward the realization of the need for an Armenian senior citizens home in the Bay Area. Once established, plans to expand the facilities into an intermediate care home and convalescent hospital for Armenians in perpetuity. **CONTACT PERSON:** Edward Minasian, Executive Director.

Massachusetts

(96)
ARMENIAN WOMEN'S WELFARE ASSOCATION, INC.
431 POND STREET   (617) 522-7850
JAMAICA PLAIN, MASSACHUSETTS 02130   (617) 522-2600
ACRONYM: A.W.W.A. **DATE FOUNDED:** 1915. **DIRECTORS & OFFICERS:** Verkin T. Selian, President; Anna Demerjian, Vice President; Lucy Equmlian, Treasurer; Sophie Tolajian, Recording Secretary; Haiqouhi Daqley, Corresponding Secretary; Nancy Kasarjian, Assistant Treasurer; Alice O. Kasparian, Trustee Chairperson. **NO. OF CHAPTERS IN THE U.S.A.:** Four chapters in Boston, Belmont, Watertown, and Worcester in Massachusetts. **PURPOSE & ACTIVITIES OF ORGANIZATION:** A charitable organization of devoted, volunteer Armenian women. The home accommodates 83 residents and is always full to capacity. It enjoys a fine reputation, as one of the best nursing facilities. Since its inception in 1915, membership has been limited to women only. The organization is independent of church or political affiliation. The home is a haven for the sick and elderly who need care. **CONTACT PERSON:** Verkin T. Selian, President.

New Jersey

(97)
HOME FOR THE ARMENIAN AGED
70 MAIN STREET
EMERSON, NEW JERSEY 07630   (201) 261-6662 (201) 261-6663
DATE FOUNDED: 1938. **DIRECTORS & OFFICERS:** Armenak Mardirossian, Chairman & President; Zareh Kapikian, Vice President and Vice Chairman; Garo Spenjian, Treasurer; Isabelle Bolsetzian, Recording Secretary. **PURPOSE & ACTIVITIES OF ORGANIZATION:** Care for the elderly, nursing and boarding. **PUBLICATION:** Hyedoun. **CONTACT PERSON:** Armenak Mardirossian, President.

New York

(98)
NEW YORK ARMENIAN HOME FOR THE AGED
ARMENIAN WELFARE ASSOCIATION INC.
137-31 45 AVENUE
FLUSHING, NEW YORK 11355   (212) 461-1504

DIRECTORS & OFFICERS: Leon Karibian, Chairman; Paul B. Chaputian, Vice Chairman; Harry Hintlian, Treasurer; Shah Arslan, Recording Secretary; Thomas C. Gallo, Corresponding Secretary; Margaret C. T. Kyrkostas, Administrator. **PURPOSE & ACTIVITIES OF ORGANIZATION:** Throughout its history, the New York Armenian Home for the Aged has sought to provide the finest care possible for the elderly in an environment that reflects their Armenian heritage. The home continues to base its very existence on the needs of the elderly who enter its doors. **PUBLICATION:** New York Armenian Home for the Aged Newsletter. **LIBRARY:** Yes. **CONTACT PERSON:** Margaret C. T. Kyrkostas, Administrator.

Armenian Studies and Research Centers
California

(99)
ARMENOLOGICAL STUDIES, RESEARCH AND EXHIBITS
P.O. BOX 742
ENCINO, CALIFORNIA 91316

DATE FOUNDED: 1974. **NO. OF CHAPTERS IN THE U.S.A.:** Two chapters in California and Massachusetts. **PURPOSE & ACTIVITIES OF ORGANIZATION:** To collect books, literature, maps, coins, stamps, etc., relating to Armenia; do research and prepare publications on selected Armenian subjects; distribute such publications to libraries, government agencies, universities, etc. **BOOK SELLING SERVICE:** Available. **CONTACT PERSON:** Melkon Armen Khandjian.

Massachusetts

(100)
NATIONAL ASSOCIATION FOR ARMENIAN STUDIES
AND RESEARCH
175 MOUNT AUBURN STREET
CAMBRIDGE, MASSACHUSETTS 02138   (617) 876-7630

(101)
SOCIETY FOR ARMENIAN STUDIES
DEPT. OF NEAR EASTERN LANGUAGES
HARVARD UNIVERSITY
6 DIVINITY AVENUE # 103
CAMBRIDGE, MASSACHUSETTS 02138   **(617) 495-5757**
CONTACT PERSON: Dr. Kevork B. Bardakjian.

(102)
ZORYAN INSTITUTE FOR CONTEMPORARY ARMENIAN
RESEARCH AND DOCUMENTATION, INC.
85 FAYERWEATHER STREET
CAMBRIDGE, MASSACHUSETTS 02138   **(617) 497-6713**
DATE FOUNDED: 1982. **DIRECTORS & OFFICERS:** Levon Charkou-
dian, Chairman; Tatul Sonents Papazian, Treasurer; Leon Sarkisian,
Clerk; Gerard Libaridian, Director. **PURPOSE & ACTIVITIES OF
ORGANIZATION:** To do research, document, and publish on the Arme-
nian experience in the modern world; analyze and understand the struc-
tures, institutions, and dynamics of Armenian society through a
multi-disciplinary approach. **PUBLICATION:** Zoryan Institute Bulletin.
SCHOLARSHIPS, GRANTS, LOANS: Available. **BOOK SELLING
SERVICE:** Available. **LIBRARY:** Yes. **CONTACT PERSON:** Laura Yardumian, Administrative Assistant.

Pennsylvania

(103)
ARMENIAN HISTORICAL RESEARCH ASSOCIATION, INC.
30 NORTHWOOD ROAD
NEWTOWN SQUARE, PENNSYLVANIA 19073   **(215) 356-0635**
ACRONYM: A.H.R.A. **DATE FOUNDED:** 1961. **DIRECTORS & OFFI-
CERS:** Charles N. Mahjoubian, Chairman & President; Rev. Dr. Peter
Doghramji, Vice Chairman & Vice President; Aram Kabakjian, Treasurer;
Nazar Y. Daghlian, Recording Secretary; Helen Sevag, Corresponding
Secretary. **PURPOSE & ACTIVITIES OF ORGANIZATION:** Research
promotion by professionals and members; education of public by lec-
tures and discussions; special newspaper advertisements; book reviews
by members; promotion of joint effort and activity with other organiza-
tions; acceptance of fees and gifts to support its work. **PUBLICATION:**
Armenian Historical Research Association Newsletter. **BOOK SELLING
SERVICE:** Available.

Professional Organizations
California

(104)
ARMENIAN BUSINESS ALLIANCE OF CALIFORNIA
5621 SUNSET BLVD.
LOS ANGELES, CALIFORNIA 90028   **(213) 667-9070**

(105)
ARMENIAN BUSINESS DEVELOPMENT AND TRAINING CENTER
5250 SANTA MONICA BLVD. SUITE 312
LOS ANGELES, CALIFORNIA 90029 (213) 666-8282 (213) 666-6286
DATE FOUNDED: 1983. **DIRECTORS & OFFICERS:** Garo Kamarian, Director; Meline Melconian, Corresponding Secretary; **PURPOSE & ACTIVITIES OF ORGANIZATION:** The center has trained staff who assist in problem solving in the areas of management, finance, taxation, marketing, etc. This technical assistance is provided in training seminars or individual business counseling sessions. **CONTACT PERSON:** Garo Kamarian, Director.

(106)
ARMENIAN NUMISMATIC SOCIETY
8511 BEVELRY PARK PLACE
PICO RIVERA, CALIFORNIA 90660   **(213) 695-0380**
DATE FOUNDED: 1971. **DIRECTORS & OFFICERS:** Luther Eskijian, President; Wartan Gowenian, Treasurer; Y. T. Nercessian, Executive Director. **PURPOSE & ACTIVITIES OF ORGANIZATION:** To study Armenian coins, bank notes, medals, and publish literature relating to these items. **PUBLICATION:** Armenian Numismatic Journal. **BOOK SELLING SERVICE:** Available. **CONTACT PERSON:** Y. T. Nercessian, Secretary.

(107)
ARMENIAN PROFESSIONAL SOCIETY
215 MARINERS VIEW LANE
LA CANADA, CALIFORNIA 91011   **(818) 790-7271**
ACRONYM: A.P.S. **DATE FOUNDED:** 1958. **DIRECTORS & OFFICERS:** Garo Minassian, President; Peniamin Chavdarian, Vice President; Bea Nairi, Treasurer; Seda Marootian, Executive Director; Harry Markarian, Second Vice President. **NO. OF CHAPTERS IN THE U.S.A.:** One chapter in San Francisco. **PURPOSE & ACTIVITIES OF ORGANIZATION:**

The Armenian Professional Society is a non-sectarian, non-partisan, and non-political organization. Its purpose is to foster fellowship among Armenian professionals and provide a meeting place for members who share the same cultural, educational and social interests. It fosters research and acknowledges achievements in science, the arts and other academic areas. The society encourages Armenian students to attain university education and to proceed into post-graduate and research work. It provides scholarship funds and grants-in-aid for promising Armenian students at the graduate level. **SCHOLARSHIPS, GRANTS, LOANS:** Available. **CONTACT PERSON:** Seda Marootian, Executive Secretary.

(108)
ARMENIAN PROFESSIONAL SOCIETY OF THE BAY AREA
C/O DR. CHRISTINE POOCHIGIAN
2529 HAYWARD DRIVE
BURLINGAME, CALIFORNIA 94010   **(415) 692-4898**

(109)
ASSOCIATION OF TEACHERS IN ARMENIAN SCHOOLS OF CALI-FORNIA
C/O LILLIE MERIGIAN
17924 TARZANA STREET
ENCINO, CALIFORNIA 91316   **(818) 780-1418**

District of Columbia
Washington D.C.

(110)
GEORGETOWN ARMENIAN LAW STUDENT ASSOCIATION
GEORGETOWN UNIVERSITY LAW CENTER
600 NEW JERSEY AVENUE, N.W.
WASHINGTON, D.C. 20001   **(202) 332-9314**
ACRONYM: G.A.L.S.A. **DATE FOUNDED:** 1982. **DIRECTORS & OFFI-CERS:** Raffi K. Hovannisian, President; Van Krikorian, Treasurer; Meline Haratunian, Recording Secretary; Jane Minasian, Public Relations. **PURPOSE & ACTIVITIES OF ORGANIZATION:** To serve Armenian interests at the law center; increase awareness of Armenian culture and history among fellow students; serve as an avenue of communication between the law center community and Armenian communities throughout the country; and study Armenian issues from both international and domestic law perspectives. **CONTACT PERSON:** Raffi K. Hovannisian.

Maryland

(111)
ARMENIAN RUGS SOCIETY
C/O 6930 WISCONSIN AVENUE
CHEVY CHASE, MARYLAND 20815   **(301) 654-4044**
DATE FOUNDED: 1980. **DIRECTORS & OFFICERS:** A. T. Gregorian, Chairman; Arthur T. Gregorian, President; Harold Bedoukian, Vice President; James M. Keshishian, Treasurer; Loretta Boxdorfer, Recording and Corresponding Secretary. **PURPOSE & ACTIVITIES OF ORGANIZATION:** The A.R.S. is a non-profit association devoted to diffusion of the arts, crafts and science related to Armenian rugs, carpets and textiles. One specific goal of the A.R.S. is to seek rugs and textiles with Armenian inscriptions, to create a data bank of these rugs and make them available by reproductions to scholars and collectors. **BOOK SELLING SERVICE:** Available. **CONTACT PERSON:** James M. Keshishian, Treasurer; and A. T. Gregorian, Chairman.

Massachusetts

(112)
ARMENIAN AMERICAN MEDICAL ASSOCIATION
20 CLARENDON ROAD
BELMONT, MASSACHUSETTS 02178   **(617) 489-4070**
ACRONYM: A.A.M.A. **DATE FOUNDED:** 1971. **DIRECTORS & OFFICERS:** Paul Y. Hasserjian, M.D., President; Donald Shushan, M.D., Vice President; Harry Azadian, M.D., Treasurer; Chares Nargozian, M.D., Recording Secretary. **PURPOSE & ACTIVITIES OF ORGANIZATION:** To develop bonds of friendship among physicians of Armenian parentage by meeting at least twice a year; to assist young Armenian Americans desiring medical education; to assist newly arriving physicians or those starting practice. **SCHOLARSHIPS, GRANTS, LOANS:** Available. **CONTACT PERSON:** Chares Nargozian, M.D., Secretary.

(113)
ARMENIAN ARTISTS ASSOCIATION OF AMERICA
59 BIGELOW AVENUE
P.O. BOX 140
WATERTOWN, MASSACHUSETTS 02172   **(617) 923-9174**
ACRONYM: A.A.A.A. **DATE FOUNDED:** 1983. **DIRECTORS & OFFICERS:** John Terzian, Chairman & President; Richard H. Tashjian, Vice Chairman and Vice President; John Dasho, Treasurer; Zoya Ormatian,

Recording and Corresponding Secretary; George Ormatian, Executive Director. **PURPOSE & ACTIVITIES OF ORGANIZATION:** To bring together artists of Armenian descent in the various arts media; to foster and promote artists of Armenian descent in America and abroad; to plan and execute art exhibits by the active members; to promote interest in and knowledge of artistic fields through lectures and other functions; to exchange information with Armenian artists abroad as well as to exchange artists, and to establish scholarships. **SCHOLARSHIPS, GRANTS, LOANS:** Available. **CONTACT PERSON:** Richard H. Tashjian, Vice Chairman.

New York

(114)
THE ARMENIAN NATIONAL EDUCATION COMMITTEE
138 EAST 39th STREET
NEW YORK, NEW YORK 10016   (212) 689-7231 (212) 689-7810
ACRONYM: A.N.E.C. **DATE FOUNDED:** 1959. **DIRECTORS & OFFICERS:** Albert Bagian, Chairman; Vahe Amirian, Vice Chairman; His Eminence Archbishop Mesrob Ashjian, President; Osky Cascone, Treasurer; Hourig Papazian-Sahagian, Executive Director and Corresponding Secretary. **AFFILIATION TO OTHER ORGANIZATIONS:** Co-sponsored by the Eastern Prelacy of Armenian Apostolic Church of North America and Armenian Relief Society of North America, Regional Executive. **PURPOSE & ACTIVITIES OF ORGANIZATION:** A.N.E.C. seeks to instill an unquenchable spirit in each student, based on the knowledge of the Armenian language and culture. A.N.E.C. is committed to improve the effectiveness and quality of Armenian one-day and day-schools under its jurisdiction, in the eastern and mid-western U.S.A. and Canada. A.N.E.C. is composed of an all-volunteer board of professionals who have demonstrated deep concern for Armenian education in their respective communities. A.N.E.C. commissions, produces, recommends and disseminates educational materials and textbooks to network schools, conducts teacher-training seminars, organizes student festivals and other regional activities and sponsors experimental schools, academies and educational programs. **LIBRARY:** Yes. **BOOK SELLING SERVICE:** Available. **ONE-DAY/SATURDAY SCHOOL:** Yes. **CONTACT PERSON:** Hourig Papazian-Sahagian, Executive Director.

(115)
ARMENIAN NETWORK OF AMERICA, INC.
211 EAST 53rd STREET SUITE 2A
NEW YORK, NEW YORK 10022   **(212) 838-0860**

ACRONYM: A.N.A. **DATE FOUNDED:** 1983. **DIRECTORS & OFFICERS:** Levon Boyajian, President; Michael Kasparian, Vice President; Edele Hovnanian, Treasurer; Alice Amirian, Recording Secretary. **PURPOSE & ACTIVITIES OF ORGANIZATION:** The Network emphasizes the connection between career pursuits and Armenian identity, by creating a network of college youth, young professionals and established career people to promote community leadership and enhance participation of Armenians in the American society. Programs include; a computerized clearing house of information on Armenians in professions and businesses, and formation of a network of Armenian professional societies. **SCHOLARSHIP, GRANTS, LOANS:** Available. **CONTACT PERSON:** Levon Boyajian, President.

Pennsylvania

(116)
THE ARMENIAN AMERICAN MEDICAL AND DENTAL ASSOCIATION OF GREATER PHILADELPHIA
904 CLOVER HILL ROAD
WYNNEWWOOD, PENNSYLVANIA 19096   **(215) 649-6761**

ACRONYM: A.A.M.D.A. **DATE FOUNDED:** 1983. **DIRECTORS & OFFICERS:** Dr. Simon Simonian, President; Dr. Vahaken Tachjian, Vice President; Dr. Arthur Odabashian, Treasurer; Dr. Gabriel Tatarian, Recording Secretary; Dr. Seta Masseredjian-Apelian, Corresponding Secretary; Dr. Hratch Kasparian, Chairman. **PURPOSE & ACTIVITIES OF ORGANIZATION:** To assist Armenian Americans embarking in medical and dental careers; to enhance the members in professional and scientific growth; to enhance health awareness within the Armenian community.

Armenian Apostolic Churches Affilated with the Eastern Prelacy

BISHOP MESROB ASHJIAN, PRELATE
PRELACY OF THE ARMENIAN APOSTOLIC CHURCH OF AMERICA
139 EAST 39th STREET, NEW YORK, NEW YORK 10016
TEL.: (212) 689-7810

Connecticut

(117)
SAINT STEPHEN'S ARMENIAN APOSTOLIC CHURCH
167 TREMONT STREET
P.O. BOX 263
NEW BRITAIN, CONNECTICUT 06051   (203) 229-8322
CLERGYMAN: Rev. Sahag Andekian, Pastor.

Illinois

(118)
ALL SAINTS' ARMENIAN APOSTOLIC CHURCH
1701 NORTH GREENWOOD
GLENVIEW, ILLINOIS 60025   (312) 769-1059
CLERGYMAN: Archpriest Sempad Der Mksian, Pastor

(119)
SAINT GREGORY THE ILLUMINATOR ARMENIAN APOSTOLIC
CHURCH
1732 MAPLE STREET
GRANITE CITY, ILLINOIS 62040   (618) 451-7884
CLERGYMAN: Rev. Zaven Poladian, Pastor. PUBLICATION: Newsletter.

(120)
SAINT PAUL ARMENIAN APOSTOLIC CHURCH
645 SOUTH LEWIS AVENUE
WAUKEGAN, ILLINOIS 60085   (312) 244-4573
CONTACT PERSON: Charles Nordigian, Chairman.

Maryland

(121)
SOURP KHATCH ARMENIAN APOSTOLIC CHURCH
4906 FLINT DRIVE
CHEVY CHASE, MARYLAND 20816   (301) 229-8742

CLERGYMAN: Rev. Sahag Vertanesian, Pastor. PUBLICATION: Mashtots. DATE CONSECRATED: 1964. SATURDAY/SUNDAY SCHOOL: Yes. BOOK SELLING SERVICE: Available. LIBRARY: Yes. CONTACT PERSON: Rev. Sahag Vertanesian, Pastor.

Massachusetts

(122)
HOLY TRINITY ARMENIAN APOSTOLIC CHURCH
635 GROVE STREET
WORCESTER, MASSACHUSETTS 01605   (617) 852-2414
CLERGYMAN: Rev. Vazken Bekiarian, Pastor.

(123)
SAINT ASDVADZADZIN ARMENIAN APOSTOLIC CHURCH
211 CHURCH STREET
WHITINSVILLE, MASSACHUSETTS 01588   (617) 234-3677
CLERGYMAN: Rev. Gomidas Der Torossian, Pastor. DATE FOUNDED: 1953. DATE CONSECRATED: 1957. SUNDAY-SCHOOL: Yes. CONTACT PERSON: Rev. Gomidas Der Torossian.

(124)
SAINT GREGORY ARMENIAN APOSTOLIC CHURCH
135 GOODWIN STREET
INDIAN ORCHARD, MASSACHUSETTS 01151   (413) 543-4763
CLERGYMAN: Rev. Antranig Baljian, Pastor.

(125)
SAINT GREGORY ARMENIAN APOSTOLIC CHURCH OF MERRI-MACK VALLEY
158 MAIN STREET
NORTH ANDOVER, MASSACHUSETTS 01845   (617) 685-5038
CLERGYMAN: Rev. Arshag Daghlian, Pastor. DATE FOUNDED: 1970. DATE CONSECRATED: 1970. SATURDAY/SUNDAY-SCHOOL: Yes.

(126)
SAINT STEPHEN'S ARMENIAN APOSTOLIC CHURCH
38 ELTON AVENUE
WATERTOWN, MASSACHUSETTS 02172   (617) 924-7562
CLERGYMAN: Archpriest Torkom Hagopian, Pastor.

Michigan

(127)
SAINT SARKIS ARMENIAN APOSTOLIC CHURCH
19300 FORD ROAD
DEARBORN, MICHIGAN 48128   **(313) 336-6200**
CLERGYMAN: Rev. Dr. Gorun Shrikian, Pastor. **DATE FOUNDED:** 1932. **PUBLICATION:** The Illuminator. **SATURDAY/SUNDAY-SCHOOL:** Yes. **BOOK SELLING SERVICE:** Available. **SCHOLAR-SHIPS, GRANTS, LOANS:** Available. **LIBRARY.** Yes. **CONTACT PERSON:** Rev. Dr. Gorun Shrikian, Pastor.

New Jersey

(128)
SAINTS VARTANANTZ ARMENIAN APOSTOLIC CHURCH OF NEW JERSEY
461 BERGEN BLVD.
RIDGEFIELD, NEW JERSEY 07657   **(201) 943-2950**
CLERGYMAN: Archpriest Rev. Fr. Vahrich Shirinian, Pastor. **DATE FOUNDED:** 1959. **PUBLICATION:** Vartanantz. **SATURDAY/SUNDAY-SCHOOL:** Yes. **BOOK SELLING SERVICE:** Available. **LIBRARY:** Yes. **CONTACT PERSON:** Rev. Father Vahrich Shirinian.

New York

(129)
THE ARMENIAN APOSTOLIC CHURCH OF AMERICA EASTERN PRE-LACY
138 EAST 39th STREET
NEW YORK, NEW YORK 10016   **(212) 689-7810**
CLERGYMAN: Bishop Mesrop Ashjian, Prelate. **PUBLICATION:** Outreach. **CONTACT PERSON:** Rev. Khoren Habeshian, Executive Secretary.

(130)
HOLY CROSS ARMENIAN APOSTOLIC CHURCH
101 SPRING AVENUE
TROY, NEW YORK 12180   **(518) 274-1477**
CLERGYMAN: Rev. Khatchig Meguerdichian.

(131)
SAINT HAGOP ARMENIAN APOSTOLIC CHURCH OF NIAGARA FALLS
300 9th STREET
NIAGARA FALLS, NEW YORK 14303   **(716) 282-9377**
CONTACT PERSON: H. Ishkhanian, Chairman.

(132)
SAINT ILLUMINATOR'S ARMENIAN APOSTOLIC CATHEDRAL
221 EAST 27th STREET
NEW YORK, NEW YORK 10016   **(212) 689-5880**
CLERGYMAN: Archpriest Moushegh Der Kaloustian. **PUBLICATION:**
Mayr Yegeghetsi.

(133)
SAINT JOHN THE BAPTIST ARMENIAN APOSTOLIC CHURCH
372 WEST MATSON AVENUE
SYRACUSE, NEW YORK 13205   **(315) 492-9983**
CLERGYMAN: Rev. Khatchig Meguerdichian.

(134)
SAINT SARKIS ARMENIAN APOSTOLIC CHURCH
42nd AVENUE and 213th STREET
BAYSIDE, NEW YORK 11361   **(212) 224-2275**
CLERGYMAN: Archpriest Asoghik Kelejian, Pastor.

Ohio

(135)
HOLY CROSS ARMENIAN APOSTOLIC CHURCH
4402 WALLINGS ROAD
NORTH ROYALTON, OHIO 44133   **(216) 831-8938 (216) 237-3560**
CONTACT PERSON: Krikor Topalian, Chairman.

Oklahoma

(136)
SAINT GREGORY ARMENIAN APOSTOLIC CHURCH
9104 ROLLING GREEN
OKLAHOMA CITY, OKLAHOMA 73136   **(405) 271-6582**
CONTACT PERSON: Dr. Robert Armen Magarian, Chairman.

Pennsylvania

(137)
SAINT GREGORY THE ILLUMINATOR ARMENIAN APOSTOLIC
CHURCH
8701 RIDGE AVENUE   **(215) 482-9200**
PHILADELPHIA, PEENSYLVANIA 19128   **(215) 482-3344**

CLERGYMAN: Archpriest Arsen Hagopian, Pastor. **DATE FOUNDED:**

1927. **DATE CONSECRATED:** 1928. **PUBLICATION:** Illuminator. **SAT-URDAY/SUNDAY-SCHOOL:** Yes. **BOOK SELLING SERVICE:** Available.

Rhode Island

(138)
SAINTS VARTANANTZ ARMENIAN APOSTOLIC CHURCH
402 BROADWAY
PROVIDENCE, RHODE ISLAND 02909   **(401) 831-6399**

CLERGYMAN: Archpriest Dr. Mesrob Tashjian. **DATE FOUNDED:** 1890.
DATE CONSECRATED: 1945. **PUBLICATION:** Gantegh. **SATURDAY/SUNDAY-SCHOOL:** Yes. **LIBRARY:** Yes. **CONTACT PERSON:** Archpriest Dr. Mesrob Tashjian.

Wisconsin

(139)
SAINT HAGOP'S ARMENIAN APOSTOLIC CHURCH
4100 NORTH NEWMAN ROAD
RACINE. WISCONSIN 53406   **(414) 886-4037**

CONTACT PERSON: Matthew Mikaelian, Chairman.

Armenian Apostolic Churches
Affilated with the Western Prelacy

THE MOST REV. ARCHBISHOP DATEV SARKISSIAN, PRELATE.
WESTERN PRELACY OF THE ARMENIAN APOSTOLIC CHURCH

4401 RUSSELL AVENUE, LOS ANGELES, CALIFORNIA 90027
(213) 663-8273 (213) 663-8274

California

(140)
ARMENIAN APOSTOLIC CHURCH OF AMERICA WESTERN PRE-LACY
4401 RUSSELL AVENUE
LOS ANGELES, CALIFORNIA 90027 (213) 663-8273 (213) 663-8274
PUBLICATION: Hromgla.

(141)
ARMENIAN APOSTOLIC CHURCH OF ORANGE COUNTY
5372 DUNCANNON AVENUE
WESTMINSTER, CALIFORNIA 92683   **(714) 894-4669**

CLERGYMAN: Rev. Ashod Kochian. DATE FOUNDED: 1973. PUBLI-
CATION: Lradoo. CONTACT PERSON: Ashod Kochian, Pastor, and
Hagop Melkonian, Chairman.

(142)
HOLY CROSS ARMENIAN APOSTOLIC CATHEDRAL
900 WEST LINCOLN AVENUE
MONTEBELLO, CALIFORNIA 90640   (213) 727-1114
CLERGYMAN: Very Rev. Fr. Nareg Shirikian, Pastor, and Rev. Fr.
Papken Manuelian. DATE FOUNDED: 1981. DATE CONSECRATED:
1984. PUBLICATION: Yes. SATURDAY/SUNDAY-SCHOOL: Yes.
BOOK SELLING SERVICE: Available. CONTACT PERSON: Rev. Fr.
Papken Manuelian, Pastor.

(143)
HOLY MARTYRS ARMENIAN APOSTOLIC CHURCH
5300 WHITE OAK AVENUE
ENCINO, CALIFORNIA 91316   (818) 981-6159
CLERGYMAN: Rev. Vartan Arakelian, Pastor. PUBLICATION: Hovid.

(144)
HOLY TRINITY ARMENIAN APOSTOLIC CHURCH
2226 EAST VENTURA AVENUE
P.O. BOX 1865
FRESNO, CALIFORNIA 93721   (209) 486-1142 (209) 486-1141
CLERGYMAN: Rev. Hrant Serabian, Pastor. PUBLICATION: Voice.
DATE FOUNDED: 1914. DATE CONSECRATED: 1914. SUNDAY-
SCHOOL: Yes. SCHOLARSHIPS, GRANTS, LOANS: Available.
LIBRARY: Yes.

(145)
SAINT GARABED ARMENIAN APOSTOLIC CHURCH
1614 NORTH ALEXANDRIA AVENUE
LOS ANGELES, CALIFORNIA 90027 (213) 666-0507 (213) 662-4222
CLERGYMAN: Rev. Vatche Naccachian, Pastor. PUBLICATION: Saint
Garabed Armenian Apostolic Church Bulletin.

(146)
SAINT GREGORY ARMENIAN APOSTOLIC CHURCH
51 COMMONWEALTH AVENUE
SAN FRANCISCO, CALIFORNIA 94118   (415) 751-4140
CLERGYMAN: Rev. Datev Kaloustian, Pastor. DATE FOUNDED: 1952.
DATE CONSECRATED: 1966. PUBLICATION: Looys. SATURDAY-
SCHOOL: Yes.

(147)
SAINT MARY'S ARMENIAN APOSTOLIC CHURCH
500 SOUTH CENTRAL AVENUE
GLENDALE, CALIFORNIA 91204   **(818) 244-2402**
CLERGYMAN: Archpriest Anoushavan Artinian, Pastor. **PUBLICATION:**
Saint Mary's Armenian Apostolic Church Bulletin.

Armenian Apostolic Churches
Affiliated with the Eastern Diocese
THE MOST REV. ARCHBISHOP TORKOM MANOOGIAN, PRIMATE
DIOCESE OF THE ARMENIAN CHURCH OF NORTH AMERICA

SAINT VARTAN ARMENIAN CATHEDRAL
630 SECOND AVENUE, NEW YORK, NEW YORK 10016
(212) 686-0710

Connecticut
(148)
ARMENIAN CHURCH OF THE HOLY ASCENSION
1460 HUNTINGTON TURNPIKE
TRUMBULL, CONNECTICUT 06611   **(203) 372-5770**
CLERGYMAN: Fr. Untzag Nalbandian, Pastor. **DATE FOUNDED:** 1931.
DATE CONSECRATED: New church, 1984. **PUBLICATION:** Ani. **SAT-
URDAY/SUNDAY-SCHOOL:** Yes. **LIBRARY:** Yes.

(149)
HOLY RESURRECTION ARMENIAN CHURCH
1910 STANLEY STREET
NEW BRITAIN, CONNECTICUT 06053   **(203) 223-7875**
CLERGYMAN: Rev. Vartan Der Assadourian, Pastor.

(150)
SAINT GEORGE ARMENIAN APOSTOLIC CHURCH
22 WHITE STREET
HARTFORD, CONNECTICUT 06114   **(203) 524-5647**
CLERGYMAN: Rev. Yeprem Kelegian, Pastor.

District of Columbia
Washington D.C.
(151)
SAINT MARY'S ARMENIAN APOSTOLIC CHURCH
4125 FESSENDEN STREET N.W.
WASHINGTON, D.C. 20016   **(202) 363-1923 (301) 942-2434**

CLERGYMAN: Rev. Fr. Vertanes Kalayjian, Pastor. DATE FOUNDED: 1930. DATE CONSECRATED: 1960. PUBLICATION: Shnorhali. SAT-URDAY/SUNDAY-SCHOOL: Yes. BOOK SELLING SERVICE: Available. SCHOLARSHIPS, GRANTS, LOANS: Available. LIBRARY: Yes. CONTACT PERSON: Rev. Vertanes Kalayjian, Pastor.

Florida

(152)
ARMENIAN CHURCH OF SOUTH FLORIDA
P.O. BOX "O"
POMPANO BEACH, FLORIDA 33061   (305) 491-1600
CLERGYMAN: Rev. Zaven Arzoumanian, Pastor.

(153)
SAINT JOHN THE BAPTIST ARMENIAN APOSTOLIC CHURCH
120 N.E. 16th STREET
MIAMI, FLORIDA 33132   (305) 371-4484
CLERGYMAN: Rev. Fr. Terenig Kondralina, Pastor. DATE FOUNDED: 1948. DATE CONSECRATED: 1953. SUNDAY-SCHOOL: Yes. CONTACT PERSON: Louise Mahakian.

Illinois

(154)
HOLY SHOGHAGAT ARMENIAN CHURCH
400 HUNTWOOD ROAD
BELLEVILLE, ILLINOIS 62221   (618) 233-9453

(155)
SAINT GEORGE ARMENIAN CHURCH
1015 McAREE ROAD
WAUKEGAN, ILLINOIS 60085   (312) 244-0424

(156)
SAINT GREGORY THE ILLUMINATOR ARMENIAN CHURCH
6700 WEST DIVERSEY AVENUE
CHICAGO, ILLINOIS 60636   (312) 637-1711
CLERGYMAN: Rev. Vahram Hazarian, Pastor.

(157)
SAINT JAMES ARMENIAN CHURCH
816 CLARK STREET
EVANSTON, ILLINOIS 60201   (312) 864-6263

CLERGYMAN: Very Rev. Varoujan Kabaradjian, Pastor.

(158)
SAINTS JOACHIM AND SAINT ANNE ARMENIAN CHURCH
12600 SOUTH RIDGELAND
PALOS HEIGHTS, ILLINOIS 60463 (312) 388-9765

Massachusetts

(159)
CHURCH OF OUR SAVIOUR ARMENIAN APOSTOLIC CHURCH
87 SALISBURY STREET
WORCESTER, MASSACHUSETTS 01609 (617) 756-2931
CLERGYMAN: Rev. Aved Terzian. **PUBLICATION:** Soorhantag.

(160)
HOLY CROSS ARMENIAN CHURCH
54 EAST HAVERHILL
LAWRENCE, MASSACHUSETTS 01841 (617) 683-9942
CLERGYMAN: Very Rev. Baret Yeretzian, Pastor.

(161)
HOLY TRINITY ARMENIAN APOSTOLIC CHURCH OF GREATER BOSTON
145 BRATTLE STREET
CAMBRIDGE, MASSACHUSETTS 02138 (617) 354-0632
CLERGYMAN: Rev. Mampre Kouzonian, Pastor. **PUBLICATION:** Dadjar.

(162)
SAINT GREGORY THE ILLUMINATOR ARMENIAN APOSTOLIC CHURCH
110 MAIN STREET
HAVERHILL, MASSACHUSETTS 01830 (617) 372-9227
CLERGYMAN: Deacon Krikor Zamroutian, Visiting Deacon-in-Charge.
DATE FOUNDED: 1943. **DATE CONSECRATED:** 1945. **PUBLICATION:**
Loosavorich. **BOOK SELLING SERVICE:** Available. **LIBRARY:** Yes.
CONTACT PERSON: Zaven Gostanian, Parish Council Chairman.

(163)
SAINT JAMES ARMENIAN APOSTOLIC CHURCH
465 MT. AUBURN STREET
WATERTOWN, MASSACHUSETTS 02172 (617) 923-8860
CLERGYMAN: Rev. Dajad A. Davidian, Pastor. **DATE FOUNDED:** 1928.

DATE CONSECRATED: 1937. **PUBLICATION:** Looys. **SATURDAY/ SUNDAY-SCHOOL:** Yes. **CONTACT PERSON:** Rev. Dajad A. Davidian, Pastor.

(164)
SAINT MARK ARMENIAN CHURCH
2427 WILBRAHAM ROAD
SPRINGFIELD, MASSACHUSETTS 01129   **(413) 734-8691**
CLERGYMAN: Very Rev. Mesrob Semerjian. **PUBLICATION:** Sanahin.

(165)
SAINTS VARTANANTZ ARMENIAN CHURCH
180 OLDE WESTFORD ROAD
CHELMSFORD, MASSACHUSETTS 01824   **(617) 256-7234**
CLERGYMAN: Rev. Ghevont Samoorian, Pastor.

Michigan

(166)
SAINT JOHN'S ARMENIAN APOSTOLIC CHURCH
22001 NORTHWESTERN HIGHWAY
SOUTHFIELD, MICHIGAN 48075   **(313) 569-3405**
CLERGYMAN: The Very Rev. Paren Avedikian, Pastor.

New Jersey

(167)
HOLY CROSS ARMENIAN APOSTOLIC CHURCH
318 27th STREET
UNION CITY, NEW JERSEY 07087   **(201) 864-2480**
CLERGYMAN: Rev. Carnig Hallajian, Pastor.

(168)
SAINT LEON ARMENIAN APOSTOLIC CHURCH
12-61 SADDLE RIVER ROAD
FAIR LAWN, NEW JERSEY 07410   (201) 791-2862 (201) 791-1583
CLERGYMAN: Rev. Paree Metjian, Pastor. **DATE FOUNDED:** 1942. **DATE CONSECRATED:** 1944. **PUBLICATION:** Lradoo. **WEDNESDAY/ SUNDAY-SCHOOL:** Yes. **BOOK SELLING SERVICE:** Available. **LIBRARY:** Yes. **CONTACT PERSON:** Barbara Hovsepian or Varsen Torosian.

(169)
SAINT MARY ARMENIAN APOSTOLIC CHURCH
200 WEST MT. PLEASANT AVENUE
LIVINGSTON, NEW JERSEY 07039   (201) 992-8255 (201) 533-9794

CLERGYMAN: Very Rev. Fr. Houssing Bagdasian, Pastor. DATE FOUNDED: 1926. DATE CONSECRATED: New church, 1982. PUBLI- CATION: Gantegh. SATURDAY/SUNDAY-SCHOOL: Yes. BOOK SELLING SERVICE: Available. CONTACT PERSON: Fr. Houssig Bagdasian, Pastor.

(170)
SAINT THOMAS ARMENIAN APOSTOLIC CHURCH
P.O. BOX 53 (HWY 9W at EAST CLINTON AVE.)
TENAFLY, NEW JERSEY 07670   (201) 567-5446
CLERGYMAN: Rev. Arnak Kasparian, Pastor. PUBLICATION: Beacon. SATURDAY/SUNDAY SCHOOL: Yes. BOOK SELLING SERVICE: Available. CONTACT PERSON: Rev. Arnak Kasparian, Pastor.

New York

(171)
ARMENIAN CHURCH OF NORTHERN WESTCHESTER
P.O. BOX 114
LAKE PEEKSKILL, NEW YORK 10537   (914) 528-4567
CLERGYMAN: Rev. Onnig Terzian, Deacon-in-Charge.

(172)
ARMENIAN CHURCH OF WESTCHESTER
SAINT JAMES ARMENIAN CHURCH
55 LINCOLN AVENUE
PURCHASE, NEW YORK 10528   (914) 253-9077
CLERGYMAN: Rev. Karekin Kasparian, Pastor.

(173)
ARMENIAN CHURCH OF WESTERN QUEENS
(ALL SAINTS EPISCOPAL CHURCH)
43-12 46th STREET
SUNNYSIDE, NEW YORK 11104   (212) 939-2275
CLERGYMAN: Rev. Mamigon Vosganian, Pastor.

(174)
HOLY CROSS ARMENIAN CHURCH
580 WEST 187th STREET
NEW YORK, NEW YORK 10033   (212) 927-4020
CLERGYMAN: Rev. Fr. Guregh Kalfayan. DATE FOUNDED: 1929. DATE CONSECRATED: 1929. PUBLICATION: Zuartnotz. CONTACT PERSON: Alice Demirdjian, Secretary.

(175)
HOLY MARTYR'S ARMENIAN APOSTOLIC CHURCH
209-15 HORACE HARDING EXPRESS WAY
BAYSIDE, NEW YORK 11364   **(212) 225-0235**
CLERGYMAN: Rev. Michael Buttero, Pastor. **PUBLICATION:** Nareg.

(176)
SAINT GREGORY THE ILLUMINATOR ARMENIAN CHURCH
12 CORBETT AVENUE
BINGHAMTON, NEW YORK 13903   **(607) 722-8801**
CLERGYMAN: Very Rev. Fr. Sooren Chinchinian, **DATE FOUNDED:**
1928. **PUBLICATION:** Sunrise. **SUNDAY-SCHOOL:** Yes.

(177)
SAINT GREGORY THE ILLUMINATOR ARMENIAN CHURCH
630 SECOND AVENUE
NEW YORK, NEW YORK 10016   **(212) 679-1728**

(178)
SAINT PAUL'S ARMENIAN CHURCH
310 NORTH GEDDES STREET
SYRACUSE, NEW YORK 13204   **(315) 422-9047**

(179)
SAINT PETER ARMENIAN APOSTOLIC CHURCH
100 TROY-SCHENECTADY ROAD
WATERVLIET, NEW YORK 12189   (518) 274-3673 (518) 785-4816
CLERGYMAN: Rev. Garen Gdanian, Pastor. **PUBLICATION:** Loosaper.

(180)
SAINT SARKIS ARMENIAN APOSTOLIC CHURCH OF NIAGARA
FALLS
300 9th STREET
NIAGARA FALLS, NEW YORK 14303   **(716) 282-2587**
DATE FOUNDED: 1946. **DATE CONSECRATED:** 1953. **PUBLICATION:**
Saint Sarkis Armenian Apostolic Church, Parish Bulletin. **SUNDAY-
SCHOOL:** Yes. **CONTACT PERSON:** Arsen Avdoian, Chairman.

(181)
SAINT VARTAN ARMENIAN CATHEDRAL
630 SECOND AVENUE
NEW YORK, NEW YORK 10016   **(212) 686-0710**
CLERGYMAN: Rev. Fr. Arten Ashjian. **PUBLICATION:** Hayastaneayts
Yegeghestzy.

Ohio

(182)
SAINT GREGORY OF NAREG ARMENIAN CHURCH
666 RICHMOND ROAD
CLEVELAND, OHIO 44143   **(216) 381-6590**
CLERGYMAN: Rev. Diran Papazian. **PUBLICATION:** Paros.

Pennsylvania

(183)
HOLY TRINITY ARMENIAN APOSTOLIC CHURCH
101 ASHMEAD ROAD
CHELTENHAM, PENNSYLVANIA 19012   **(215) 563-1600**
CLERGYMAN: Very Rev. Haigazoun Melkonian, Pastor.

(184)
SAINT SAHAG AND SAINT MESROB ARMENIAN APOSTOLIC CHURCH
630 CLOTHIER ROAD
WYNNEWOOD, PENNSYLVANIA 19096   **(215) 642-4212**
DATE FOUNDED: 1917. **DATE CONSECRATED:** New church, 1963. **PUBLICATION:** Mer Doon. **SUNDAY-SCHOOL:** Yes. **BOOK SELLING SERVICE:** Available. **CONTACT PERSON:** Grace Ashekian, Secretary.

Rhode Island

(185)
SAINT SAHAG AND SAINT MESROB ARMENIAN APOSTOLIC CHURCH
70 JEFFERSON STREET
PROVIDENCE, RHODE ISLAND 02908   **(401) 272-7712**
CLERGYMAN: Rev. Shnork Kasparian, Pastor. **PUBLICATION:** Paros.

Texas

(186)
SAINT KEVORK ARMENIAN APOSTOLIC CHURCH
3211 SYNOTT ROAD
HOUSTON, TEXAS 77082   **(713) 558-2722**
CLERGYMAN: Rev. Fr. Nerses Jebejian, Pastor. **DATE FOUNDED:** 1964. **DATE CONSECRATED:** 1982. **PUBLICATION:** Saint Kevork Armenian Apostolic Church Bulletin. **SATURDAY/SUNDAY SCHOOL:** Yes. **BOOK SELLING SERVICE:** Available. **LIBRARY:** Yes. **CONTACT PERSON:** Rev. Fr. Nerses Jebejian, Pastor.

Virginia

(187)
SAINT JAMES ARMENIAN APOSTOLIC CHURCH
834 PEPPER AVENUE
RICHMOND, VIRGINIA 23226   **(804) 282-3818 (804) 741-1323**
CLERGYMAN: Rev. Arsen Barsamian, Pastor.

Wisconsin

(188)
HOLY RESURRECTION ARMENIAN APOSTOLIC CHURCH
909 MICHIGAN AVENUE
SOUTH MILWAUKEE, WISCONSIN 53172   **(414) 762-7460**
CLERGYMAN: Rev. Zenob Nalbandian, Pastor.

(189)
SAINT JOHN ARMENIAN CHURCH
7825 WEST LAYTON AVENUE
GREENFIELD, WISCONSIN 53220   **(414) 282-1670**
CLERGYMAN: Rev. Tateos Abdalian, Pastor. **PUBLICATION:** Ararat.

(190)
SAINT MESROB ARMENIAN APOSTOLIC CHURCH
4605 ERIE STREET
RACINE, WISCONSIN 53402   **(414) 639-0531**
CLERGYMAN: Rev. Fr. Garabed D. Kochakian, **DATE FOUNDED:** 1922.
DATE CONSECRATED: 1926. **PUBLICATION:** Varak. **SATURDAY/
SUNDAY-SCHOOL:** Yes. **SCHOLARSHIPS, GRANTS, LOANS:** Available. **LIBRARY:** Yes. **CONTACT PERSON:** Rev. Fr. Garabed D. Kochakian, Pastor.

Armenian Apostolic Churches
Affiliated with the Western Diocese
THE MOST REV. ARCHBISHOP VACHE HOVSEPIAN, PRIMATE
WESTERN DIOCESE OF THE ARMENIAN CHURCH OF NORTH
AMERICA
1201 NORTH VINE STREET
HOLLYWOOD, CALIFORNIA 90038
(213) 466-5265

Arizona

(191)
ARMENIAN CHURCH OF MARICOPA COUNTY
P.O. BOX 214
PHOENIX, ARIZONA 85001   **(602) 973-0665 (602) 257-1234**
CONTACT PERSON: Anne Chakmakjian, Parish Council.

California

(192)
ARMENIAN APOSTOLIC CHURCH OF NORTH AMERICA
WESTERN DIOCESE
1201 NORTH VINE STREET
LOS ANGELES, CALIFORNIA 90038   **(213) 466-5265**

(193)
ARMENIAN APOSTOLIC CHURCH OF SANTA CLARA VALLEY
11370 SOUTH STELLING ROAD
CUPERTINO, CALIFORNIA 95014   **(408) 257-6743**
CLERGYMAN: Rev. Fr. Vazken Movsesian, Parish Priest. **DATE FOUNDED:** 1964. **PUBLICATION:** Armenian Apostolic Church of Santa Clara Valley Newsletter. **SATURDAY/SUNDAY SCHOOL:** Yes. **LIBRARY.** Yes. **CONTACT PERSON:** Rev. Fr. Vazken Movsesian, Parish Priest.

(194)
ARMENIAN CHURCH OF THE DESERT
P.O. BOX 2700
PALM DESERT, CALIFORNIA 92261   **(619) 396-2355**
CONTACT PERSON: Ara Herbekian.

(195)
SAINT GREGORY ARMENIAN APOSTOLIC CHURCH
2215 EAST COLORADO BLVD.
PASADENA, CALIFORNIA 91107   **(818) 449-1523**
CLERGYMAN: Very Rev. Fr. Moushegh Tashjian, Parish Priest. **DATE FOUNDED:** 1945. **DATE CONSECRATED:** 1964. **PUBLICATION:** Shoghagat. **SATURDAY/SUNDAY-SCHOOL:** Yes. **LIBRARY.** Yes. **CONTACT PERSON:** Very Rev. Fr. Moushegh Tashjian, Parish Priest.

(196)
SAINT JAMES ARMENIAN APOSTOLIC CHURCH
4950 WEST SLAUSON AVENUE
LOS ANGELES, CALIFORNIA 90056   **(213) 295-4588**
CLERGYMAN: Very Rev. Arshag Khatchadourian, Parish Priest.

(197)
SAINT JAMES ARMENIAN APOSTOLIC CHURCH
3240 "B" STREET
SACRAMENTO, CALIFORNIA 95816 (916) 443-3633 (916) 443-1171
CLERGYMAN: Rev. Artoon Sempadian, Parish Priest.

(198)
SAINT JOHN ARMENIAN CATHEDRAL
1201 NORTH VINE STREET
LOS ANGELES, CALIFORNIA 90038   **(213) 466-5265**
CLERGYMAN: Rev. Vartan Tatevossian, Parish Priest.

(199)
SAINT JOHN ARMENIAN APOSTOLIC CHURCH
4473-30th STREET
SAN DIEGO, CALIFORNIA 92116   (619) 562-1533 (619) 284-7179
CLERGYMAN: The Rev. Fr. Levon Avak Kahanah Arakelian, Pastor.
DATE FOUNDED: 1973. **PUBLICATION:** Voice. **SATURDAY/SUNDAY-
SCHOOL:** Yes. **LIBRARY:** Yes. **CONTACT PERSON:** The Rev. Fr.
Levon A. Kahanah Arakelian.

(200)
SAINT JOHN ARMENIAN APOSTOLIC CHURCH
275 OLYMPIC WAY
SAN FRANCISCO, CALIFORNIA 94131   **(415) 661-1142**
CLERGYMAN: Rev. Aris Shirvanian, Parish Priest.

(201)
SAINT MARY ARMENIAN CHURCH OF YETTEM
14395 AVENUE 384
YETTEM, CALIFORNIA 93670   (209) 528-6892 (209) 591-9996
CLERGYMAN: Rev. Fr. Vartan Kasparian, Parish Priest. **DATE
FOUNDED:** 1904. **DATE CONSECRATED:** 1911, new church, 1946.
PUBLICATION: Saint Mary Armenian Church of Yettem Bulletin. **SUN-
DAY-SCHOOL:** Yes. **BOOK SELLING SERVICE:** Available. **SCHOLAR-
SHIPS, GRANTS, LOANS:** Available. **LIBRARY:** Yes. **CONTACT
PERSON:** Rev. Fr. Vartan Kasparian, Parish Priest.

(202)
SAINT PAUL ARMENIAN CHURCH
3767 NORTH FIRST STREET
FRESNO, CALIFORNIA 93726   **(209) 226-6343**

CLERGYMAN: Archpriest Shahe Altounian, Parish Priest. **DATE CONSECRATED:** 1979. **PUBLICATION:** Tertig. **SUNDAY-SCHOOL:** Yes. **BOOK SELLING SERVICE:** Available. **LIBRARY:** Yes. **CONTACT PERSON:** Archpriest Shahe Altounian, Parish Priest.

(203)
SAINT PETER ARMENIAN APOSTOLIC CHURCH
17231 SHERMAN WAY
VAN NUYS, CALIFORNIA 91406   **(818) 344-4860**

CLERGYMAN: Fr. Shahe Avak Kahana Semerdjian, Parish Priest. **DATE FOUNDED:** 1958. **DATE CONSECRATED:** 1966. **PUBLICATION:** Pari-Loor. **SATURDAY/SUNDAY-SCHOOL:** Yes. **LIBRARY.** Yes.

(204)
SAINT SARKIS ARMENIAN APOSTOLIC CHURCH
700 SOUTH LA VERNE AVENUE
EAST LOS ANGELES, CALIFORNIA 90022   **(213) 269-0907**

CLERGYMAN: Rev. Vartan Dulgarian, Parish Priest. **PUBLICATION:** Gantegh.

(205)
SAINT VARTAN ARMENIAN APOSTOLIC CHURCH
650 SPRUCE STREET
OAKLAND, CALIFORNIA 94610   **(415) 893-1671**

CLERGYMAN: Rev. Mesrob Sarafian, Parish Priest.

(206)
SAINTS SAHAG-MESROB ARMENIAN APOSTOLIC CHURCH
P.O. BOX 205
1249 "F" STREET
REEDLEY, CALIFORNIA 93654   **(209) 638-2740**

CLERGYMAN: Rev. Fr. Datev Tatoulian, Parish Priest. **DATE FOUNDED:** 1923. **DATE CONSECRATED:** 1924 **PUBLICATION:** Saints Sahag-Mesrob Armenian Apostolic Church Bulletin. **SUNDAY-SCHOOL:** Yes. **LIBRARY:** Yes. **CONTACT PERSON:** Rev. Fr. Datev Tatoulian, Parish Priest.

Washington State

(207)
THE ARMENIAN CHURCH OF SEATTLE
P.O. BOX 1266   **(206) 746-8198**
MERCER ISLAND, WASHINGTON 98040   **(206) 232-2932**

DATE FOUNDED: 1981. **PUBLICATION:** The Armenian Church of Seattle Newsletter. **CONTACT PERSON:** Onnig Zerounian, Chairman & Parish Council.

Armenian Evangelical Churches
ARMENIAN EVANGELICAL
UNION
1743 WEST VARTIKIAN AVENUE
FRESNO, CALIFORNIA 93711
(209) 431-7718   (209) 435-0500

California

(208)
ARMENIAN BROTHERHOOD BIBLE CHURCH
1480 EAST WASHINGTON BLVD.
PASADENA, CALIFORNIA 91104   (818) 794-8717 (818) 797-8985
CLERGYMAN: Rev. Joseph Matossian, Pastor. **DATE FOUNDED:** 1971.
SATURDAY/SUNDAY-SCHOOL: Yes.

(209)
ARMENIAN CHURCH OF THE NAZARENE
411 EAST ACACIA AVENUE
GLENDALE, CALIFORNIA 91205   (818) 244-9920
CLERGYMAN: Rev. Habib Alajaji. **DATE FOUNDED:** 1979. **PUBLICA-**
TION: Armenian Church of Nazarene Newsletter. **SATURDAY/SUN-**
DAY-SCHOOL: Yes. **BOOK SELLING SERVICE:** Available. **CONTACT:**
Church Office.

(210)
ARMENIAN EVANGELICAL BRETHREN CHURCH
3200 LONDON
LOS ANGELES, CALIFORNIA 90026   (213) 483-7265

(211)
ARMENIAN EVANGELICAL BRETHREN CHURCH
1576 EAST WASHINGTON BLVD.
PASADENA, CALIFORNIA 91104   (818) 794-9834 (818) 794-7804
CLERGYMAN: Rev. Vahram Touryan, Pastor. **DATE FOUNDED:** 1933.
DATE CONSECRATED: 1960. **SATURDAY/SUNDAY-SCHOOL:** Yes.

(213)
ARMENIAN EVANGELICAL CHURCH OF HOLLYWOOD
4904 FOUNTAIN AVENUE
LOS ANGELES, CALIFORNIA 90029   (818) 794-0232
CLERGYMAN: Rev. H. Abraham Chaparian, Pastor.

(215)
ARMENIAN PENTECOSTAL CHURCH
1220 WEST WHITTIER BLVD.
MONTEBELLO, CALIFORNIA 90640 **(213) 728-8179**
CLERGYMAN: The Rev. Ardavast Minassian, Pastor.

(216)
BETHEL ARMENIAN EVANGELICAL CHURCH
1620 IRVING STREET
SAN FRANCISCO, CALIFORNIA 94122 **(415) 836-4443**
CLERGYMAN: Rev. James Kazarian, and Rev. Hovagimian.

(217)
CALVARY ARMENIAN CONGREGATIONAL CHURCH
725 BROTHERHOOD WAY
SAN FRANCISCO, CALIFORNIA 94132 **(415) 566-0717**
CLERGYMAN: The Rev. L. Nishan Bakalian, Pastor. **DATE FOUNDED:** 1926. **PUBLICATION:** Calvary Messenger. **SUNDAY-SCHOOL:** Yes. **CONTACT PERSON:** The Rev. L. Nishan Bakalian, Pastor.

(218)
FIRST ARMENIAN PRESBYTERIAN CHURCH
430 SOUTH FIRST STREET
FRESNO, CALIFORNIA 93702 **(209) 237-6638**
CLERGYMAN: Rev. Bernard Guekguezian, Senior Pastor. **DATE FOUNDED:** 1897. **DATE CONSECRATED:** 1897. **PUBLICATION:** Lifeline. **SATURDAY/SUNDAY-SCHOOL:** Yes. **LIBRARY:** Yes. **CONTACT PERSON:** Anita Console, Secretary.

(219)
IMMANUEL ARMENIAN CONGREGATIONAL CHURCH
9516 DOWNEY AVENUE
DOWNEY, CALIFORNIA 90240 **(213) 862-7012**
CLERGYMAN: Rev. Edward Tovmassian, Pastor. **PUBLICATION:** Immanuel.

(220)
PILGRIM ARMENIAN CONGREGATIONAL CHURCH
3673 NORTH FIRST STREET
FRESNO, CALIFORNIA 93726 **(209) 229-2915**
CLERGYMAN: Rev. Roger A. D. Minassian, Pastor. **PUBLICATION:** Pilgrims Progress. **DATE FOUNDED:** 1901. **DATE CONSECRATED:** 1901. **SUNDAY-SCHOOL:** Yes. **LIBRARY:** Yes. **CONTACT PERSON:** Rev. Roger Minassian.

(221)
SAINT NAREG CHURCH OF THE NAZARENE
113 SOUTH 4th STREET
MONTEBELLO, CALIFORNIA 90640   **(213) 721-6490**
CLERGYMAN: Rev. Krikor Haleblian, Pastor. **DATE FOUNDED:** 1981.
DATE CONSECRATED: 1981. **SUNDAY-SCHOOL:** Yes. **CONTACT**
PERSON: Rev. Krikor Haleblian, Pastor.

(222)
UNITED ARMENIAN CONGREGATIONAL CHURCH
3480 CAHUENGA BLVD.
LOS ANGELES, CALIFORNIA 90068   **(213) 851-5265**
CLERGYMAN: Rev. Berdj Djambazian, Pastor.

Illinois

(223)
ARMENIAN CONGREGATIONAL CHURCH OF CHICAGO
5430 NORTH SHERIDAN ROAD
CHICAGO, ILLINOIS 60640   **(312) 784-2962**
CLERGYMAN: Rev. Barkev N. Darakjian, Pastor. **DATE FOUNDED:**
1916. **PUBLICATION:** Lantern. **SUNDAY-SCHOOL:** Yes. **CONTACT**
PERSON: Rev. Barkev N. Darakjian.

Massachusetts

(224)
THE ARMENIAN EVANGELICAL CHURCH OF THE MARTYRS
20-22 ORMOND STREET
WORCESTER, MASSACHUSETTS 01609   **(617) 753-7650**
CLERGYMAN: Rev. Manasseh Shnorhokian, Pastor. **DATE FOUNDED:**
1892. **SUNDAY SCHOOL:** Yes. **SCHOLARSHIPS, GRANTS, LOANS:**
Available. **CONTACT PERSON:** Hrant Tashjian, Moderator.

(225)
ARMENIAN MEMORIAL CONGREGATIONAL CHURCH
32 BIGELOW AVENUE
WATERTOWN, MASSACHUSETTS 02172   **(617) 923-0498**

CLERGYMAN: Rev. Ron Tovmassian, Pastor. **DATE CONSECRATED:**
1949. **PUBLICATION:** Armenian Memorial Congregational Church Bulletin. **SUNDAY-SCHOOL:** Yes. **CONTACT PERSON:** Rev. Ron Tovmassian.

(226)
FIRST ARMENIAN CHURCH OF BELMONT
380 CONCORD AVENUE
BELMONT, MASSACHUSETTS 02178   **(617) 484-4779**

CLERGYMAN: The Rev. Vartan Hartunian, Pastor. DATE FOUNDED: 1892. DATE CONSECRATED: 1908. PUBLICATION: First Armenian church of Belmont Bulletin. SUNDAY-SCHOOL: Yes. BOOK SELLING SERVICE: Available. SCHOLARSHIPS, GRANTS, LOANS: Available. LIBRARY: Yes. CONTACT PERSON: Rev. Vartan Hartunian, Pastor.

Michigan

(227)
ARMENIAN CONGREGATIONAL CHURCH OF GREATER DETROIT
26210 WEST 12 MILE ROAD
P.O. BOX 531
SOUTHFIELD, MICHIGAN 48034   (313) 352-0680
CLERGYMAN: The Rev. Dr. Vahan Tootikian, Pastor. DATE FOUNDED: 1917. DATE CONSECRATED: New church, 1967. PUBLICATION: Armenian Congregational Church Bulletin. SATURDAY/SUNDAY-SCHOOL: Yes: LIBRARY: Yes. CONTACT PERSON: The Rev. Dr. Vahan H. Tootikian, Minister.

New Hampshire

(228)
ARARAT ARMENIAN CONGREGATIONAL CHURCH
4 SALEM STREET
SALEM, NEW HAMPSHIRE 03079   (603) 898-7042
CLERGYMAN: Rev. John Mokkosian, Pastor. DATE FOUNDED: 1912. DATE CONSECRATED: 1913. PUBLICATION: Mount Ararat News. SUNDAY-SCHOOL: Yes. LIBRARY: Yes. CONTACT PERSON: Rev. John Mokkosian, Pastor.

New Jersey

(229)
ARMENIAN PRESBYTERIAN CHURCH
140 FOREST AVENUE
PARAMUS, NEW JERSEY 07652   (201) 265-8585
CLERGYMAN: Rev. Karl Avakian, Pastor.

New York

(230)
THE ARMENIAN EVANGELICAL CHURCH OF NEW YORK
152 EAST 34th STREET
NEW YORK, NEW YORK 10016   (212) 685-3177
CLERGYMAN: The Rev. Herald G. Hassessian. DATE FOUNDED: 1896. PUBLICATION: The Armenian Evangelical Church of New York Bulletin.

(231)
UNITED ARMENIAN CALVARY CONGREGATIONAL CHURCH
P.O. BOX 805
9th AND EAGLE STREETS
TROY, NEW YORK 12180   (518) 237-6137
CLERGYMAN: Rev. William J. Hammann, Pastor.

Pennsylvania
(232)
ARMENIAN MARTYRS' CONGREGATIONAL CHURCH
100 NORTH EDMONDS AVENUE   (215) 446-3330
HAVERTOWN, PENNSYLVANIA 19083   (215) 853-3000

CONTACT PERSON: The Rev. Dr. Soghomon Nuyujukian, Pastor.

Rhode Island
(233)
ARMENIAN EUPHRATES EVANGELICAL CHURCH
13 FRANKLIN STREET
PROVIDENCE, RHODE ISLAND 02903   (401) 751-4568
CLERGYMAN: Rev. John Zarifian, Pastor. **DATE FOUNDED:** 1889.
DATE CONSECRATED: 1892. **PUBLICATION:** Armenian Euphrates
Evangelical Church Newsletter. **SUNDAY-SCHOOL:** Yes. **CONTACT
PERSON:** Rev. John Zarifian, Pastor.

Armenian Roman Catholic Churches
HOLY CROSS ARMENIAN CATHOLIC CHURCH
100 MT. AUBURN STREET
CAMBRIDGE, MASSACHUSETTS 02138
(617) 547-2122

California
(234)
ARMENIAN CATHOLIC CHURCH QUEEN OF MARTYRS
1339 PLEASANT AVENUE
LOS ANGELES, CALIFORNIA 90033   (213) 261-9898
CLERGYMAN: The Rev. Michael Akian, Pastor.

Massachusetts

(235)
HOLY CROSS ARMENIAN CATHOLIC CHURCH
P.O. BOX 15
100 MOUNT AUBURN STREET
CAMBRIDGE, MASSACHUSETTS 02138   (617) 547-2122
CLERGYMAN: Fr. Luke Arakelian.

Michigan

(236)
SAINT VARTAN ARMENIAN CATHOLIC CHURCH
8541 GREENFIELD ROAD
DETROIT, MICHIGAN 48228   (313) 584-3345

CLERGYMAN: Monsignor Joseph Kalajian. DATE FOUNDED: 1948.
PUBLICATION: Vartenic. SATURDAY/SUNDAY-SCHOOL: Yes. BOOK
SELLING SERVICE: Available: LIBRARY: Yes. CONTACT PERSON:
Monsignor Joseph Kalajian.

New Jersey

(237)
SACRED HEART ARMENIAN CATHOLIC CHURCH
44 MARY STREET
PATERSON, NEW JERSEY 07503   (201) 523-0447
CLERGYMAN: Rev. Elias Boustany.

Pennsylvania

(238)
SAINT MARK'S ARMENIAN CATHOLIC CHURCH
400 HAVERFORD ROAD
WYNNEWOOD, PENNSYLVANIA 19096   (215) 896-7789

CLERGYMAN: Most Rev. Nerses Setian, Pastor. DATE FOUNDED:
1924. PUBLICATION: Saint Mark's Armenian Catholic Church Newsletter. CONTACT PERSON: Patrick J. Dempsey.

Sunday-Schools
California

(239)
ARMENIAN APOSTOLIC CHURCH OF SANTA CLARA VALLEY SUN-
DAY-SCHOOL
11370 SOUTH STELLING
CUPERTINO, CALIFORNIA 95014   (408) 257-6743

DATE FOUNDED: 1964. SPONSORING ORGANIZATION: Armenian
Apostolic Church of Santa Clara Valley. SUBJECTS OFFERED: Arme-
nian language, culture, history and religious education. GRADE LEV-
ELS: Beginning, intermediate, advanced, and adult. ENROLLMENT: 25

girls, 15 boys, total: 40. **CONTACT PERSON:** Susan Movsesian, Superintendent.

(240)
ARMENIAN BROTHERHOOD BIBLE CHURCH SUNDAY-SCHOOL
1480 EAST WASHINGTON BLVD.
PASADENA, CALIFORNIA 91104   **(818) 794-8717**
SUBJECTS OFFERED: Armenian language, and religious education.
GRADE LEVELS: Beginning, intermediate, advanced, and adult.
ENROLLMENT: 60 girls, 45 boys, total: 105. **CONTACT PERSON:**
Kevork Kouyoumjian, Superintendent.

(241)
ARMENIAN CHURCH OF THE NAZARENE SUNDAY-SCHOOL
411 EAST ACACIA AVENUE
GLENDALE, CALIFORNIA 91205   **(818) 244-9920**
DATE FOUNDED: 1980. **SPONSORING ORGANIZATION:** Armenian
Church of the Nazarene. **SUBJECTS OFFERED:** Armenian language
and religious education. **GRADE LEVELS:** Beginning. **ENROLLMENT:**
Total: 45. **CONTACT:** Church Office.

(242)
ARMENIAN EVANGELICAL BRETHREN CHURCH SUNDAY-SCHOOL
1576 EAST WASHINGTON BLVD.
PASADENA, CALIFORNIA 91104   **(818) 794-9834 (818) 794-7804**
DATE FOUNDED: 1965. **SPONSORING ORGANIZATION:** Armenian
Evangelical Brethren Church. **SUBJECTS OFFERED:** Armenian language, culture, history, and religious education. **GRADE LEVELS:**
Beginning, intermediate, advanced, and adult. **ENROLLMENT:** 46 girls,
42 boys, total: 88. **CONTACT PERSON:** Ashken Aroyan, Principal.

(243)
CALVARY ARMENIAN CONGREGATIONAL CHURCH SUNDAY
SCHOOL
725 BROTHERHOOD WAY
SAN FRANCISCO, CALIFORNIA 94132   **(415) 566-0717**
DATE FOUNDED: 1926. **SPONSORING ORGANIZATION:** Calvary
Armenian Congregational Church. **SUBJECTS OFFERED:** Religious
education. **GRADE LEVELS:** Beginning, intermediate, and youth group.
ENROLLMENT: 18 girls, 14 boys, total: 32. **CONTACT PERSON:** Rev.
Laurence Nishan Bakalian.

(244)
HOLY CROSS ARMENIAN APOSTOLIC CATHEDRAL SUNDAY-SCHOOL
900 WEST LINCOLN AVENUE
MONTEBELLO, CALIFORNIA 90640   **(213) 727-1114**
DATE FOUNDED: 1979. SPONSORING ORGANIZATION: Holy Cross Armenian Cathedral. SUBJECTS OFFERED: Armenian language, history, religious education, and religious songs. GRADE LEVELS: Beginning, intermediate and advanced. ENROLLMENT: 60 girls, 55 boys, total: 115. CONTACT PERSON: Rev. Fr. Papken Manuelian, Pastor.

(245)
HOLY TRINITY ARMENIAN APOSTOLIC CHURCH SUNDAY-SCHOOL
P.O. BOX 1865
2226 EAST VENTURA AVENUE
FRESNO, CALIFORNIA 93721   **(209) 486-1142 (209) 486-1141**

(246)
PILGRIM ARMENIAN CONGREGATIONAL CHURCH
SUNDAY SCHOOL
3673 NORTH FIRST STREET
FRESNO, CALIFORNIA 93710   **(209) 229-2915**
DATE FOUNDED: 1901. SPONSORING ORGANIZATION: Pilgrim Armenian Congregational Church. SUBJECTS OFFERED: Armenian culture, history, and religious education. GRADE LEVELS: Beginning, intermediate, advanced and adult. ENROLLMENT: 55 girls, 70 boys, total: 125. CONTACT PERSON: Joan Hensleit, Director of Christian Education.

(247)
SAINT GREGORY ARMENIAN APOSTOLIC CHURCH SUNDAY-SCHOOL
2215 EAST COLORADO BLVD.
PASADENA, CALIFORNIAN 91107   **(818) 449-1523**

SPONSORING ORGANIZATION: Saint Gregory Armenian Church. SUBJECTS OFFERED: Armenian history, folk dance, songs, and church history. GRADE LEVELS: Beginning and intermediate. ENROLLMENT: Total: 80. CONTACT PERSON: Very Rev. Fr. Moushegh Tashjian, Parish Priest.

(248)
SAINT JOHN ARMENIAN APOSTOLIC CHURCH SUNDAY-SCHOOL
4473-30th STREET
SAN DIEGO, CALIFORNIA 92116   **(619) 562-1533 (619) 284-7179**

DATE FOUNDED: 1977. SPONSORING ORGANIZATION: Saint John Armenian Apostolic Church. SUBJECTS OFFERED: Armenian language, culture, and religious education. GRADE LEVELS: Beginning, and intermediate. **ENROLLMENT:** 14 girls, 11 boys, total: 25. **CONTACT PERSON:** Berjouhi Ghazil, Director.

(249)
SAINT MARY ARMENIAN CHURCH OF YETTEM SUNDAY-SCHOOL
14395 AVENUE 384
YETTEM, CALIFORNIA 93670   (209) 528-6892 (209) 591-9996
DATE FOUNDED: 1944. **SPONSORING ORGANIZATION:** Saint Mary Armenian Church of Yettem. **SUBJECTS OFFERED:** Armenian culture, history, and religious education. **GRADE LEVELS:** Beginning, intermediate, and advanced. **ENROLLMENT:** Total: 34. **CONTACT PERSON:** Bea Soxman, Superintendent.

(250)
SAINT NAREG CHURCH OF THE NAZARENE
113 SOUTH 4th STREET
MONTEBELLO, CALIFORNIA 90640   (213) 721-6490
DATE FOUNDED: 1983. **SPONSORING ORGANIZATION:** Saint Nareg Church of the Nazarene. **SUBJECTS OFFERED:** Religious education and English language. **GRADE LEVELS:** Beginning, intermediate, advanced and adult. **ENROLLMENT:** Total: 20. **CONTACT PERSON:** Krikor Haleblian, Pastor, and Bedros Hamalian, Director.

(251)
SAINT PAUL ARMENIAN CHURCH SUNDAY-SCHOOL
3767 NORTH FIRST STREET
FRESNO, CALIFORNIA 93726   (209) 226-6343
DATE FOUNDED: 1949. **SPONSORING ORGANIZATION:** Saint Paul Armenian Church. **SUBJECTS OFFERED:** Armenian language, culture, history and religious education. **GRADE LEVELS:** Beginning, intermediate, advanced and adult. **ENROLLMENT:** 90 girls, 60 boys, total: 150. **CONTACT PERSON:** Archpriest Shahe Altounian, Parish Priest.

(252)
SAINT PETER ARMENIAN APOSTOLIC CHURCH SUNDAY-SCHOOL
17231 SHERMAN WAY
VAN NUYS, CALIFORNIA 91406   (818) 344-4860
DATE FOUNDED: 1958. **SPONSORING ORGANIZATION:** Saint Peter Armenian Church. **SUBJECTS OFFERED:** Armenian language, culture, history, religious education and English language. **GRADE LEVELS:** Beginning and intermediate. **ENROLLMENT:** Total: 90. **CONTACT PERSON:** Fr. Shahe Avak Kahana Semerdjian, Pastor.

(253)
SAINTS SAHAG-MESROB ARMENIAN APOSTOLIC CHURCH SUN-DAY-SCHOOL
1249 "F" STREET
REEDLEY, CALIFORNIA 93654   (209) 638-2740 (209) 638-7483
DATE FOUNDED: 1925. **SPONSORING ORGANIZATION:** Saints Sahag-Mesrob Armenian Church. **SUBJECTS OFFERED:** Armenian language, culture, history, and religious education. **GRADE LEVELS:** Beginning, intermediate, advanced and adult. **CONTACT PERSON:** Rev. Fr. Datev Tatoulian, Parish Priest.

Connecticut

(254)
SAINT STEPHEN'S ARMENIAN APOSTOLIC CHURCH SUNDAY-SCHOOL
167 TREMONT STREET
NEW BRITAIN, CONNECTICUT 06051   (203) 523-5712

District of Columbia
Washington D.C.

(255)
SAINT MARY'S ARMENIAN APOSTOLIC CHURCH SUNDAY-SCHOOL
4125 FESSENDEN STREET N.W.
WASHINGTON, D.C. 20016   (202) 363-1923 (301) 942-2434
DATE FOUNDED: 1960. **SPONSORING ORGANIZATION:** Saint Mary's Armenian Apostolic Church. **SUBJECTS OFFERED:** Armenian language, culture, history, religious education, songs, and dance. **GRADE LEVELS:** Beginning, intermediate and advanced. **ENROLLMENT:** Total: 75. **CONTACT PERSON:** Rev. Vertanes Kalayjian, Pastor.

Florida

(256)
SAINT JOHN THE BAPTIST ARMENIAN APOSTOLIC CHURCH SUN-DAY-SCHOOL
120 N.E. 16th STREET
MIAMI, FLORIDA 33132   (305) 371-4484
DATE FOUNDED: 1953. **SPONSORING ORGANIZATION:** Young Women's Guild of Saint John The Baptist Armenian Apostolic Church. **SUBJECTS OFFERED:** Armenian language, culture, history and religious

education. **GRADE LEVELS:** Beginning and intermediate. **ENROLL-MENT:** 10 girls, 10 boys, total: 20. **CONTACT PERSON:** Audrey Pilafian, Superintendent.

Illinois

(257)
ALL SAINTS' ARMENIAN APOSTOLIC CHURCH SUNDAY-SCHOOL
1701 NORTH GREENWOOD
GLENVIEW, ILLINOIS 60025   **(312) 438-7484 (312) 769-1059**
CONTACT PERSON: Diana Kokouzian.

(258)
ARMENIAN CONGREGATIONAL CHURCH OF CHICAGO SUNDAY-SCHOOL
5430 NORTH SHERIDAN ROAD
CHICAGO, ILLINOIS 60640   **(312) 784-2962**

DATE FOUNDED: 1940. **SPONSORING ORGANIZATION:** Armenian Congregational Church of Chicago. **SUBJECTS:** Religious education. **GRADE LEVELS:** Beginning and intermediate. **ENROLLMENT:** Total: 20. **CONTACT PERSON:** Karoon Gueyikian, Superintendent.

(259)
SAINT GREGORY THE ILLUMINATOR ARMENIAN APOSTOLIC CHURCH
SUNDAY-SCHOOL
1732 MAPLE STREET
GRANITE CITY, ILLINOIS 62040   **(618) 452-0424**
CONTACT PERSON: Rita Garabedian.

(260)
SAINT PAUL ARMENIAN APOSTOLIC CHURCH SUNDAY-SCHOOL
921 GAGE LANE
LAKE FOREST, ILLINOIS 60045   **(312) 234-4026**
CONTACT PERSON: Katherine Mikaelian.

Maryland

(261)
HAMASDEGH ARMENIAN SUNDAY-SCHOOL
4906 FLINT DRIVE
CHEVY CHASE, MARYLAND 20816   **(301) 229-6880**

DATE FOUNDED: 1969. SPONSORING ORGANIZATION: Soorph Khatch Armenian Apostolic Church. SUBJECTS OFFERED: Armenian language, culture, history, religious education, English language and dance. GRADE LEVELS: Beginning and intermediate. ENROLLMENT: 55 girls, 45 boys, total: 100. CONTACT PERSON: Sahag Dardarian.

Massachusetts

(262)
ARMENIAN EVANGELICAL CHURCH OF THE MARTYRS SUNDAY-SCHOOL
22-20 ORMOND STREET
WORCESTER, MASSACHUSETTS 01609   **(617) 753-7650**

DATE FOUNDED: 1892. SPONSORING ORGANIZATION: Armenian Evangelical Church of the Martyrs. SUBJECTS OFFERED: Religious education and English language. GRADE LEVELS: Beginning and intermediate. ENROLLMENT: Total: 5. CONTACT PERSON: Linda Bogosian.

(263)
ARMENIAN MEMORIAL CONGREGATIONAL CHURCH SUNDAY-SCHOOL
32 BIGELOW AVENUE
WATERTOWN, MASSACHUSETTS 02172   **(617) 923-0498**

SPONSORING ORGANIZATION: Armenian Memorial Congregational Church. SUBJECTS OFFERED: Religious education. GRADE LEVELS: Beginning and intermediate. ENROLLMENT: 20 girls, 20 boys, total: 40. CONTACT PERSON: Rev. Ron Tovmassian, Minister.

(264)
FIRST ARMENIAN CHURCH OF BELMONT SUNDAY-SCHOOL
380 CONCORD AVENUE
BELMONT, MASSACHUSETTS 02178(617) 484-4779 (617) 484-0776

DATE FOUNDED: 1960. SPONSORING ORGANIZATION: First Armenian Church of Belmont. SUBJECTS OFFERED: Armenian language, culture, history, religious education, English language and Christianity. GRADE LEVELS: Beginning, intermediate, and high school. ENROLLMENT: 40 girls, 40 boys, total: 80. CONTACT PERSON: The Rev. Joanne G. Hartunian, Minister to Youth.

(265)
HOLY TRINITY ARMENIAN APOSTOLIC CHURCH SUNDAY-SCHOOL
635 GROVE STREET
WORCESTER, MASSACHUSETTS 01615   **(617) 842-2438**

CONTACT PERSON: Nvart Asadoorian.

(266)
SAINT ASDVADZADZIN ARMENIAN APOSTOLIC CHURCH SUNDAY-SCHOOL
211 CHURCH STREET
WHITINSVILLE, MASSACHUSETTS 01588   **(617) 234-8724**
CONTACT PERSON: Debbie Bedrosian.

(267)
SAINT GREGORY ARMENIAN APOSTOLIC CHURCH SUNDAY-SCHOOL
135 GOODWIN STREET
INDIAN ORCHARD, MASSACHUSETTS 01151   **(413) 598-8760**
CONTACT PERSON: Alice Hagopian.

(268)
SAINT GREGORY ARMENIAN APOSTOLIC CHURCH OF MERRI-MACK VALLEY
SUNDAY-SCHOOL
158 MAIN STREET
NORTH ANDOVER, MASSACHUSETTS 01845   **(617) 685-5038**
DATE FOUNDED: 1970. SPONSORING ORGANIZATION: Armenian Relief Society. SUBJECTS OFFERED: Armenian language, culture, history and religious education. GRADE LEVELS: Beginning and intermediate. ENROLLMENT: 20 girls, 10 boys, total: 30. CONTACT PERSON: Nora Daghlian.

(269)
SAINT JAMES ARMENIAN APOSTOLIC CHURCH SUNDAY-SCHOOL
465 MT. AUBURN STREET
WATERTOWN, MASSACHUSETTS 02172   **(617) 923-8860**
DATE FOUNDED: 1936. SPONSORING ORGANIZATION: Saint James Armenian Apostolic Church. SUBJECTS OFFERED: Armenian language, culture, history and religious education. GRADE LEVELS: Beginning, intermediate, advanced, and adult. ENROLLMENT: 158 girls, 143 boys, total: 301. CONTACT PERSON: Rev. Dajad A. Davidian, Pastor.

(270)
SAINT STEPHEN'S ARMENIAN APOSTOLIC CHURCH SUNDAY-SCHOOL
38 ELTON AVENUE
WATERTOWN, MASSACHUSETTS 02172   **(617) 899-4040**
CONTACT PERSON: Margaret Stepanian.

Michigan

(271)
ARMENIAN CONGREGATIONAL CHURCH OF GREATER DETROIT SUNDAY-SCHOOL
26210 WEST 12 MILE ROAD
SOUTHFIELD, MICHIGAN 48034   **(313) 352-0680**

DATE FOUNDED: 1917. **SPONSORING ORGANIZATION:** Armenian Congregational Church of Greater Detroit. **SUBJECTS OFFERED:** Armenian language, culture, history, and religious education. **GRADE LEVELS:** Beginning, intermediate, advanced and adult. **ENROLLMENT:** 40 girls, 45 boys, total: 85. **CONTACT PERSON:** Rev. Dr. Vahan H. Tootikian.

(272)
SAINT SARKIS ARMENIAN APOSTOLIC CHURCH
19300 FORD ROAD
DEARBORN, MICHIGAN 48128   **(313) 383-2453**

New Hampshire

(273)
ARARAT ARMENIAN CONGREGATIONAL CHURCH SUNDAY-SCHOOL
4 SALEM STREET
SALEM, NEW HAMPSHIRE 03079   **(603) 898-7042**

SPONSORING ORGANIZATION: Ararat Armenian Congregational Church. **SUBJECTS OFFERED:** Religious education and English language. **GRADE LEVELS:** Beginning, intermediate, advanced, and adult. **ENROLLMENT:** Total: 50. **CONTACT PERSON:** Rev. John Mokkosian Pastor.

New Jersey

(274)
ARARATIAN ARMENIAN SUNDAY-SCHOOL
200 WEST MOUNT PLEASANT AVENUE
LIVINGSTON, NEW JERSEY 07039   **(201) 533-9794**

DATE FOUNDED: 1950. **SPONSORING ORGANIZATION:** Saint Mary Armenian Apostolic Church. **SUBJECTS OFFERED:** Armenian language, culture, history and religious education. **GRADE LEVELS:** Beginning, intermediate, advanced and adult. **ENROLLMENT:** 42 girls, 35 boys, total: 77. **CONTACT PERSON:** Dr. Richard Kopp, Superintendent.

(275)
NAREG ARMENIAN SUNDAY-SCHOOL
461 BERGEN BLVD.
RIDGEFIELD, NEW JERSEY 07657   (201) 943-2950 (201) 943-9650
DATE FOUNDED: 1959. **SPONSORING ORGANIZATION:** Saints Vartanantz Armenian Apostolic Church. **SUBJECTS OFFERED:** Armenian language, culture, history, religious education and English language. **GRADE LEVELS:** Beginning and intermediate. **ENROLLMENT:** Total: 101. **CONTACT PERSON:** Archpriest Vahrich Shirinian and Michael Mirakian.

(276)
SAINT LEON ARMENIAN APOSTOLIC CHURCH SUNDAY-SCHOOL
12-61 SADDLE RIVER ROAD
FAIR LAWN, NEW JERSEY 07410   **(201) 791-2862**
DATE FOUNDED: 1847. **SPONSORING ORGANIZATION:** Saint Leon Armenian Apostolic Church. **SUBJECTS OFFERED:** Armenian language, culture, history, and religious education. **GRADE LEVELS:** Beginning, intermediate and advanced. **ENROLLMENT:** 45 girls, 55 boys, total: 100. **CONTACT PERSON:** Berjdouhi Feredjian, Superintendent.

(277)
SAINT THOMAS ARMENIAN APOSTOLIC CHURCH SUNDAY-SCHOOL
P.O. BOX 53
TENAFLY, NEW JERSEY 07670   **(201) 567-5446**
DATE FOUNDED: 1958. **SPONSORING ORGANIZATION:** Saint Thomas Armenian Apostolic Church. **SUBJECTS OFFERED:** Armenian language, culture, history, religious education and dance. **ENROLLMENT:** Total: 125. **CONTACT PERSON:** Louise Kalemkerian.

New York

(278)
HOLY CROSS ARMENIAN APOSTOLIC CHURCH
101 SPRING AVENUE
TROY, NEW YORK 12180   **(518) 869-3411**
CONTACT PERSON: Lucy Sarkissian.

(279)
SAINT GREGORY THE ILLUMINATOR ARMENIAN CHURCH SUNDAY-SCHOOL
12 CORBETT AVE.
BINGHAMTON, NEW YORK 13903   **(607) 722-8801**

DATE FOUNDED: 1953. **SPONSORING ORGANIZATION:** Saint Gregory the Illuminator Armenian Church. **SUBJECTS OFFERED:** Armenian language and religious education. **GRADE LEVELS:** Beginning. **ENROLLMENT:** 7 girls, 3 boys, total: 10. **CONTACT PERSON:** Adrienne Khachadourian, Superintendent.

(280)
SAINT ILLUMINATOR'S ARMENIAN APOSTOLIC CATHEDRAL
221 EAST 27th STREET
NEW YORK, NEW YORK 10016 (718) 762-6696
CONTACT PERSON: Peter Jelalian.

(281)
SAINT SARKIS ARMENIAN APOSTOLIC CHURCH OF NIAGARA FALLS
SUNDAY-SCHOOL
300 9th STREET
NIAGARA FALLS, NEW YORK 14303 (716) 282-2587
CONTACT PERSON: Arsen Avdoian.

Pennsylvania

(282)
SAINT GREGORY THE ILLUMINATOR ARMENIAN APOSTOLIC CHURCH
SUNDAY-SCHOOL
8701 RIDGE AVENUE (215) 428-9200
PHILADELPHIA, PENNSYLVANIA 19128 (215) 428-3344

DATE FOUNDED: 1927. **SPONSORING ORGANIZATION:** Saint Gregory the Illuminator Armenian Apostolic Church. **SUBJECTS OFFERED:** Armenian language, culture, history, religious education and English language. **GRADE LEVELS:** Beginning and intermediate. **ENROLLMENT:** 25 girls, 40 boys, total: 65. **CONTACT PERSON:** Harbig Garabedian.

(283)
SAINT SAHAG AND SAINT MESROB SUNDAY-SCHOOL
630 CLOTHIER ROAD
WYNNEWOOD, PENNSYLVANIA 19096 (215) 642-4212
DATE FOUNDED: 1925. **SPONSORING ORGANIZATION:** Saint Sahag and Saint Mesrob Armenian Church. **SUBJECTS OFFERED:** Armenian language, culture and religious education. **GRADE LEVELS:** Beginning and intermediate. **ENROLLMENT:** 65 girls, 45 boys, total: 110. **CONTACT PERSON:** Adrienne H. Riser, Superintendent.

Rhode Island

(284)
ARMENIAN EUPHRATES EVANGELICAL CHURCH SUNDAY-SCHOOL
13 FRANKLIN STREET
PROVIDENCE, RHODE ISLAND 02903   **(401) 751-4568**

DATE FOUNDED: 1892. **SPONSORING ORGANIZATION:** Armenian Euphrates Evangelical Church. **SUBJECTS OFFERED:** Religious education. **GRADE LEVELS:** Beginning, intermediate, advanced, and nursery. **ENROLLMENT:** 12 girls, 8 boys, total: 20. **CONTACT PERSON:** Peggy Tatewosian, Superintendent.

(285)
SAINTS VARTANANTZ ARMENIAN APOSTOLIC CHURCH SUNDAY-SCHOOL
402 BROADWAY
PROVIDENCE, RHODE ISLAND 02909   **(401) 831-6399**

SPONSORING ORGANIZATION: Saints Vartanantz Armenian Apostolic Church. **SUBJECTS OFFERED:** Armenian language, culture, history and religious education. **GRADE LEVELS:** Beginning, intermediate, and advanced. **CONTACT PERSON:** Archpriest Dr. Mesrob Tashjian.

Texas

(285-A)
SAINT KEVORK ARMENIAN APOSTOLIC CHURCH SUNDAY-SCHOOL
3211 SYNOTT ROAD
HOUSTON, TEXAS 77082   **(713) 558-2722**

DATE FOUNDED: 1981. **SUBJECTS OFFERED:** Religious education, dance and songs. **GRADE LEVELS:** Beginning, intermediate, advanced and adult. **ENROLLMENT:** 30 girls, 40 boys, total: 70. **CONTACT PERSON:** Fr. Nersess Jebejian, Pastor and Superintendent.

Wisconsin

(286)
SAINT HAGOP'S ARMENIAN APOSTOLIC CHURCH SUNDAY-SCHOOL
4100 NORTH NEWMAN ROAD
RACINE, WISCONSIN 53406   **(414) 639-8606**

CONTACT PERSON: Helen Nelson.

(287)
SAINT MESROB ARMENIAN APOSTOLIC CHURCH SUNDAY-SCHOOL
4605 ERIE STREET
RACINE, WISCONSIN 53402 (414) 639-0531
DATE FOUNDED: 1935. **SPONSORING ORGANIZATION:** Diocese of the Armenian Church, Department of Religious Education. **SUBJECTS OFFERED:** Armenian language, culture, history, religious education and English language. **GRADE LEVELS:** Beginning, intermediate and advanced. **ENROLLMENT:** 28 girls, 27 boys, total: 55. **CONTACT PERSON:** Donna Barootian, Superintendent.

Theological Schools
California

(288)
ARMENIAN BIBLE COLLEGE
1605 EAST ELIZABETH STREET
PASADENA, CALIFORNIA 91104 (818) 791-2575
DATE FOUNDED: 1982. **DIRECTOR OF PROGRAM:** Dr. Yeghia Babikian. **DEGREES OFFERED:** Single courses and Diplomas. **CURRICULUM AND INSTRUCTORS:** Three year curriculum in Armenian Studies, English Language, Biblical Knowledge, Biblical Doctrine, Church History, Music, Ministerian Services and related sciences. **SCHOLARSHIPS, GRANTS, LOANS:** Available. **PUBLICATION:** Harvest. **CONTACT PESON:** Dr. Yeghia Babikian, Director.

(289)
FULLER THEOLOGICAL SEMINARY
ARMENIAN THEOLOGICAL STUDIES PROGRAM
135 NORTH OAKLAND AVENUE
PASADENA, CALIFORNIA 91010 (818) 449-1745
DATE FOUNDED: 1983. **DIRECTOR OF PROGRAM.** Dr. Krikor Haleblian. **DEGREES OFFERED:** Graduate Program (Ph.D.), Graduate Program (M.A.), and Single Courses. **SCHOLARSHIPS, GRANTS, LOANS:** Available. **CONTACT PERSON:** Dr. Krikor Haleblian.

New York

(290)
SAINT NERSESS ARMENIAN SEMINARY
150 STRATTON ROAD
NEW ROCHELLE, NEW YORK 10804 (914) 636-2003
CONTACT PERSON: Deacon Michael Chevian.

Section Three

NEWSPAPERS AND PERIODICALS

Newspapers
(Daily, Weekly, Monthly)

Journals and Magazines
(General Interest)

Organization Bulletins and Newsletters

Church Bulletins and Newsletters

Armenian Studies and Research Periodicals

School Bulletins and Newsletters

Newspapers
Daily, Weekly, Monthly
California

(291)
ARMENIAN OBSERVER, 1970-
ARMENIAN OBSERVER
6646 HOLLYWOOD BLVD. SUITE 207
LOS ANGELES, CALIFORNIA 90028   **(213) 467-6767**
EDITOR & PUBLISHER: Osheen Keshisian. **FREQUENCY:** Weekly.
LANGUAGE: English. **CONTENTS:** The Armenian Observer, an English
language Armenian weekly, began publication on Wednesday, December 23, 1970, in Los Angeles. An independent publication, covers the
local Armenian scene, national as well as the international news related
to the Armenian people and Armenian affairs. **CONTACT PERSON:**
Osheen Keshishian, Publisher and Editor.

(292)
ASBAREZ, 1908-
ASBAREZ PUBLISHING CO.
419 WEST COLORADO STREET
GLENDALE, CALIFORNIA 91204   **(818) 500-9363**
EDITOR: Vahe Gourjian & Serge Samoniantz. **PUBLISHER:** Asbarez
Publishing Co. **FREQUENCY:** Daily. **SUBSCRIPTION RATE:** $60. **CIR-CULATION:** 3,000. **LANGUAGE:** Armenian and English. **CONTENTS:**
Asbarez is the daily newspaper of the Armenian Revolutionary Federation which covers international, national, and local news and events for
the Armenian cause and the Armenian people worldwide. **CONTACT PERSON:** Vahe Gourjian, Managing Editor.

(293)
THE CALIFORNIA COURIER, 1958-
THE CALIFORNIA COURIER
1610 NORTH WILCOX AVENUE
LOS ANGELES, CALIFORNIA 90028   **(213) 464-8337**
EDITOR: Harut Sassounian. **PUBLISHER:** George Mason. **FRE-QUENCY:** Weekly. **SUBSCRIPTION RATE:** $25. **CIRCULATION:** 3,000.
LANGUAGE: English. **CONTENTS:** Covers news, stories, community
events, political, cultural, athletic, artistic, social events, editorials and
commentaries.

(294)
KACH NAZAR, 1970-

KACH NAZAR
1127 EAST BROADWAY
GLENDALE, CALIFORNIA 91205   **(818) 246-0125**

EDITOR & PUBLISHER: Hovanes Balayan. **LANGUAGE:** Armenian and English. **CONTENTS:** Armenian satirical periodical. Covers local and international news related to the Armenians. **CONTACT PERSON:** Hovanes Balayan.

(295)
LRAPER, 1936-

LRAPER
P.O. BOX 38821
LOS ANGELES, CALIFORNIA 90038   **(213) 467-9681**

(296)
MASSIS ARMENIAN WEEKLY, 1981-

SOCIAL DEMOCRATIC HUNCHAKIAN PARTY, WESTERN DISTRICT
1060 NORTH ALLEN AVENUE Suite 101
PASADENA, CALIFORNIA 91104   **(818) 797-7680**

EDITOR: Dr. Artin Sagherian. **PUBLISHER:** Social Democratic Hunchakian Party. **FREQUENCY:** Weekly. **SUBSCRIPTION RATE:** $30. **CIRCULATION:** 1,000. **LANGUAGE:** Armenian. **CONTENTS:** Covers news and editorials about Armenian and international subjects, news about the activities of the Armenians in Los Angeles, news and sports news from the Soviet Armenia. **CONTACT PERSON:** Krikor Khodarian, Managing Editor.

(298)
NOR GYANK, 1978-

NOR GYANK
825 EAST COLORADO STREET
GLENDALE, CALIFORNIA 91205   **(818) 240-9996**

(299)
NOR OR, 1922-

NOR OR
7466 BEVERLY BLVD. #201
LOS ANGELES, CALIFORNIA 90036 (213) 933-8248 (213) 933-3298

EDITOR: Editorial Board. **PUBLISHER:** Nor Or Publishers Association Inc. **FREQUENCY:** Semi-weekly. **LANGUAGE:** Armenian. **CONTENTS:**

Nor Or is the official publication of the Armenian Democratic Liberal Organization, Western District. Covers local and national news related to Armenians.

(300)
NOR SEROOND, 1975-

NOR SEROOND
3923 EDENHURST AVENUE
LOS ANGELES, CALIFORNIA 90039   **(213) 661-6328**

EDITOR & PUBLISHER: Sidewan Nairi. **FREQUENCY:** Monthly. **SUBSCRIPTION RATE:** $15. **CIRCULATION:** 1,600. **LANGUAGE:** Armenian, sometimes English (one page).

(301)
PAROS, 1984-

PAROS
6646 HOLLYWOOD BLVD.
LOS ANGELES, CALIFORNIA 90028   **(213) 462-0976**

EDITOR: Souren Boursalyan. **FREQUENCY:** Bi-weekly. **SUBSCRIPTION RATE:** $20. **CIRCULATION:** 2,000. **LANGUAGE:** Eastern Armenian. **CONTENTS:** Covers news and views, literature, sports, women, medical, general topics, community activities. **CONTACT PERSON:** Souren Boursalyan.

Massachusetts

(302)
THE ARMENIAN MIRROR-SPECTATOR, 1932-

THE ARMENIAN MIRROR-SPECTATOR
468 MOUNT AUBURN STREET
WATERTOWN, MASSACHUSETTS 02172   **(617) 924-4420**

EDITOR: Ara Kalaydjian. **PUBLISHER:** Armenian Democratic Liberal Organization; Baikar Association, Inc. **FREQUENCY:** Weekly. **LANGUAGE:** English.

(303)
ARMENIAN WEEKLY, 1933-

ARMENIAN WEEKLY
80 BIGELOW AVENUE
WATERTOWN, MASSACHUSETTS 02172   **(617) 926-3974**

EDITOR: Kevork Donabedian. **PUBLISHER:** Hairenik Association, Inc. **FREQUENCY:** Weekly. **LANGUAGE:** English.

(304)
BAIKAR ARMENIAN WEEKLY, 1922-

BAIKAR WEEKLY
468 MOUNT AUBURN STREET
WATERTOWN, MASSACHUSETTS 02172   (617) 924-4420

EDITOR: Krikor Keusseyan. **PUBLISHER:** Baikar Association, Inc. **FRE-QUENCY:** Weekly. **LANGUAGE:** Armenian. **CONTENTS:** Baikar is the official newspaper of the Armenian Democratic Liberal Organization. Covers cultural and political articles.

(305)
HAIRENIK, 1899-

ARMENIAN REVOLUTIONARY FEDERATION OF AMERICA
80 BIGELOW AVENUE
WATERTOWN, MASSACHUSETTS 02172   (617) 926-3974

EDITOR: Kevork Donabedian. **PUBLISHER:** Hairenik Association, Inc. **FREQUENCY:** Daily. **LANGUAGE:** Armenian (daily), English (weekly). **CONTENTS:** The oldest Armenian newspaper in the United States. Covers Armenian community news and Armenian Revolutionary Federation activities.

New York

(306)
THE ARMENIAN REPORTER, 1967-

ARMENIAN REPORTER PUBLISHING CO.
67-07 UTOPIA PARKWAY
FRESH MEADOW, NEW YORK 11365   (718) 380-3636

EDITOR: Edward K. Boghosian. **PUBLISHER:** Armenian Reporter Publishing Co., Inc. **FREQUENCY:** Weekly. **SUBSCRIPTION RATE:** $35. **CIRCULATION:** 4,800. **LANGUAGE:** English. **BOOK SELLING SERVICE:** Available. **CONTENTS:** News of the Armenian community in the nation and world-wide. **CONTACT PERSON:** Edward K. Boghosian.

Journals and Magazines
California

(307)
ABRIL MAGAZINE, 1977-

ABRIL BOOKSTORE AND PUBLISHING CO.
5450 SANTA MONICA BLVD.
LOS ANGELES, CALIFORNIA 90029   (213) 467-9483

EDITOR: Haroutoun Yeretzian. **PUBLISHER:** Abril Bookstore and Publishing Co. **FREQUENCY:** Monthly. **LANGUAGE:** Armenian. **CONTENTS:** Articles about Armenian culture.

(308)
NAVASART, 1982-

NAVASART
515 WEST BROADWAY #D
Inside Crown Foods Market
GLENDALE, CALIFORNIA 91204   (818) 241-5933

EDITOR: Armen Donoyan. **PUBLISHER:** Navasart Foundation. **FREQUENCY:** Monthly. **SUBSCRIPTION RATE:** $25. **CIRCULATION:** 1,700. **LANGUAGE:** Armenian. **BOOK SELLING SERVICE:** Available. **CONTENTS:** Armenian literary and cultural magazine. **CONTACT PERSON:** Armen Donoyan.

(309)
RAINBOW, 1984-

RAINBOW
409 WESTERN AVENUE
GLENDALE, CALIFORNIA 91201   (818) 243-6827

EDITOR & PUBLISHER: Hrant Avedisian. **FREQUENCY:** Quarterly. **SUBSCRIPTION RATE:** $10. **CIRCULATION:** 1,700. **LANGUAGE:** Armenian. **BOOK SELLING SERVICE:** Available. **CONTENTS:** Literature and the arts articles. **CONTACT PERSON:** Hrant Avedisian, Editor.

(310)
SEVAN MAGAZINE, 1982-

SEVAN MAGAZINE
5300 SANTA MONICA BLVD. SUITE 207
LOS ANGELES, CALIFORNIA 90029   (213) 460-4843

EDITOR: Madlen Karadjhyan. **PUBLISHER:** Vart Nazarian. **FREQUENCY:** Bi-weekly. **SUBSCRIPTION RATE:** $25. **CIRCULATION:** 1,500. **LANGUAGE:** Armenian. **CONTENTS:** Covers Armenian community activities, literature and the arts articles.

Massachusetts

(311)
THE ARMENIAN REVIEW, 1948-

THE ARMENIAN REVIEW, INC.
36 ELTON AVENUE
WATERTOWN, MASSACHUSETTS 02172   (617) 926-4037

EDITOR: Gerard J. Libaridian. **PUBLISHER:** The Armenian Review, Inc. **FREQUENCY:** Quarterly. **SUBSCRIPTION RATE:** $15. **CIRCULATION:** 1,000. **LANGUAGE:** English. **CONTENTS:** Multi-disciplinary academic journal devoted to all periods of Armenian history and culture. **CONTACT PERSON:** Gerard J. Libaridian.

New Jersey

(312)

ARARAT LITERARY QUARTERLY, 1959-

ARMENIAN GENERAL BENEVOLENT UNION OF AMERICA
585 SADDLE RIVER ROAD
SADDLE BROOK, NEW JERSEY 07662   **(201) 797-7600**

EDITOR: Leo Hamalian. **PUBLISHER:** Armenian General Benevolent Union of America. **FREQUENCY:** Quarterly. **SUBSCRIPTION RATE:** $10 for one year, $19 for two years, $28 for three years. **CIRCULATION:** 2,000. **LANGUAGE:** English. **CONTENTS:** A literary quarterly, featuring Armenian subjects, prominent writers such as W. Saroyan, and new writers of Armenian origin. **CONTACT PERSON:** Terry Chisnolm, Director of Publications.

(313)

ERITASSART HAYASTAN, 1903-

SOCIAL DEMOCRATIC HUNCHAKIAN PARTY OF AMERICA
353 FOREST AVENUE
PARAMUS, NEW JERSEY 07652   **(201) 262-5363**

EDITOR: Arsen Jerejian. **PUBLISHER:** Social Democratic Hunchakian Party of America. **FREQUENCY:** Monthly. **SUBSCRIPTION RATE:** $15. **CIRCULATION:** 1,100. **LANGUAGE:** Armenian. **CONTENTS:** Each issue contains articles about Armenian culture, history, national rights, events, past and present of the Social Democratic Hunchakian Party, and articles related to the advancement of the mother country, Armenia.

(314)

HOOSHARAR MIOUTUNE, 1912-

ARMENIAN GENERAL BENEVOLENT UNION OF AMERICA
585 SADDLE RIVER ROAD
SADDLE BROOK, NEW JERSEY 07662   **(201) 797-7600**

EDITOR: Antranik L. Poladian. **PUBLISHER:** Armenian General Benevolent Union of America. **FREQUENCY:** Monthly. **SUBSCRIPTION RATE:** $10. **CIRCULATION:** 5,000. **LANGUAGE:** Armenian. **CONTENTS:** Communiques and reports pertaining to the activities of A.G.B.U.; review of cultural, historical, literary and educational activities. **CONTACT PERSON:** Antranik L. Poladian.

(315)

HOOSHARAR, 1914-

ARMENIAN GENERAL BENEVOLENT UNION OF AMERICA
585 SADDLE RIVER ROAD
SADDLE BROOK, NEW JERSEY 07662   **(201) 797-7600**

EDITOR: Terry Chisnolm. **PUBLISHER:** Armenian General Benevolent Union of America. **FREQUENCY:** Ten times a year. **SUBSCRIPTION RATE:** $10. **CIRCULATION:** 6,500. **LANGUAGE:** English. **BOOK SELLING SERVICE:** Available. **CONTENTS:** Covers members' activities in sports, culture, drama, dance and education, plus outside reviews of film, art, literature, and profiles of people. **CONTACT PERSON:** Terry Chisnolm, Director of Publications.

(316)
PHOENIX, 1971-

PHOENIX
P.O. BOX 132
DUMONT, NEW JERSEY 07628   **(201) 385-8225**
EDITOR: Pierre Papazian. **FREQUENCY:** Quarterly. **SUBSCRIPTION RATE:** $10. **LANGUAGE:** English. **CONTENTS:** Phoenix is a newsletter of fact, opinion, and analysis of Armenian and international affairs.

Organization
Bulletins and Newsletters
California

(317)
A.A.I.C. ALUMNI MONITOR, 1983-

AMERICAN ARMENIAN INTERNATIONAL COLLEGE
1950 THIRD STREET
LA VERNE, CALIFORNIA 91759   **(714) 593-0432**
FREQUENCY: Six times a year. **SUBSCRIPTION RATE:** Free. **CIRCULATION:** 500. **LANGUAGE:** Armenian and English. **CONTENTS:** Covers alumni news, college events, events of interests to the Alumni Association, and community news. **CONTACT PERSON:** Hovsep Kanimian.

(318)
ABACA NEWSLETTER, 1982-

ARMENIAN BUSINESS ALLIANCE OF CALIFORNIA
5621 SUNSET BLVD.
LOS ANGELES, CALIFORNIA 90028   **(213) 667-9070**

(319)
ARARAT HYELIGHTS, 1983-

ARARAT HOME OF LOS ANGELES
3730 WEST 27th STREET
LOS ANGELES, CALIFORNIA 90018   **(213) 733-5502**
EDITOR: Rosine De Cervantes and Diane Ansorian. **PUBLISHER:**

Ararat Home of Los Angeles. **FREQUENCY:** Quarterly. **SUBSCRIPTION RATE:** Free. **CIRCULATION:** 17,000. **LANGUAGE:** English. **CONTENTS:** Covers news of the Ararat Home and Hospital, its personalities, events, and news in general.

(320)
ARMENIAN DIRECTORY YELLOW PAGES, 1980-
UNIARTS
1745 GARDENA AVENUE SUITE 102
GLENDALE, CALIFORNIA 91204   **(818) 244-1167**
PUBLISHER: Uniarts Publishing Co. **FREQUENCY:** Annual. **LANGUAGE:** Armenian and English. **CONTENTS:** Covers American business advertisements in Los Angeles and Orange Counties, as well as residential listings in Southern California. **CONTACT PERSON:** Bernard Berberian, Publisher.

(321)
THE ARMENIAN HORIZON, 1980-
U.C.L.A. ARMENIAN STUDENTS ASSOCIATION
308 WESTWOOD PLAZA-BOX 533
LOS ANGELES, CALIFORNIA 90024
EDITORS: Mark Malkasian and Barlow Der Mugrdechian. **PUBLISHER:** U.C.L.A. Armenian Students Association. **FREQUENCY:** Quarterly. **SUBSCRIPTION RATE:** Free. **CIRCULATION:** 5,000. **LANGUAGE:** English and Armenian. **CONTENTS:** A newspaper devoted to covering the news of the Armenian community in depth. Special articles covering Armenian students, written by Armenian students. **CONTACT PERSON:** Barlow Der Mugrdechian.

(322)
ARMENIAN MUSICAL STUDIES NEWSLETTER, 1980-
ARMENIAN MUSICAL STUDIES PROGRAM
U.S.C. SCHOOL OF MUSIC
UNIVERSITY PARK
LOS ANGELES, CALIFORNIA 90089-0851   **(213) 743-8901**
EDITOR: Dr. Ohannes Salibian. **PUBLISHER:** Armenian Musical Studies Program. **FREQUENCY:** Two times a year. **LANGUAGE:** English. **CONTENTS:** Armenian musical studies development, intended to inform the general and academic audience about the U.S.C. Program for Armenian Musical Studies. **CONTACT PERSON:** Dr. Ohannes Salibian.

(323)
ARMENIAN NATIONAL COMMITTEE, WESTERN REGION BULLETIN, 1980-
ARMENIAN NATIONAL COMMITTEE
419-A WEST COLORADO STREET
GLENDALE, CALIFORNIA 91204   (818) 243-0197
EDITOR: Tom Lanman. **PUBLISHER:** Armenian National Committee, Western Region. **FREQUENCY:** Quarterly. **SUBSCRIPTION RATE:** Free. **CIRCULATION:** 22,000. **LANGUAGE:** Armenian and English. **CONTENTS:** Report on A.N.C. Western Region activities and political activities of interest to the Armenian community in the U.S.A. **CONTACT PERSON:** Tom Lanman, Editor.

(324)
ARMENIAN NUMISMATIC JOURNAL, 1975-
ARMENIAN NUMISMATIC SOCIETY
8511 BEVERLY PARK PLACE
PICO RIVERA, CALIFORNIA 90660   (213) 695-0380
EDITOR: Y. T. Nercessian. **PUBLISHER:** Armenian Numismatic Society. **FREQUENCY:** Quarterly. **SUBSCRIPTION RATE:** 1st year $7, 2nd year $6. **CIRCULATION:** 130. **LANGUAGE:** Armenian and English. **BOOK SELLING SERVICE:** Available. **CONTENTS:** Articles related to Armenian numismatics, and abstracts on Armenian numismatic literature. **CONTACT PERSON:** Y. T. Nercessian.

(325)
THE BUGLE, 1984-
MESROBIAN ALUMNI ASSOCIATION
C/O 600 NORTH 21st
MONTEBELLO, CALIFORNIA 90640   (213) 721-6230
PUBLISHER: Mesrobian Alumni Association. **FREQUENCY:** Monthly. **SUBSCRIPTION RATE:** Free. **CIRCULATION:** 1,000. **LANGUAGE:** English. **CONTENTS:** Summary of the Alumni activities, descriptions of upcoming events, present positions of alumni. **CONTACT PERSON:** Shahen Hariapetian, Editorial Board.

(326)
GAYDZ
ARMENIAN GENERAL BENEVOLENT UNION
589 NORTH LARCHMONT BLVD.
LOS ANGELES, CALIFORNIA 90004   (213) 467-2428
EDITOR: Gia Aivazian and Lucie Fattal. **PUBLISHER:** Armenian General

Benevolent Union. **FREQUENCY:** Bi-monthly. **LANGUAGE:** Armenian and English.

(327)
HARVEST, 1982-
ARMENIAN BIBLE COLLEGE
1605 EAST ELIZABETH STREET
PASADENA, CALIFORNIA 91104   **(818) 791-2575**
EDITOR: Yeghia Babikian. **PUBLISHER:** Armenian Bible College. **FRE-QUENCY:** Bi-monthly. **SUBSCRIPTION RATE:** Free. **CIRCULATION:** 2,500. **LANGUAGE:** Armenian and English. **CONTENTS:** It is the news-letter of the Armenian Bible College published essentially for promotional as well as cultural, educational and religious purposes. **CONTACT PER-SON:** Yeghia Babikian, Director.

(328)
HYE SHARZHOOM, 1979-
CALIFORNIA STATE UNIVERSITY, FRESNO
ARMENIAN STUDIES PROGRAM
FRESNO, CALIFORNIA 93740   **(209) 294-2832**
EDITOR: Flora Tchaderjian and Dickran Kouymjian. **PUBLISHER:** Arme-nian Studies Program, California State University at Fresno. **FRE-QUENCY:** Quarterly. **LANGUAGE:** Armenian and English. **CONTENTS:** Hye Sharzhoom is the official publication of C.S.U.F. Armenian Students Organization and the Armenian Studies Program. Includes articles about Armenian culture, history and book reviews.

(329)
JOURNAL OF THE SOCIETY FOR ARMENIAN STUDIES, 1984-
SOCIETY FOR ARMENIAN STUDIES
DEPARTMENT OF NEAR EASTERN LANGUAGES AND CULTURES
UNIVERSITY OF CALIFORNIA LOS ANGELES
405 HILGARD AVENUE
LOS ANGELES, CALIFORNIA 90024   **(213) 823-1307**
EDITOR: Prof. Avedis Sanjian. **PUBLISHER:** Society for Armenian Studies. **FREQUENCY:** Annual. **LANGUAGE:** English. **SUBSCRIPTION RATE:** $15. **CONTENTS:** A scholarly journal.

(329-A)
MASHTOTS, 1976-
AMERICAN ARMENIAN INTERNATIONAL COLLEGE
1950 THIRD STREET
LA VERNE, CALIFORNIA 91750   **(714) 593-2595**   **(714) 593-2594**
EDITOR: Editorial Board. **PUBLISHER:** American Armenian Interna-

tional College. **FREQUENCY:** Monthly. **SUBSCRIPTION RATE:** Free. **CIRCULATION:** 5,000. **LANGUAGE:** Armenian and English. **CONTENTS:** Educational and professional articles; A.A.I.C. news and activities; book reviews and biographies of benefactors. **CONTACT PERSON:** Dr. Garbis Der Yeghiayan, College Dean.

(330)
THE SAN DIEGO ARMENIAN

ARMENIAN AMERICAN ASSOCIATION
4175 FAIRMOUNT AVENUE
SAN DIEGO, CALIFORNIA 92105   **(619) 280-1105**

EDITOR: Jack Bournazian. **PUBLISHER:** Armenian American Association of San Diego. **FREQUENCY:** Monthly. **LANGUAGE:** Armenian and English.

(331)
VARAK, 1953-

GENERAL SOCIETY OF VASBOURAGAN
C/O LILYAN CHOOLJIAN
6071 EAST BUTLER AVENUE
FRESNO, CALIFORNIA 93727   **(209) 251-7272**

EDITOR: Lilyan Chooljian. **PUBLISHER:** General Society of Vasbouragan. **FREQUENCY:** Bi-annual. **SUBSCRIPTION RATE:** $10. **CIRCULATION:** 300. **LANGUAGE:** Armenian and English. **CONTENTS:** Articles of interest to all Vanetzies regarding the history, archaeology, the people of Vasbouragan, and the accomplishments of their descendents today, in order to perpetuate the appreciation of a very rich heritage. **CONTACT PERSON:** Contact any member of the Central Executive Committee or local chapters.

District of Columbia
Washington D.C.

(332)
ARMENIAN ASSEMBLY JOURNAL, 1972-

ARMENIAN ASSEMBLY OF AMERICA, INC.
122 C STREET, N.W. #350
WASHINGTON, D.C. 20001   **(202) 393-3434   (800) 368-5895**

EDITOR: Susan Carlin. **PUBLISHER:** Armenian Assembly of America. **FREQUENCY:** Quarterly. **SUBSCRIPTION RATE:** Free. **CIRCULATION:** 7,000. **LANGUAGE:** English. **CONTENTS:** The Armenian Assembly's newsletter focuses on the organization's activities with a view toward identifying issues of concern to Armenian-Americans.

(333)
FASCA NEWSLETTER, 1981-
FEDERATION OF ARMENIAN STUDENT CLUBS OF AMERICA
122 C STREET, N.W. #350
WASHINGTON, D.C. 20001   **(202) 393-3434   (800) 368-5895**
EDITOR: Laurens Ayvazian. **PUBLISHER:** Federation of Armenian Student Clubs of America. **FREQUENCY:** Semi-annual. **SUBSCRIPTION RATE:** Free. **CIRCULATION:** 2,000. **LANGUAGE:** English. **CONTENTS:** News of Armenian college club activities; information on scholarships, Armenian academic life, and grant opportunities. **CONTACT PERSON:** Laurens Ayvazian.

Maryland

(334)
ARMENIAN RUGS SOCIETY NEWSLETTER, 1980-
ARMENIAN RUGS SOCIETY
6930 WISCONSIN AVENUE
CHEVY CHASE, MARYLAND 20815   **(301) 654-4044**
PUBLISHER: Armenian Rugs Society. **FREQUENCY:** Quarterly. **SUBSCRIPTION RATE:** Included in the membership. **CIRCULATION:** 110. **LANGUAGE:** English. **BOOK SELLING SERVICE:** Available. **CONTACT PERSON:** James M. Keshishian, Treasurer.

Massachusetts

(335)
ARA NEWSLETTER, 1979-
ARMENIAN RENAISSANCE ASSOCIATION
67 LEONARD STREET
BELMONT, MASSACHUSETTS 02178   **(617) 489-1365**
PUBLISHER: Armenian Renaissance Association. **FREQUENCY:** Quarterly. **SUBSCRIPTION RATE:** Free. **CIRCULATION:** 1,000. **LANGUAGE:** Armenian and English. **CONTENTS:** Covers chapter activities, educational and social services, and cultural articles. **CONTACT PERSON:** Martha Hananian.

(336)
ARMENIAN ARTISTS ASSOCIATION OF AMERICA NEWSLETTER
ARMENIAN ARTISTS ASSOCIATION OF AMERICA
59 BIGELOW AVENUE
P.O. BOX 140
WATERTOWN, MASSACHUSETTS 02172   **(617) 923-9174**
PUBLISHER: Armenian Artists Association of America. **SUBSCRIPTION**

RATE: Free. **CIRCULATION:** 1,000. **LANGUAGE:** English. **CONTENTS:** Covers organization's activities.

(337)
ARMENIAN LIBRARY AND MUSEUM OF AMERICA NEWSLETTER, 1972-
ARMENIAN LIBRARY AND MUSEUM OF AMERICA
380 CONCORD AVENUE
BELMONT, MASSACHUSETTS 02178   **(617) 484-4780**
PUBLISHER: Armenian Library and Museum of America. **FREQUENCY:** Three to four times a year. **SUBSCRIPTION RATE:** Free. **LANGUAGE:** English. **CIRCULATION:** 500. **CONTENTS:** Covers organization's acquisitions, news and activities. **CONTACT PERSON:** Angele Hovsepian, Secretary.

(338)
HAI SIRD, 1939-
ARMENIAN RELIEF SOCIETY OF NORTH AMERICA
38 ELTON STREET
WATERTOWN, MASSACHUSETTS 02172   **(617) 926-5892**
EDITOR: Arpie Balian. **PUBLISHER:** Armenian Relief Society, Inc. **FREQUENCY:** Annual. **LANGUAGE:** Armenian, English, and French. **CONTENTS:** Reports from the Armenian Relief Society Central Executive and its regional offices, as well as contemporary issues.

(339)
KERMANIG, 1930-
UNION OF MARASH ARMENIANS CENTRAL COMMITTEE
P.O. BOX 95, NEW TOWN BRANCH
BOSTON, MASSACHUSETTS 02258
EDITOR: Ara Kalaydjian. **PUBLISHER:** Union of Marash Armenians. **FREQUENCY:** Quarterly. **LANGUAGE:** Armenian and English.

(340)
NOR ARABKIR DEGHEGADOU, 1942-
ARABKIR UNION, INC.
P.O. BOX 42
WATERTOWN, MASSACHUSETTS 02172

(341)
SOCIETY FOR ARMENIAN STUDIES NEWSLETTER, 1976-
BOSTON COLLEGE
SLAVIC & EASTERN LANGUAGES
CARNEY #236
CHESTNUT HILL, MASSACHUSETTS 02167　　　　**(617) 552-3912**

EDITOR: Michael J. Connolly. **PUBLISHER:** Society for Armenian Studies. **FREQUENCY:** Three times a year. **LANGUAGE:** English. **CONTENTS:** Includes information on the activities of the Society, its members, the state of Armenology studies, and listings of publications. **CONTACT PERSON:** Michael J. Connolly, Editor.

(342)
ZORYAN INSTITUTE BULLETIN, 1983-
THE ZORYAN INSTITUTE
85 FAYERWEATHER STREET
CAMBRIDGE, MASSACHUSETTS 02138　　　　**(617) 497-6713**

EDITOR: Mark Ayanian. **PUBLISHER:** The Zoryan Institute. **FREQUENCY:** Three to six times a year. **SUBSCRIPTION RATE:** Complementary. **CIRCULATION:** 2,000. **LANGUAGE:** English. **BOOK SELLING SERVICE:** Available. **CONTENTS:** Covers information on research, documentation, public discussions, and publications sponsored by the institute as well as description of recent archival acquisitions. **CONTACT PERSON:** Mark Ayanian.

Michigan

(343)
MIOUTIUN, 1969-
CULTURAL SOCIETY OF ARMENIANS FROM INSTANBUL
3106 GLENVIEW
ROYAL OAK, MICHIGAN 48073

PUBLISHER: Cultural Society of Armenians from Istanbul. **FREQUENCY:** Quarterly. **LANGUAGE:** Armenian.

Minnesota

(344)
ARMENIAN CULTURAL ORGANIZATION OF MINNESOTA NEWSLETTER

ARMENIAN CULTURAL ORGANIZATION OF MINNESOTA
1015 IVES LANE
PLYMOUTH, MINNESOTA 55441　　　　**(612) 545-5894**

CONTACT PERSON: Arek Tathevossian, President.

New Jersey

(345)
A.G.A.U. BULLETIN, 1921-
ARMENIAN GENERAL ATHLETIC UNION
116 38th STREET
UNION CITY, NEW JERSEY 07087   **(201) 865-0057**

EDITOR: Mike Megerdichian. **PUBLISHER:** Armenian General Athletic Union, U.S.A., Inc. **FREQUENCY:** Semi-monthly. **LANGUAGE:** English. **CONTENTS:** Covers news on Armenian American athletes.

(346)
A.M.A.A. NEWS, 1969-
ARMENIAN MISSIONARY ASSOCIATION OF AMERICA
140 FOREST AVENUE
PARAMUS, NEW JERSEY 07652   **(201) 265-2607/8**

EDITOR: G. H. Chopourian, Ph.D. **PUBLISHER:** Armenian Missionary Association of America, Inc. **FREQUENCY:** Bi-monthly. **LANGUAGE:** Armenian and English. **CONTENTS:** Promotional, informational, and inspirational newsletter.

(347)
HYDOUN
HOME FOR THE ARMENIAN AGED
70 MAIN STREET
EMERSON, NEW JERSEY 07630   **(201) 261-6626**

PUBLISHER: Home for the Armenian Aged. **FREQUENCY:** Semi-annual. **LANGUAGE:** Armenian and English. **CONTENTS:** General activities at the Home, including pictures. **CONTACT PERSON:** Leah Tegnazian.

(347-A)
SOCIETY FOR ARMENIAN STUDIES OCCASIONAL PAPERS, 1981-
SOCIETY FOR ARMENIAN STUDIES
GLASSBORO STATE COLLEGE
DEPARTMENT OF HISTORY
GLASSBORO, NEW JERSEY 08028   **(607) 445-5000**
CONTACT PERSON: Robert Hewson.

New York

(348)
ARMENIAN ARCHITECTURAL ARCHIVES
ARMENIAN EDUCATIONAL COUNCIL INC.
BRUNSWICK HILLS, EAST ROAD
TROY, NEW YORK 12180   **(518) 274-4526**
EDITOR: Inter-Documentation Co., Holland. **CONTENTS:** This documented photographic collection of Armenian architecture is designed to be a resource for research in architectural history. The series will have six or more issues, two of which with nearly 12,000 photos in microfiche are now being distributed to universities around the world.

(349)
ARMENIAN STUDENTS' ASSOCIATION OF AMERICA NEWSLETTER
ARMENIAN STUDENTS' ASSOCIATION OF AMERICA
P.O. BOX 1557
NEW YORK, NEW YORK 10116
FREQUENCY: Quarterly.

(350)
ARMENIAN STUDIES AT COLUMBIA UNIVERSITY NEWSLETTER
COLUMBIA UNIVERSITY
CENTER FOR ARMENIAN STUDIES
500 KENT HALL BOX A
NEW YORK, NEW YORK 10027   (718) 520-6951   (212) 280-2013
EDITOR: Eleanor H. Tejirian. **PUBLISHER:** Armenian Studies Center at Columbia University. **CONTENTS:** Covers activities of the Center.

(351)
KEGHARD, 1977-
ARMENIAN CHURCH YOUTH ORGANIZATION
630 SECOND AVENUE
NEW YORK, NEW YORK 10016   **(212) 686-0710**
OR
JAMES MAGARIAN, EXECUTIVE SECRETARY
99 LONG POND ROAD
TYNGSBOROUGH, MASSACHUSETTS 01879   **(617) 256-7234**
EDITOR: James Magarian, Executive Secretary. **FREQUENCY:** Annual. **LANGUAGE:** English. **CONTENTS:** Includes photos and articles reflecting the past year in A.C.Y.O.A.

(352)
KIROUKIRK, 1960-

THE ARMENIAN LITERARY SOCIETY
114 FIRST STREET
YONKERS, NEW YORK 10704   **(914) 237-5751**   **(914) 761-2127**

EDITOR: Editorial Council. **PUBLISHER:** The Armenian Literary Society.
FREQUENCY: Quarterly. **SUBSCRIPTION RATE:** Free. **CIRCULATION:**
1,500. **LANGUAGE:** Armenian and English. **BOOK SELLING SERVICE:**
Available. **CONTACT PERSON:** K. Magarian.

(353)
MENK, 1977-

ARMENIAN CULTURAL ASSOCIATION HAMAZKAYIN
P.O. BOX 804
WOODSIDE, NEW YORK 11377   **(914) 268-2521**

(354)
NEW YORK ARMENIAN HOME FOR THE AGED NEWSLETTER

NEW YORK ARMENIAN HOME FOR THE AGED
137-31 45 AVENUE
FLUSHING, NEW YORK 11355   **(212) 461-1504**

FREQUENCY: Semi-annual. **SUBSCRIPTION RATE:** Free. **CIRCULA-
TION:** 3,500. **LANGUAGE:** English. **CONTENTS:** Covers activities of the
Home and donations.

(355)
NOR-SEBASTIA, 1928-

PAN-SEBASTIA REHABILITATION UNION
P.O. BOX 198
MADISON SQUARE STATION
NEW YORK, NEW YORK 10159   **(212) 679-1728**

EDITOR: Krikor Vosganian. **PUBLISHER:** Pan-Sebastia Rehabilitation
Union. **FREQUENCY:** Three to four times a year. **SUBSCRIPTION
RATE:** Free. **CIRCULATION:** 1,000. **LANGUAGE:** Armenian and Eng-
lish. **CONTENTS:** Covers news from and about the compatriots, its
branches, Armenia and Holy Etchmiadzin. **CONTACT PERSON:** Zareh
Kapikian.

Ohio

(356)
ANNUAL OF ARMENIAN LINGUISTICS, 1979-

PROF. JOHN GREPPIN
CLEVELAND STATE UNIVERSITY
CLEVELAND, OHIO 44115   **(216) 687-3967**   **(216) 687-3951**

EDITORS: Prof. John Greppin, Cleveland; Academician G. B. Djahukian, Yerevan; Prof. Eric Hamp, Chicago; Rudiger Schmitt, Saarbrucken, West Germany; Prof. G. Bolognesi, Milan, Italy; A.A. Khachaturian, Yerevan. FREQUENCY: Annual. SUBSCRIPTION RATE: $14 for two years. CIRCULATION: 200. LANGUAGE: English, French, German, and Italian. CONTENTS: A scholarly publication for an audience with some academic background in linguistics or allied studies. CONTACT PERSON: Prof. John A. C. Greppin.

(357)
PAP OUKHTI, 1935-
EDUCATIONAL ASSOCIATION OF MALATIA
12813 GAY AVENUE
CLEVELAND, OHIO 44105

EDITOR: Gevork Melitenetsi. PUBLISHER: Educational Association of Malatia, Central Executive Board. FREQUENCY: Quarterly. LANGUAGE: Armenian. CONTENTS: A literary magazine.

Pennsylvania

(359)
ARMENIAN HISTORICAL RESEARCH ASSOCIATION NEWSLETTER
ARMENIAN HISTORICAL RESEARCH ASSOCIATION
30 NORTHWOOD ROAD
NEWTOWN SQUARE, PENNSLYVANIA 19073   (215) 356-0635

EDITOR: Dr. Charles N. Mahjoubian. PUBLISHER: Armenian Historical Research Association. FREQUENCY: Semi-annual. LANGUAGE: Armenian and English.

Church
Bulletins and Newsletters
California

(360)
ARMENIAN APOSTOLIC CHURCH OF SANTA CLARA VALLEY NEWSLETTER, 1967-
ARMENIAN APOSTOLIC CHURCH OF SANTA CLARA VALLEY
11370 SOUTH STELLING
CUPERTINO, CALIFORNIA 95015   (408) 257-6743

EDITOR: Venus Phillips. PUBLISHER: Armenian Apostolic Church of Santa Clara Valley. FREQUENCY: Monthly. SUBSCRIPTION RATE: Donation. CIRCULATION: 500. LANGUAGE: Armenian and English. CONTENTS: Covers events pertaining to the parish, as well as educational articles.

(361)
CALVARY MESSENGER
CALVARY ARMENIAN CONGREGATIONAL CHURCH
725 BROTHERHOOD WAY
SAN FRANCISCO, CALIFORNIA 94132 (415) 566-0717
PUBLISHER: Calvary Armenian Congregational Church. **CONTENTS:**
Covers church news and activities.

(362)
GANTEGH, 1963-
SAINT SARKIS ARMENIAN CHURCH
700 SOUTH LA VERNE AVENUE
EAST LOS ANGELES, CALIFORNIA 90022 (213) 269-0907
EDITOR: Fr. Vartan Kahana Dulgarian, Pastor. **PUBLISHER:** Saint
Sarkis Armenian Church. **LANGUAGE:** Armenian and English. **CON-
TENTS:** Covers church's news.

(363)
HOOSHARAR, 1980-
ARMENIAN CHURCH OF THE NAZARENE
411 EAST ACACIA AVENUE
GLENDALE, CALIFORNIA 91205 (818) 244-9920
PUBLISHER: Armenian Church of the Nazarene. **FREQUENCY:**
Monthly. **CIRCULATION:** 225. **LANGUAGE:** Armenian. **BOOK SELLING
SERVICE:** Available. **CONTENTS:** Devotional short articles from the
Pastor or an individual. Also includes news and activities of the church
and its auxiliaries. **CONTACT PERSON:** Church Office.

(364)
HOVID, 1964-
HOLY MARTYRS ARMENIAN APOSTOLIC CHURCH
5300 WHITE OAK AVENUE
ENCINO, CALIFORNIA 91316 (818) 981-6159
EDITOR: Rev. Vartan Arakelian. **PUBLISHER:** Holy Martyrs Armenian
Apostolic Church. **FREQUENCY:** Bi-monthly. **LANGUAGE:** Armenian
and English. **CONTENTS:** Covers religious and educational topics as
well as news releases about weddings, baptisms, and funerals.

(365)
HROMGLA, 1982-
**THE ARMENIAN APOSTOLIC CHURCH OF AMERICA WESTERN PRE-
LACY**
4401 RUSSELL AVENUE
LOS ANGELES, CALIFORNIA 90027 (213) 663-8273

EDITOR: Levon Khacherian, Chief Editor. PUBLISHER: The Armenian Apostolic Church of America, Western Prelacy. FREQUENCY: Annual. LANGUAGE: Armenian and English. CONTENTS: Covers religious and cultural topics.

(366)
IMMANUEL

IMMANUEL ARMENIAN CONGREGATIONAL CHURCH
9516 DOWNEY AVENUE
DOWNEY, CALIFORNIA 90240   (213) 862-7012

EDITOR: Rev. Edward S. Tovmassian, Pastor. PUBLISHER: Immanuel Armenian Congregational Church. FREQUENCY: Monthly (except in July and August). LANGUAGE: English. CONTENTS: Covers church news and announcements.

(367)
LIFELINE

FIRST ARMENIAN PRESBYTERIAN CHURCH
430 SOUTH FIRST STREET
FRESNO, CALIFORNIA 93702   (209) 237-6638

EDITOR: Anita Console, Secretary. PUBLISHER: First Armenian Presbyterian Church. FREQUENCY: Monthly. LANGUAGE: Armenian and English. CONTENTS: Covers various church activities and announcements.

(368)
LOOYS

SAINT GREGORY ARMENIAN APOSTOLIC CHURCH
51 COMMONWEALTH AVENUE
SAN FRANCISCO, CALIFORNIA 94118   (415) 751-4150

EDITOR: Rev. Fr. Datev Kaloustian. PUBLISHER: Saint Gregory Armenian Apostolic Church. FREQUENCY: Bi-monthly. SUBSCRIPTION RATE: Free. CIRCULATION: 900. LANGUAGE: Armenian and English. CONTENTS: Covers religious and church related activities of the community. CONTACT PERSON: Rev. Fr. Datev Kaloustian, Pastor.

(369)
MOTHER CHURCH, 1979-

THE ARMENIAN APOSTOLIC CHURCH OF NORTH AMERICA WESTERN DIOCESE
1201 NORTH VINE STREET
LOS ANGELES, CALIFORNIA 90038   (213) 466-5265

EDITOR: The Very Rev. Fr. Sipan Mekhsian. FREQUENCY: Monthly.

LANGUAGE: Armenian and English. **CONTENTS:** Covers official communiques, spiritual messages, theology, religion, literature, diocesan acitivities, and news from parishes.

(370)
OSHAGAN
SAINT JAMES ARMENIAN APOSTOLIC CHURCH
4950 WEST SLAUSON AVENUE
LOS ANGELES, CALIFORNIA 90065   **(213) 295-4588**
PUBLISHER: Saint James Armenian Apostolic Church. **LANGUAGE:** Armenian and English. **CONTENTS:** Covers church news and activities.

(371)
PARI-LOOR, 1957-
SAINT PETER ARMENIAN APOSTOLIC CHURCH
17231 SHERMAN WAY
VAN NUYS, CALIFORNIA 91406   **(818) 344-4860**
EDITOR: Fr. Shahe Avak Kahana Semerdjian. **PUBLISHER:** Saint Peter Armenian Apostolic Church. **FREQUENCY:** Bi-monthly. **SUBSCRIPTION RATE:** Free. **CIRCULATION:** 1,300. **CONTENTS:** The Pari-Loor is published every other month as a service to its parishioners and friends. It provides reports and happenings on various church organizations as well as activities within the church. **CONTACT PERSON:** Fr. Shahe Semerdjian, Pastor.

(372)
PILGRIMS PROGRESS
PILGRIM ARMENIAN CONGREGATIONAL CHURCH
3673 NORTH FIRST STREET
FRESNO, CALIFORNIA 93726   **(209) 229-2915**
EDITOR: Rev. Roger Minassian, Pastor. **PUBLISHER:** Pilgrim Armenian Congregational Church. **FREQUENCY:** Weekly. **LANGUAGE:** English. **CONTENTS:** Covers weekly church news.

(373)
SAINT GARABED ARMENIAN APOSTOLIC CHURCH BULLETIN
SAINT GARABED ARMENIAN APOSTOLIC CHURCH
1614 NORTH ALEXANDRIA AVENUE
LOS ANGELES, CALIFORNIA 90027   **(213) 666-0507**
EDITOR: Rev. Vatche Naccachian. **PUBLISHER:** Saint Garabed Armenian Apostolic Church. **FREQUENCY:** Quarterly. **LANGUAGE:** Armenian and English. **CONTENTS:** Religious articles and announcements.

(374)

SAINT MARY ARMENIAN CHURCH OF YETTEM BULLETIN, 1973-

SAINT MARY ARMENIAN CHURCH
14395 AVENUE 384
YETTEM, CALIFORNIA 93670   **(209) 528-6892**

EDITOR: Rev. Fr. Vartan Kasparian. **PUBLISHER:** Saint Mary Armenian Church of Yettem. **FREQUENCY:** Monthly. **SUBSCRIPTION RATE:** Free. **CIRCULATION:** 315. **LANGUAGE:** Armenian and English. **BOOK SELLING SERVICE:** Available. **CONTENTS:** Covers general news of interest to the functioning of the church parish, parish council, ladies society, youth, Sunday school, community, and so forth. **CONTACT PERSON:** Rev. Fr. Vartan Kasparian, Parish Priest.

(375)

SAINT MARY'S ARMENIAN APOSTOLIC CHURCH BULLETIN

SAINT MARY'S ARMENIAN APOSTOLIC CHURCH
500 SOUTH CENTRAL AVENUE
GLENDALE, CALIFORNIA 91204   **(818) 244-2402**

(376)

SAINTS SAHAG AND MESROB ARMENIAN APOSTOLIC CHURCH BULLETIN

SAINTS SAHAG AND MESROB ARMENIAN APOSTOLIC CHURCH
1249 "F" STREET
P.O. BOX 205
REEDLEY, CALIFORNIA 93654   **(209) 638-2740**

(377)
SHOGHAGAT

SAINT GREGORY ARMENIAN APOSTOLIC CHURCH
2215 EAST COLORADO BLVD.
PASADENA, CALIFORNIA 91107   **(818) 449-1523**

EDITOR: Very Rev. Fr. Moushegh Tashjian. **PUBLISHER:** Saint Gregory Armenian Apostolic Church. **FREQUENCY:** Bi-monthly. **SUBSCRIPTION RATE:** Free. **CIRCULATION:** 700. **LANGUAGE:** Armenian and English. **CONTENTS:** Shoghagat contains much news on church organizations and their activities, both in Armenian and English languages. It also contains Diocesan news, pictures of parish activities and many informative subjects about the Armenian Church, festive days and Armenian traditions. **CONTACT PERSON:** Very Rev. Fr. Moushegh Tashjian.

(378)
TERTIG, 1969-

SAINT PAUL ARMENIAN CHURCH
3767 NORTH FIRST STREET
FRESNO, CALIFORNIA 93726   **(209) 226-6343**

EDITOR: Archpriest Shahe Altounian. **PUBLISHER:** Saint Paul Armenian Church. **FREQUENCY:** Weekly. **SUBSCRIPTION RATE:** Free. **CIRCULATION:** 600. **LANGUAGE:** Armenian and English. **BOOK SELLING SERVICE:** Available. **CONTENTS:** Gives the news of upcoming events, activities, and weekly messages, sermon topics and religious services. **CONTACT PERSON:** Archpriest Shahe Altounian.

(379)
VOICE, 1950-

HOLY TRINITY ARMENIAN APOSTOLIC CHURCH
P.O. BOX 1865
2222 EAST VENTURA AVENUE
FRESNO, CALIFORNIA 93718   **(209) 486-1141 (209) 486-1142**

EDITOR: Rev. Hrant Serabian, Pastor. **PUBLISHER:** Holy Trinity Armenian Apostolic Church. **FREQUENCY:** Weekly. **LANGUAGE:** Armenian and English. **CONTENTS:** Covers church news and activities.

(380)
VOICE, 1983-

SAINT JOHN ARMENIAN APOSTOLIC CHURCH
4473 30th STREET
SAN DIEGO, CALIFORNIA 92116   **(619) 562-1533 (619) 562-9399**

EDITOR & PUBLISHER: Rev. Levon and Yerelzgin Grace Arakelian. **FREQUENCY:** Bi-monthly. **SUBSCRIPTION RATE:** Free. **CIRCULATION:** 500. **LANGUAGE:** English and Armenian. **CONTENTS:** Includes parish life, function, moral, religious, and educational short essays and stories; advocates unity and the one big family ideal. **CONTACT PERSON:** Rev. Levon Arakelian.

Connecticut

(381)
ANI, 1984-

ARMENIAN CHURCH OF THE HOLY ASCENSION
1460 HUNTINGTION TURNPIKE
TRUMBULL, CONNECTICUT 06611   **(203) 372-5770**

EDITOR: Theresa Harabedian. **PUBLISHER:** Armenian Church of the Holy Ascension. **FREQUENCY:** Monthly. **SUBSCRIPTION RATE:** Free.

CIRCULATION: 250. **LANGUAGE:** Armenian and English. **CONTACT PERSON:** Theresa Harabedian.

(382)
LOOSAPER, 1964-
SAINT STEPHEN'S ARMENIAN APOSTOLIC CHURCH
P.O. BOX 263
167 TREMONT STREET
NEW BRITAIN, CONNECTICUT 06051   **(203) 229-8322**
EDITOR: Rev. Sahag Andekian, Pastor. **PUBLISHER:** Saint Stephen's Armenian Apostolic Church. **FREQUENCY:** Monthly. **LANGUAGE:** Armenian and English. **CONTENTS:** Covers church news, religious articles, church donations, upcoming community events, prelacy messages and editorials.

District of Columbia
Washington D.C.

(383)
SHNORHALE, 1960-
SAINT MARY'S ARMENIAN APOSTOLIC CHURCH
4125 FESSENDEN STREET, N.W.
WASHINGTON, D.C. 20016   **(202) 363-1923**
EDITOR: Rev. Vertanes Kalayjian, Pastor. **PUBLISHER:** Saint Mary's Armenian Apostolic Church. **FREQUENCY:** Bi-monthly. **SUBSCRIPTION RATE:** Free. **CIRCULATION:** 800. **LANGUAGE:** Armenian and English. **BOOK SELLING SERVICE:** Available. **CONTENTS:** Covers pastoral messages, parish activities, news and activities related to the Armenian American community, religious, cultural, and educational articles. **CONTACT PERSON:** Gary Avedikian, Bookstore Manager.

Illinois

(384)
GHEVONT YERETS CHURCH BULLETIN, 1970-
ARCHPRIEST FR. SARKIS ANDREASSIAN
1353 WEST CATALPA AVENUE
CHICAGO, ILLINOIS 60640   **(312) 769-1059**
EDITOR: Archpriest Rev. Sarkis Andreassian and Maro Stathopoulos, Assistant. **PUBLISHER:** Hovig Alexanian. **FREQUENCY:** Quarterly. **LANGUAGE:** Armenian and English. **CONTENTS:** Articles about Armenian culture and community news.

(385)
LANTERN, 1940-
ARMENIAN CONGREGATIONAL CHURCH OF CHICAGO
5430 NORTH SHERIDAN ROAD
CHICAGO, ILLINOIS 60640 (312) 784-2962

EDITOR: Rev. Barkev N. Darakjian. **PUBLISHER:** Armenian Congregational Church of Chicago. **FREQUENCY:** Quarterly. **SUBSCRIPTION RATE:** Free. **CIRCULATION:** 300. **LANGUAGE:** Armenian and English. **CONTENTS:** Church news and religious articles. **CONTACT PERSON:** Rev. Barkev N. Darakjian, Pastor and Editor.

(386)
SAINT GREGORY THE ILLUMINATOR ARMENIAN APOSTOLIC CHURCH NEWSLETTER, 1961-
SAINT GREGORY THE ILLUMINATOR ARMENIAN APOSTOLIC CHURCH
1732 MAPLE STREET
GRANITE CITY, ILLINOIS 62040 (618) 451-7884

EDITOR: Rev. Khoren Habeshian, Pastor. **PUBLISHER:** Saint Gregory the Illuminator Armenian Apostolic Church. **FREQUENCY:** Bi-monthly. **LANGUAGE:** Armenian and English.

Maryland

(387)
MASHTOTS, 1969-
SOURP KHATCH HOLY CROSS ARMENIAN CHURCH
4906 FLINT DRIVE
CHEVY CHASE, MARYLAND 20816 (301) 229-8742

EDITOR: Rev. Sahag Vertanesian. **PUBLISHER:** Sourp Khatch Holy Cross Armenian Church. **FREQUENCY:** Bi-monthly. **SUBSCRIPTION RATE:** Free. **CIRCULATION:** 525. **LANGUAGE:** Armenian and English. **BOOK SELLING SERVICE:** Available. **CONTENTS:** Covers community news with official messages, sermons, religious news and information. **CONTACT:** Church Office.

Massachusetts

(388)
ARAX, 1963-
SAINT ASDVADZADZIN ARMENIAN APOSTOLIC CHURCH
211 CHURCH STREET
WHITINSVILLE, MASSACHUSETTS 01588 (617) 234-3677

FREQUENCY: Monthly. **LANGUAGE:** Armenian and English.

(389)
ARMENIAN MEMORIAL CONGREGATIONAL CHURCH BULLETIN
ARMENIAN MEMORIAL CONGREGATIONAL CHURCH
32 BIGELOW AVENUE
WATERTOWN, MASSACHUSETTS 02172   (617) 923-0498
EDITOR: Rev. Ron Tovmassian. **PUBLISHER:** Armenian Memorial Church. **FREQUENCY:** Monthly. **SUBSCRIPTION RATE:** Free. **CIRCULATION:** 500. **LANGUAGE:** English. **CONTENTS:** Religious articles by the Pastor, articles from various church organizations, community news, church concerns, church calendar, reproductions of sermons preached recently, and inspirational poems and stories. **CONTACT PERSON:** Rev. Ron Tovmassian.

(390)
DADJAR, 1966-
HOLY TRINITY ARMENIAN APOSTOLIC CHURCH OF GREATER BOSTON
145 BRATTLE STREET
CAMBRIDGE, MASSACHUSETTS 02138   (617) 354-0632
EDITOR: Rev. Mampre Kouzonian, Pastor. **PUBLISHER:** Holy Trinity Armenian Apostolic Church. **FREQUENCY:** Monthly. **LANGUAGE:** Armenian and English. **CONTENTS:** Covers church activities.

(391)
FIRST ARMENIAN CHURCH OF BELMONT BULLETIN
FIRST ARMENIAN CHURCH OF BELMONT
380 CONCORD AVENUE
BELMONT, MASSACHUSETTS 02178   (617) 484-4779
EDITOR: The Rev. Vartan Hartunian. **PUBLISHER:** First Armenian Church of Belmont. **FREQUENCY:** Monthly. **SUBSCRIPTION RATE:** Free. **CIRCULATION:** 500. **LANGUAGE:** English. **BOOK SELLING SERVICE:** Available. **CONTENTS:** Covers any and all news relating to life of the church, monthly schedule of events, pastoral letter, scripture of the month, thoughts of the month, church news, poems, and events. **CONTACT PERSON:** The Rev. Vartan Hartunian.

(392)
LOOSAVORICH, 1974-
SAINT GREGORY THE ILLUMINATOR ARMENIAN APOSTOLIC CHURCH
110 MAIN STREET
HAVERHILL, MASSACHUSETTS 01830   (617) 372-9227
EDITOR: Deacon Krikor Zamroutian. **PUBLISHER:** Saint Gregory the

Illuminator Armenian Apostolic Church. **FREQUENCY:** Bi-monthly. **SUB-SCRIPTION RATE:** Free. **CIRCULATION:** 250. **LANGUAGE:** Armenian and English. **BOOK SELLING SERVICE:** Available. **CONTENTS:** Reports from church organizations, functions held in the church, Christmas and Easter Yughakins, messages from the diocese, deaths, weddings, and christenings, etc. **CONTACT PERSON:** Zarty Chilingirian, Secretary.

(393)
LOOYS, 1953-
SAINT JAMES ARMENIAN APOSTOLIC CHURCH
465 MOUNT AUBURN STREET
WATERTOWN, MASSACHUSETTS 02172   **(617) 923-8860**

EDITOR: Haig H. Tommayan. **PUBLISHER:** Saint James Armenian Apostolic Church. **FREQUENCY:** Monthly. **SUBSCRIPTION RATE:** Free. **CIRCULATION:** 2,100. **LANGUAGE:** Armenian and English. **CONTENTS:** Covers church chronicle, church activities, and educational articles on Armenian church and heritage.

(394)
SANAHIN, 1962-
SAINT JOHN THE DIVINE ARMENIAN APOSTOLIC CHURCH
64 DRESDEN STREET
SPRINGFIELD, MASSACHUSETTS 01109   **(413) 734-8692**

EDITOR: Rev. Mesrob Semerjian, Pastor. **PUBLISHER:** Saint John the Divine Armenian Apostolic Church. **FREQUENCY:** Monthly. **LANGUAGE:** Armenian and English. **CONTENTS:** Covers church activities and news.

(395)
SOORHANTAG
CHURCH OF OUR SAVIOUR ARMENIAN APOSTOLIC CHURCH
87 SALISBURY STREET
WORCESTER, MASSACHUSETTS 01609   **(617) 756-2931**

EDITOR: Deacon Daniel Kachakian and Rev. Yeghishe Gigirian. **PUBLISHER:** Church of Our Saviour Armenian Apostolic Church. **FREQUENCY:** Bi-monthly. **LANGUAGE:** Armenian and English. **CONTENTS:** Cultural articles and church news.

Michigan

(396)
ARMENIAN CONGREGATIONAL CHURCH OF GREATER DETROIT BULLETIN, 1975-
ARMENIAN CONGREGATIONAL CHURCH OF GREATER DETROIT
P.O. BOX 531
26210 WEST 12 MILE ROAD
SOUTHFIELD, MICHIGAN 48034   (313) 352-0680
EDITOR: Rev. Dr. Vahan H. Tootikian. **PUBLISHER:** Armenian Congregational Church. **FREQUENCY:** Monthly. **SUBSCRIPTION RATE:** Free. **CIRCULATION:** 350. **LANGUAGE:** English.

(397)
ILLUMINATOR, 1960-
SAINT SARKIS ARMENIAN APOSTOLIC CHURCH
19300 FORD ROAD
DEARBORN, MICHIGAN 48128   (313) 336-6200
EDITOR: Rev. Dr. Gorun Shrikian. **PUBLISHER:** Saint Sarkis Armenian Apostolic Church. **FREQUENCY:** Bi-monthly. **SUBSCRIPTION RATE:** Free. **CIRCULATION:** 1,200. **LANGUAGE:** Armenian and English. **BOOK SELLING SERVICE:** Available. **CONTENTS:** Religious articles, lists of the Saints and feast days of the Armenian church, community and church related news, etc. **CONTACT PERSON:** Geno Sarkisian, Secretary.

(398)
VARTENIK
SAINT VARTAN ARMENIAN CATHOLIC CHURCH
8541 GREENFIELD ROAD
DEARBORN, MICHIGAN 48128   (313) 336-6200

New Hampshire

(399)
MOUNT ARARAT NEWS, 1981-
ARARAT ARMENIAN CONGREGATIONAL CHURCH
4 SALEM STREET
SALEM, NEW HAMPSHIRE 03079   (603) 898-7042
EDITOR: Rev. John Mokkosian and Nancy Asadoorian. **PUBLISHER:** Ararat Armenian Congregational Church. **FREQUENCY:** Monthly. **LANGUAGE:** English. **CONTENTS:** Covers church activities and events.

New Jersey

(400)
BEACON, 1960-
SAINT THOMAS ARMENIAN APOSTOLIC CHURCH
P.O. BOX 53
TENAFLY, NEW JERSEY 07670   **(201) 567-5446**

EDITOR: Rev. Arnak Kasparian. **PUBLISHER:** Saint Thomas Armenian Church. **FREQUENCY:** Monthly. **SUBSCRIPTION RATE:** Free. **CIRCULATION:** 850. **LANGUAGE:** Armenian and English. **CONTENTS:** Covers church activities.

(401)
GANTEGH, 1950-
SAINT MARY ARMENIAN CHURCH
200 WEST MOUNT PLEASANT AVENUE
LIVINGSTON, NEW JERSEY 07039   **(201) 533-9794**

PUBLISHER: Saint Mary Armenian Church. **FREQUENCY:** Monthly. **SUBSCRIPTION RATE:** Free. **CIRCULATION:** 246. **LANGUAGE:** Armenian and English. **BOOK SELLING SERVICE:** Available. **CONTENTS:** Covers message from the pastor, news concerning parish, reports from church organizations, religious articles, cultural, and current events, etc. **CONTACT PERSON:** Pastor or Church Secretary.

(402)
THE HERALD
ARMENIAN PRESBYTERIAN CHURCH
140 FOREST AVENUE
PARAMUS, NEW JERSEY 07652   **(201) 265-8585**

(403)
LRADOO, 1953-
SAINT LEON ARMENIAN APOSTOLIC CHURCH
12-61 SADDLE RIVER ROAD
FAIR LAWN, NEW JERSEY 07410   **(201) 791-2862**

EDITOR: Vivian Hovsepian. **PUBLISHER:** Saint Leon Armenian Apostolic Church. **FREQUENCY:** Monthly. **SUBSCRIPTION RATE:** Free. **CIRCULATION:** 560. **LANGUAGE:** Armenian and English. **CONTENTS:** Lradoo is the main publication of the church. Covers messages from the pastor, organizational news, what happenings in the parish, parish registry of baptisms, weddings, funerals, and upcoming events.

(404)
SAINTS VARTANANTZ NEWSLETTER, 1959-
SAINTS VARTANANTZ ARMENIAN APOSTOLIC CHURCH OF NEW JERSEY
461 BERGEN BLVD.
RIDGEFIELD, NEW JERSEY 07657   **(201) 943-2950**
EDITOR: Rev. Fr. Vahrich Shirinian. **PUBLISHER:** Saints Vartanantz Armenian Apostolic Church of New Jersey. **SUBSCRIPTION RATE:** Free. **CIRCULATION:** 1,200. **LANGUAGE:** Armenian and English. **CONTACT:** Church Office.

New York

(405)
THE ARMENIAN EVANGELICAL CHURCH OF NEW YORK BULLETIN, 1912-
THE ARMENIAN EVANGELICAL CHURCH OF NEW YORK
152 EAST 34th STREET
NEW YORK, NEW YORK 10016   **(212) 685-3177**
EDITOR: Rev. Herald A. G. Hassessian. **PUBLISHER:** The Armenian Evangelical Church of New York. **FREQUENCY:** Monthly, except for July and August. **SUBSCRIPTION RATE:** $5. **CIRCULATION:** 700. **LANGUAGE:** Armenian and English. **CONTENTS:** Covers pastoral messages and church related news.

(406)
THE BEMA
ARMENIAN APOSTOLIC CHURCH OF NORTH AMERICA EASTERN DIOCESE
630 SECOND AVENUE
NEW YORK, NEW YORK 10016   **(212) 686-0710**
EDITOR: Editorial Board. **PUBLISHER:** Diocese of the Armenian Apostolic Church. **FREQUENCY:** Monthly. **SUBSCRIPTION RATE:** Free. Anyone who would like to be on mailing list is welcome. **LANGUAGE:** English and Armenian. **CONTENTS:** Covers events and news of the Diocese of the Armenian Church in the U.S.A. and Canada except in California.

(407)
HAYASTANEAYTS YEGEGHESTZY, 1938-
ARMENIAN APOSTOLIC CHURCH OF NORTH AMERICA EASTERN DIOCESE
630 SECOND AVENUE
NEW YORK, NEW YORK 10016   **(212) 686-0710**

EDITOR: Krikor Vosganian. **PUBLISHER:** Diocese of the Armenian Apostolic Church. **FREQUENCY:** Monthly. **LANGUAGE:** Armenian and English. **CONTENTS:** Covers news of Armenian Churches in the United States and articles about Armenian history and culture.

(408)
THE LOOSAPER, 1962-

SAINT PETER ARMENIAN APOSTOLIC CHURCH
100 TROY-SCHENECTADY ROAD
WATERVLIET, NEW YORK 12189   (518) 274-3673

EDITOR & PUBLISHER: Rev. Garen Gdanian, Pastor. **FREQUENCY:** Monthly. **LANGUAGE:** Armenian and English. **CONTENTS:** Covers church activities, coming events and community news.

(409)
MAYR YEGEGHETSI, 1940-

SAINT ILLUMINATORS ARMENIAN APOSTOLIC CATHEDRAL
221 EAST 27th STREET
NEW YORK, NEW YORK 10016   (212) 625-9012

EDITOR: Archpriest Moushegh Der Kaloustian. **PUBLISHER:** Saint Illuminators Armenian Apostolic Cathedral. **FREQUENCY:** Quarterly. **LANGUAGE:** Armenian and English. **CONTENTS:** Covers activities of the church and news about its various organizations.

(410)
NAREG, 1954-

HOLY MARTYRS ARMENIAN APOSTOLIC CHURCH
209-15 HORACE HARDING EXPRESS WAY
BAYSIDE, NEW YORK 11364   (212) 225-0235

EDITOR: Rev. Michael Buttero, Pastor. **PUBLISHER:** Holy Martyrs Armenian Apostolic Church. **LANGUAGE:** Armenian and English. **CONTENTS:** Covers church news and activities.

(411)
OUTREACH, 1979-

ARMENIAN APOSTOLIC CHURCH OF AMERICA EASTERN PRELACY
138 EAST 39th STREET
NEW YORK, NEW YORK 10016   (212) 689-7810

EDITOR: Archbishop Mesrob Ashjian and Iris Papazian. **PUBLISHER:** Prelacy of the Armenian Apostolic Church of America. **FREQUENCY:** Monthly. **SUBSCRIPTION RATE:** Free. **CIRCULATION:** 10,000 **LANGUAGE:** Armenian and English. **BOOK SELLING SERVICE:** Available. **CONTENTS:** Covers community spiritual news, special prelacy activi-

110   Newspapers and Periodicals

ties, Armenian religious and educational activities, and special articles on cultural heritage. **CONTACT PERSON:** Archbishop Mesrob Ashjian, Prelate.

(412)
SAINT SARKIS ARMENIAN APOSTOLIC CHURCH OF NIAGARA FALLS BULLETIN
SAINT SARKIS ARMENIAN APOSTOLIC CHURCH OF NIAGARA FALLS
300 9th STREET
NIAGAGA FALLS, NEW YORK 14303   **(716) 282-2587**
PUBLISHER: Saint Sarkis Armenian Apostolic Church. **FREQUENCY:** Bi-monthly. **CONTACT PERSON:** Arsen Avdonian.

(413)
SHOGHAGAT, 1961-
SAINT SARKIS ARMENIAN APOSTOLIC CHURCH OF BAYSIDE
42nd AVENUE AND 213th STREET
BAYSIDE, NEW YORK 11361   **(212) 224-2275**
EDITOR: Archpriest Fr. Asoghik Kelejian. **PUBLISHER:** Saint Sarkis Armenian Apostolic Church. **FREQUENCY:** Monthly. **LANGUAGE:** Armenian and English. **CONTENTS:** Covers church news and community activities.

(414)
SUNRISE, 1980-
SAINT GREGORY THE ILLUMINATOR ARMENIAN CHURCH
12 CORBETT AVENUE
BINGHAMTON, NEW YORK 13903   **(607) 722-8801**
EDITOR: Very Rev. Fr. Sooren Chinchinian. **PUBLISHER:** Saint Gregory Armenian Church. **FREQUENCY:** Monthly. **SUBSCRIPTION RATE:** Free. **CIRCULATION:** 200. **LANGUAGE:** English. **CONTENTS:** Deals with reports concerning parish activities, along with articles explaining the significance of the major national holidays. **CONTACT PERSON:** Jack Injajigian, Parish Council.

(415)
ZUARTNOTZ, 1929-
HOLY CROSS ARMENIAN CHURCH
580 WEST 187th STREET
NEW YORK, NEW YORK 10033   **(212) 927-4020**
EDITOR: Krikor Vosganian. **PUBLISHER:** Holy Cross Armenian Church.

SUBSCRIPTION RATE: $1. **CIRCULATION:** 1,050. **LANGUAGE:** Armenian and English. **CONTENTS:** Informs people of what goes on in the community, also includes religious articles and events in the arts and culture. **CONTACT PERSON:** Alice Demirdjian.

Ohio

(416)
PAROS, 1954-
SAINT GREGORY OF NAREG ARMENIAN CHURCH
666 RICHMOND ROAD
CLEVELAND, OHIO 44143   **(216) 381-6590**

EDITOR: The Rev. Diran Papazian, Pastor. **PUBLISHER:** Saint Gregory of Nareg Armenian Church. **FREQUENCY:** Monthly. **LANGUAGE:** Armenian and English. **CONTENTS:** Covers Armenian community religious news in Greater Cleveland.

Pennsylvania

(417)
MER DOON, 1964-
SAINT SAHAG AND SAINT MESROB ARMENIAN APOSTOLIC CHURCH
630 CLOTHIER ROAD
WYNNEWOOD, PENNSYLVANIA 19096   **(215) 642-4212**

PUBLISHER: Saint Sahag and Saint Mesrob Armenian Apostolic Church. **BOOK SELLING SERVICE:** Available.

(418)
SAINT MARK'S NEWSLETTER
SAINT MARK'S ARMENIAN CATHOLIC CHURCH
400 HAVERFORD ROAD
WYNNEWOOD, PENNSYLVANIA 19096   **(215) 896-7789**

EDITOR: Jack Zarzatian, Sr. **PUBLISHER:** Saint Mark's Armenian Catholic Church. **FREQUENCY:** Monthly. **SUBSCRIPTION RATE:** Free. **CIRCULATION:** 275. **LANGUAGE:** English. **CONTENTS:** Covers events of the Parish.

Rhode Island

(419)
ARMENIAN EUPHRATES EVANGELICAL CHURCH NEWSLETTER
ARMENIAN EUPHRATES EVANGELICAL CHURCH
13 FRANKLIN STREET
PROVIDENCE, RHODE ISLAND 02903   (401) 751-4568

(420)
GANTEGH, 1961-
SAINTS VARTANANTZ ARMENIAN APOSTOLIC CHURCH
402 BROADWAY
PROVIDENCE, RHODE ISLAND 02920   (401) 831-6399
EDITOR: Archpriest Dr. Mesrob Tashjian. **PUBLISHER:** Saints Vartanantz Armenian Apostolic Church. **FREQUENCY:** Monthly. **SUBSCRIPTION RATE:** Free. **CIRCULATION:** 750. **LANGUAGE:** Armenian and English. **CONTACT PERSON:** Archpriest Dr. Mesrob Tashjian.

(421)
PAROS, 1958-
SAINT SAHAG AND SAINT MESROB ARMENIAN APOSTOLIC CHURCH
70 JEFFERSON STREET
PROVIDENCE, RHODE ISLAND 02908   (401) 272-7712
EDITOR: Rev. Haik Donikian, Pastor. **PUBLISHER:** Saint Sahag and Saint Mesrob Armenian Apostolic Church. **FREQUENCY:** Monthly. **LANGUAGE:** Armenian and English. **CONTENTS:** Cover church activities.

Texas

(422)
SAINT KEVORK ARMENIAN APOSTOLIC CHURCH BULLETIN
SAINT KEVORK ARMENIAN APOSTOLIC CHURCH
3211 SYNOTT ROAD
HOUSTON, TEXAS 77082   (713) 558-2722
PUBLISHER: Saint Kevork Armenian Apostolic Church. **FREQUENCY:** Weekly. **LANGUAGE:** Armenian and English. **CONTENTS:** Covers church news.

Wisconsin

(423)
ARARAT, 1981-

SAINT JOHN ARMENIAN CHURCH
7825 WEST LAYTON AVENUE
GREENFIELD, WISCONSIN 53220   (414) 282-1670 (414) 421-9113

EDITOR: Lynn Kaishian. **PUBLISHER:** Saint John Armenian Church. **FREQUENCY:** Monthly. **LANGUAGE:** Armenian and English. **CONTENTS:** Religious articles, cultural and parish news, and announcements.

(424)
NAREG

SAINT HAGOP'S ARMENIAN APOSTOLIC CHURCH
4100 NORTH NEWMAN ROAD
RACINE, WISCONSIN 53406   (414) 493-8122

FREQUENCY: Bi-monthly. **LANGUAGE:** Armenian and English. **CONTENTS:** Covers church news. **CONTACT PERSON:** Matthew Mikailian, Chairman.

(425)
VARAK, 1958-

SAINT MESROB ARMENIAN APOSTOLIC CHURCH
4605 ERIE STREET
RACINE, WISCONSIN 53402   (414) 639-0531

EDITOR: Kari Akgulian. **PUBLISHER:** Saint Mesrob Armenian Apostolic Church. **FREQUENCY:** Monthly. **SUBSCRIPTION RATE:** Free. **CIRCULATION:** 250. **LANGUAGE:** Armenian and English. **CONTENTS:** Covers parish community news, activities of its organizations, educational articles of historical nature about Armenians. **CONTACT PERSON:** Kari Akgulian, Managing Editor.

Armenian Studies
and Research Periodicals
California

(426)
THE ARMENIAN HORIZON, 1980-

U.C.L.A. ARMENIAN STUDENTS ASSOCIATION
308 WESTWOOD PLAZA-BOX 533
LOS ANGELES, CALIFORNIA 90024

EDITOR: Barlow Der Mugrdechian. **PUBLISHER:** University of California, Los Angeles, Armenian Students Association. **FREQUENCY:** Quarterly. **SUBSCRIPTION RATE:** Free. **CIRCULATION:** 5,000. **LANGUAGE:** English and Armenian. **CONTENTS:** A newspaper devoted to covering the news of the Armenian community in depth. Special articles covering Armenian Students Association, written by Armenian students.

(427)
ARMENIAN MUSICAL STUDIES NEWSLETTER, 1980-

ARMENIAN MUSICAL STUDIES
U.S.C. SCHOOL OF MUSIC
UNIVERSITY PARK
LOS ANGELES, CALIFORNIA 90089   **(213) 743-8901**

EDITOR: Dr. Ohannes Salibian. **PUBLISHER:** Armenian Musical Studies Program. **FREQUENCY:** Semi-annual. **LANGUAGE:** English. **CONTENTS:** Armenian Musical Studies development, intended to inform the general and academic audience about the developments in the U.S.C. Program for Armenian Musical Studies. **CONTACT PERSON:** Dr. Ohannes Salibian.

(428)
ARMENIAN NUMISMATIC JOURNAL, 1975-

ARMENIAN NUMISMATIC SOCIETY
8511 BEVERLY PARK PLACE
PICO RIVERA, CALIFORNIA 90660   **(213) 695-0380**

EDITOR: Y. T. Nercessian. **PUBLISHER:** Armenian Numismatic Society. **FREQUENCY:** Quarterly. **SUBSCRIPTION RATE:** 1st year $7., 2nd year $6. **CIRCULATION:** 130. **LANGUAGE:** Armenian and English. **BOOK SELLING SERVICE:** Available. **CONTENTS:** Articles related to Armenian numismatics, and abstracts on Armenian numismatic literature.

(428-A)
HROMGLA, 1982-

THE ARMENIAN APOSTOLIC CHURCH OF AMERICA WESTERN PRELACY
4401 RUSSELL AVENUE
LOS ANGELES, CALIFORNIA 90027   **(213) 663-8273**

EDITOR: Levon Khacherian, Chief Editor. **PUBLISHER:** The Armenian Apostolic Church of America, Western Prelacy. **FREQUENCY:** Annual. **LANGUAGE:** Armenian and English. **CONTENTS:** Religious and cultural articles.

(429)
HYE SHARZHOOM, 1979-
CALIFORNIA STATE UNIVERSITY, FRESNO
ARMENIAN STUDIES PROGRAM
FRESNO, CALIFORNIA 93740 **(209) 294-2832**
EDITOR: Vahe K. Messerlian; Randy Baloian, Assistant Editor. **PUB-LISHER:** California State University, Fresno, Armenian Studies Program. **FREQUENCY:** Quarterly. **LANGUAGE:** Armenian and English. **CON-TENTS:** Hye Sharzhoom is the official publication of C.S.U.F. Armenian Students Organization and the Armenian Studies Program. Covers several articles about Armenian culture, history, book reviews, and Armenian Studies Program at C.S.U.F.

(429-A)
JOURNAL OF THE SOCIETY FOR ARMENIAN STUDIES, 1984-
SOCIETY FOR ARMENIAN STUDIES
DEPARTMENT OF NEAR EASTERN LANGUAGES AND CULTURES
UNIVERSITY OF CALIFORNIA LOS ANGELES
405 HILGARD AVENUE
LOS ANGELES, CALIFORNIA 90024 **(213) 825-1307**
EDITOR: Prof. Avedis Sanjian. **PUBLISHER:** Society for Armenian Studies. **FREQUENCY:** Annual. **LANGUAGE:** English. **SUBSCRIPTION RATE:** $15. **CONTENTS:** A Scholarly journal.

(430)
MASHTOTS, 1976-
AMERICAN ARMENIAN INTERNATIONAL COLLEGE
1950 THIRD STREET
LA VERNE, CALIFORNIA 91750 **(714) 593-2595**
EDITOR: Editorial Board. **PUBLISHER:** American Armenian International College. **FREQUENCY:** Monthly. **SUBSCRIPTION RATE:** Free. **CIRCULATION:** 5,000 **LANGUAGE:** Armenian and English. **CON-TENTS:** Educational and professional articles, A.A.I.C. news and activities, book reviews and biographies of benefactors. **CONTACT PERSON:** Dr. Garbis Der Yeghiayan, College Dean.

(431)
NAVASART, 1982-
NAVASART
515 WEST BROADWAY SUITE D
(INSIDE CROWN FOODS MARKET)
GLENDALE, CALIFORNIA 91204 **(818) 241-5933**
EDITOR: Armen Donoyan. **PUBLISHER:** Navasart Foundation. **FRE-**

QUENCY: Monthly. **SUBSCRIPTION RATE:** $25. **CIRCULATION:** 1,700. **LANGUAGE:** Armenian. **BOOK SELLING SERVICE:** Available. **CONTENTS:** Armenian literary and cultural magazine. **CONTACT PERSON:** Armen Donoyan, Editor.

(432)
RAINBOW, 1984-

RAINBOW
409 WESTERN AVENUE
GLENDALE, CALIFORNIA 91201   (818) 243-6827

EDITOR & PUBLISHER: Hrant Avedisian. **FREQUENCY:** Quarterly. **SUBSCRIPTION RATE:** $10. **CIRCULATION:** 1,700. **LANGUAGE:** Armenian. **BOOK SELLING SERVICE:** Available. **CONTENTS:** Literary and arts articles. **CONTACT PERSON:** Hrant Avedisian.

Massachusetts

(433)
ARMENIAN LIBRARY AND MUSEUM OF AMERICA NEWSLETTER, 1972-

ARMENIAN LIBRARY AND MUSEUM OF AMERICA
380 CONCORD AVENUE
BELMONT, MASSACHUSETTS 02178   (617) 484-4780

PUBLISHER: Armenian Library and Museum of America. **FREQUENCY:** Three to four times a year. **SUBSCRIPTION RATE:** Free. **LANGUAGE:** English. **CIRCULATION:** 500. **CONTENTS:** Covers organization's acquisitions, news, and activities.

(434)
THE ARMENIAN REVIEW, 1948-

THE ARMENIAN REVIEW
38 ELTON AVENUE
WATERTOWN, MASSACHUSETTS 02172   (617) 926-4037

EDITOR: Gerard J. Libaridian. **PUBLISHER:** The Armenian Review, Inc. **FREQUENCY:** Quarterly. **SUBSCRIPTION RATE:** $15. **CIRCULATION:** 1,000. **LANGUAGE:** English. **CONTENTS:** Multi-disciplinary academic journal devoted to all periods of Armenian history and culture. **CONTACT PERSON:** Gerard J. Libaridian.

(435)
SOCIETY FOR ARMENIAN STUDIES NEWSLETTER, 1976-

BOSTON COLLEGE
SLAVIC & EASTERN LANGUAGES
CARNEY # 236
CHESTNUT HILL, MASSACHUSETTS 02167   (617) 552-3912

EDITOR: Michael J. Connolly. **PUBLISHER:** Society for Armenian Studies. **FREQUENCY:** Three times a year. **LANGUAGE:** English. **CONTENTS:** Includes information on the activities of the Society, its members, the state of Armenology studies, and listings of publications. **CONTACT PERSON:** Michael J. Connolly, Editor.

(436)
ZORYAN INSTITUTE BULLETIN, 1983-
THE ZORYAN INSTITUTE
85 FAYERWEATHER STREET
CAMBRIDGE, MASSACHUSETTS 02138　　　　　　**(617) 497-6713**
EDITOR: Mark Ayanian. **PUBLISHER:** The Zoryan Institute. **FREQUENCY:** Three to six times a year. **SUBSCRIPTION RATE:** Complimentary. **CIRCULATION:** 2,000. **LANGUAGE:** English. **BOOK SELLING SERVICE:** Available. **CONTENTS:** Covers information on research, documentation, public discussions, and publications sponsored by the Institute as well as descriptions of recent archival acquisitions. **CONTACT PERSON:** Mark Ayanian, Editor.

New Jersey

(437)
ARARAT LITERARY QUARTERLY, 1959-
ARMENIAN GENERAL BENEVOLENT UNION OF AMERICA
585 SADDLE RIVER ROAD
SADDLE BROOK, NEW JERSEY 07662　　　　　　**(201) 797-7600**
EDITOR: Leo Hamalian. **PUBLISHER:** Armenian General Benevolent Union of America. **FREQUENCY:** Quarterly. **SUBSCRIPTION RATE:** $10 for one year, $19 for two years, $28 for three years. **CIRCULATION:** 2,000. **LANGUAGE:** English. **CONTENTS:** A literary quarterly, featuring Armenian subjects, prominent writers such as W. Saroyan, and new writers of Armenian origin. **CONTACT PERSON:** Terry Chisnolm, Director of Publications.

(437-A)
SOCIETY FOR ARMENIAN STUDIES OCCASIONAL PAPERS, 1981-
SOCIETY FOR ARMENIAN STUDIES
GLASSBORO STATE COLLEGE
DEPARTMENT OF HISTORY
GLASSBORO, NEW JERSEY 08028　　　　　　**(607) 445-5000**
CONTACT PERSON: Robert Hewson.

New York

(438)
ARMENIAN ARCHITECTURAL ARCHIVES
ARMENIAN EDUCATIONAL COUNCIL, INC.
BRUNSWICK HILLS, EAST ROAD
TROY, NEW YORK 12180   **(518) 274-4526**
EDITOR: Inter-Documentation Co., Holland. **CONTENTS:** This documented photographic collection of Armenian architecture is designed to be a resource for research in architectural history. The series will have six or more issues, two of which with nearly 12,000 photos in microfiche are now being distributed to universities around the world.

(439)
ARMENIAN STUDIES AT COLUMBIA UNIVERSITY NEWSLETTER
COLUMBIA UNIVERSITY
CENTER FOR ARMENIAN STUDIES
BOX A
500 KENT HALL
NEW YORK, NEW YORK 10027   (718) 520-6951 (212) 280-2013
EDITOR: Eleanor H. Tejirian. **PUBLISHER:** Armenian Studies Center at Columbia University. **LANGUAGE:** English. **CONTENTS:** Covers activities of the Center.

(440)
KIROUKIRK, 1960-
THE ARMENIAN LITERARY SOCIETY
114 FIRST STREET
YONKERS, NEW YORK 10704   (914) 237-5751 (914) 761-2127
EDITOR: Editorial Council. **PUBLISHER:** The Armenian Literary Society. **FREQUENCY:** Quarterly. **SUBSCRIPTION RATE:** Free. **CIRCULATION:** 1,500. **LANGUAGE:** Armenian and English. **BOOK SELLING SERVICE:** Available. **CONTACT PERSON:** K. Magarian.

Ohio

(441)
ANNUAL OF ARMENIAN LINGUISTICS, 1979-
PROF. JOHN GREPPIN
CLEVELAND STATE UNIVERSITY
CLEVELAND, OHIO 44115   (216) 687-3967 (216) 687-3951
EDITORS: Prof. John Greppin, Cleveland; Academician G. B. Djahu-

kian, Yerevan; Prof. Eric Hamp, Chicago; Rudiger Schmitt, Saarbrucken, West Germany; Prof. G. Bolognesi, Milan, Italy; A. A. Khachaturian, Yerevan. **FREQUENCY:** Annual. **SUBSCRIPTION RATE:** $14 for two years. **CONTENTS:** A scholarly publication for an audience with some academic background in linguistics or allied studies. **CONTACT PERSON:** Prof. John A. C. Greppin.

Pennsylvania

(442)
ARMENIAN HISTORICAL RESEARCH ASSOCIATION NEWSLETTER
ARMENIAN HISTORICAL RESEARCH ASSOCIATION
30 NORTHWOOD ROAD
NEWTOWN SQUARE, PENNSYLVANIA 19073   (215) 356-0635
EDITOR: Dr. Charles N. Mahjoubian. **PUBLISHER:** Armenian Historical Research Association. **FREQUENCY:** Semi-annual. **LANGUAGE:** Armenian and English.

School Bulletins and Newsletters
California

(443)
HIE TBROTZ
SAHAG-MESROB ARMENIAN CHRISTIAN SCHOOL
2501 NORTH MAIDEN LANE
ALTADENA, CALIFORNIA 91001   (818) 798-5020

(444)
KROUZIAN-ZEKARIAN ELEMENTARY SCHOOL NEWSLETTER
KROUZIAN-ZEKARIAN ELEMENTARY SCHOOL
825 BROTHERHOOD WAY   (415) 586-8686
SAN FRANCISCO, CALIFORNIA 94132   (415) 586-8687

(445)
OOSANOGH, 1979-
ARMENIAN MESROBIAN ELEMENTARY & HIGH SCHOOL
8110 PARAMOUNT BLVD.
PICO RIVERA, CALIFORNIA 90660   (213) 723-3181
PUBLISHER: Armenian Mesrobian Elementary and High School. **FREQUENCY:** Quarterly. **LANGUAGE:** Armenian and English. **CONTENTS:** Student articles on any subject.

(446)
OUR VOICE, 1980-
VAHAN & ANOUSH CHAMLIAN ARMENIAN SCHOOL
4444 LOWELL AVENUE
GLENDALE, CALIFORNIA 91214   **(818) 957-3398**
EDITOR: Khachatoorian and Pappas, English Section; Zarzavadjian and Galstian, Armenian Section. **FREQUENCY:** Semi-annual. **SUBSCRIP-TION RATE:** Free. **LANGUAGE:** Armenian and English. **CONTENTS:** Articles and pictures submitted by the students and faculty on subject matters related to the events and lessons of the academic quarter. **CONTACT PERSON:** Vartkes Ghazarian.

(447)
SEEDS, 1979-
ROSE AND ALEX PILIBOS ARMENIAN SCHOOL
1615 NORTH ALEXANDRIA AVENUE
LOS ANGELES, CALIFORNIA 90027   **(213) 668-2661**
EDITOR: Students. **PUBLISHER:** Rose and Alex Pilibos Armenian School. **LANGUAGE:** Armenian and English.

Michigan

(448)
EREPONI VISIONS
A.G.B.U. ALEX MANOOGIAN SCHOOL
22001 NORTH WESTERN HIGHWAY
SOUTHFIELD, MICHIGAN 48075   **(313) 569-2988**

New Jersey

(449)
CHAH
HOVNANIAN ARMENIAN SCHOOL
817 RIVER ROAD   **(201) 793-0913**
NEW MILFORD, NEW JERSEY 07646   **(201) 967-5940**
FREQUENCY: Semi-annual. **SUBSCRIPTION RATE:** Free. **CIRCULA-TION:** 3,000. **LANGUAGE:** Armenian and English.

Section Four

SCHOOLS

Day Schools

One Day or Saturday Schools

Day Schools
California

(450)
A.G.B.U. SAINT PETER SCHOOL
6624 LOCKHURST DRIVE
CANOGA PARK, CALIFORNIA 91307   **(818) 883-2428**

DATE FOUNDED: 1976. **PRINCIPAL:** Vartouhy Dadour. **CHAIRMAN OF THE BOARD:** Nubar Agopian. **GRADE LEVELS:** Pre-school to 10th grade. **ENROLLMENT:** 122 girls, 91 boys, total: 213. **SPONSORING ORGANIZATION:** A.G.B.U. **SCHOLARSHIPS, LOANS, GRANTS:** Available. **LIBRARY:** Yes. **CONTACT PERSON:** Varthouhy Dadour, Acting Principal.

(451)
ARMENIAN COMMUNITY SCHOOL OF FRESNO
1940 NORTH FRESNO STREET
FRESNO, CALIFORNIA 93703   **(209) 233-1800**

DATE FOUNDED: 1977. **PRINCIPAL.** Assadour Assadourian. **CHAIRMAN OF THE BOARD:** Ben Krikorian. **GRADE LEVELS:** Pre-school to 6th grade. **ENROLLMENT:** 30 girls, 53 boys, total: 83. **SPONSORING ORGANIZATION:** Community. **PUBLICATION:** Armenian Community School of Fresno Newsletter. **SCHOLARSHIPS, LOANS, GRANTS:** Available. **CONTACT PERSON:** Assadour Assadourian, Principal.

(452)
ARMENIAN MEKHITARIST FATHERS SCHOOL
4900 MARYLAND AVENUE
LA CRESCENTA, CALIFORNIA 91214   **(818) 249-6121**

(453)
ARMENIAN MESROBIAN ELEMENTARY AND HIGH SCHOOL
8110 PARAMOUNT BLVD.
PICO RIVERA, CALIFORNIA 90660   **(213) 723-3181**

DATE FOUNDED: 1965. **PRINCIPAL:** Viken Hovsepian. **CHAIRMAN OF THE BOARD:** Minas Oganessian. **GRADE LEVELS:** Pre-school to high school. **ENROLLMENT:** 179 girls, 175 boys, total: 354. **SPONSORING ORGANIZATION:** Holy Cross Armenian Apostolic Cathedral. **LIBRARY:** Yes. **CONTACT PERSON:** Viken Hovsepian, Principal.

(454)
CHARLOTTE AND ELIS MERDINIAN ARMENIAN EVANGELICAL SCHOOL
5000 COLFAX AVENUE
NORTH HOLLYWOOD, CALIFORNIA 91601   (818) 762-1022

DATE FOUNDED: 1982. PRINCIPAL: Aram Boolghoorjian. CHAIRMAN OF THE BOARD: Alice Haig. GRADE LEVELS: Pre-school to elementary. ENROLLMENT: Total: 105. SPONSORING ORGANIZATION: Armenian Evangelical School of California, Inc. LIBRARY: Yes. CONTACT PERSON: Aram Boolghoorjian or Alice Haig.

(455)
HOLY MARTYRS ELEMENTARY AND FERRAHIAN HIGH SCHOOL
5300 WHITE OAK AVENUE
ENCINO, CALIFORNIA 91316   (818) 784-6228

DATE FOUNDED: 1964. PRINCIPAL: Gabriel Injejikian. CHAIRMAN OF THE BOARD: Artoosh Satoorian. GRADE LEVELS: Pre-school to high school. ENROLLMENT: 329 girls, 316 boys, total: 645. SPONSORING ORGANIZATION: Holy Martyrs Armenian Apostolic Church. SCHOLARSHIPS, LOANS, GRANTS: Available. LIBRARY: Yes. CONTACT PERSON: Gabriel Injejikian, Principal.

(456)
KROUZIAN-ZEKARIAN ELEMENTARY SCHOOL
825 BROTHERHOOD WAY   (415) 586-8686
SAN FRANCISCO, CALIFORNIA 94132   (415) 586-8687

DATE FOUNDED: 1980. PRINCIPAL: Arsineh Oshagan. CHAIRMAN OF THE BOARD: Azad Azadkhanian. GRADE LEVELS: Pre-school to fifth grade. PUBLICATION: Krouzian-Zekarian Elementary School Newsletter. SPONSORING ORGANIZATION: Saint Gregory Armenian Apostolic Church. SCHOLARSHIPS, LOANS, GRANTS: Available. LIBRARY: Yes. CONTACT PERSON: Annig Zindarsian, Secretary.

(457)
ROSE AND ALEX PILIBOS ARMENIAN SCHOOL
1615 NORTH ALEXANDRIA AVENUE
LOS ANGELES, CALIFORNIA 90027   (213) 668-2661

DATE FOUNDED: 1969. PRINCIPAL: Hagop Hagopian. CHAIRMAN OF THE BOARD: Navasart Kazazian. GRADE LEVELS: Pre-school to 12th grade. ENROLLMENT: 420 girls, 382 boys, total: 802. SPONSORING

ORGANIZATION: Saint Garabed Armenian Apostolic Church. **PUBLI-CATION:** Seeds. **LIBRARY:** Yes. **BOOK SELLING SERVICE:** Available. **CONTACT PERSON:** Hagop Hagopian, Principal.

(458)
SAHAG MESROB ARMENIAN CHRISTIAN SCHOOL
2501 NORTH MAIDEN LANE
ALTADENA, CALIFORNIA 91001   **(818) 798-5020**
DATE FOUNDED: 1980. **PRINCIPAL:** Zabel Alahaydoyan. **CHAIRMAN OF THE BOARD:** Mike Youssefian. **GRADE LEVELS:** Kindergarten to sixth grade. **ENROLLMENT:** Total: 195. **PUBLICATION:** Hie Tbrotz. **SCHOLARSHIPS:** Available. **CONTACT PERSON:** Zabel Alahaydoyan, Principal.

(459)
SAINT GREGORY ARMENIAN SCHOOL
2215 EAST COLORADO BLVD.
PASADENA, CALIFORNIA 91107   **(818) 449-1523**
DATE FOUNDED: 1984. **CHAIRMAN OF THE BOARD:** Dr. Artin Sagherian. **GRADE LEVEL:** Kindergarten to third grade. **SPONSORING ORGANIZATION:** Saint Gregory Armenian Church. **PUBLICATION:** Shoghagat. **CONTACT PERSON:** Very Rev. Fr. Moushegh Tashjian, Parish Priest and President.

(460)
T.C.A. ARSHAG DICKRANIAN SCHOOL
1200 NORTH CAHUENGA BLVD.
LOS ANGELES, CALIFORNIA 90038 (213) 461-4377 (213) 461-4378
DATE FOUNDED: 1981. **PRINCIPAL:** Vartkes Kourouyan. **CHAIRMAN OF THE BOARD:** Prof. Avedis Sanjian. **GRADE LEVELS:** Pre-school to seventh grade. **ENROLLMENT:** 74 girls, 116 boys, total: 190. **SPONSORING ORGANIZATION:** Tekeyan Cultural Association. **CONTACT PERSON:** Ardem Khatchadourian, Secretary.

(461)
VAHAN AND ANOUSH CHAMLIAN ARMENIAN SCHOOL (Elementary & Jr. High)
4444 LOWELL AVENUE
GLENDALE, CALIFORNIA 91214   **(818) 957-3399**

DATE FOUNDED: 1976. PRINCIPAL: Vartkes Ghazarian. CHAIRMAN OF THE BOARD: Stepan Kabadyan. GRADE LEVELS: Pre-school to ninth grade. ENROLLMENT: Total: 363. SPONSORING ORGANIZA- TION: Armenian Apostolic Church of America, Western Prelacy, PUBLI- CATION: Our Voice. SCHOLARSHIPS, LOANS, GRANTS: Available. CONTACT PERSON: Vartkes Ghazarian, Principal.

(462)
VAHAN AND ANOUSH CHAMLIAN ARMENIAN SCHOOL (Pre-school)
1224 EAST CARLTON DRIVE
GLENDALE, CALIFORNIA 91205   (818) 240-7030

Massachusetts

(463)
A.G.B.U. ARMENIAN ELEMENTARY SCHOOL
465 MOUNT AUBURN STREET
WATERTOWN, MASSACHUSETTS 02172   (617) 926-1805
DATE FOUNDED: 1970. PRINCIPAL: Ellie Andreassian. CHAIRMAN OF THE BOARD: Dr. Armen Demirjian. GRADE LEVELS: Pre-school to sixth grade. ENROLLMENT: 57 girls, 46 boys, total: 103. SPONSORING ORGANIZATION: Armenian General Benevolent Union. SCHOLAR- SHIPS, LOANS, GRANTS: Available. LIBRARY: Yes. CONTACT PER- SON: Ellie Andreassian, Acting Principal.

(464)
ARMENIAN SISTERS ACADEMY
20 PELHAM ROAD
LEXINGTON, MASSACHUSETTS 02173   (617) 861-8303
DATE FOUNDED: 1982. PRINCIPAL & CHAIRMAN OF THE BOARD: Sister Alphonsa-Azadouhie Bedrossian. GRADE LEVELS: Pre-school to elementary. ENROLLMENT: Total: 84. CONTACT PERSON: A. Bedros- sian, Principal.

(464-A)
SAINT STEPHEN'S ARMENIAN NURSERY SCHOOL
47 NICHOLS AVENUE
WATERTOWN, MASSACHUSETTS 02172   (617) 926-6979

Michigan

(465)
A.G.B.U. ALEX MANOOGIAN SCHOOL
22001 NORTHWESTERN HIGHWAY
SOUTHFIELD, MICHIGAN 48075   (313) 569-2988
DATE FOUNDED: 1969. **PRINCIPAL:** Richard Norsigian. **CHAIRMAN OF THE BOARD:** Richard Apkarian. **GRADE LEVELS:** Pre-school to high school. **ENROLLMENT:** 106 girls, 115 boys, total: 221. **SPONSORING ORGANIZATION:** Armenian General Benevolent Union. **PUBLICATION:** Erepouni Vision (year book). **SCHOLARSHIPS, LOANS GRANTS:** Available. **LIBRARY:** Yes. **CONTACT PERSON:** Richard Norsigian, Principal.

(466)
A.R.S. ARMENIAN DAY SCHOOL
19310 FORD ROAD
DEARBORN, MICHIGAN 48128   (313) 336-8090
PRINCIPAL: Kari Arvanigian. **SPONSORING ORGANIZATION:** Saint Sarkis Armenian Apostolic Church and Armenian Relief Society.

New Jersey

(468)
HOVNANIAN ARMENIAN SCHOOL
817 RIVER ROAD
NEW MILFORD, NEW JERSEY 07646   (201) 967-5940
DATE FOUNDED: 1975. **PRINCIPAL:** Krikor Pidedjian. **CHAIRMAN OF THE BOARD:** Vahan Hovnanian. **GRADE LEVELS:** Pre-school to sixth grade. **ENROLLMENT:** Total: 140. **PUBLICATION:** Chah. **LIBRARY:** Yes. **CONTACT PERSON:** Krikor Pidedjian, Principal.

New York

(469)
HOLY MARTYR'S ARMENIAN DAY SCHOOL
209-15 HORACE HARDING EXPRESS WAY
BAYSIDE, NEW YORK 11364   (212) 225-4826 (212) 225-4837

DATE FOUNDED: 1969. PRINCIPAL: Sara Dadourian. CHAIRMAN OF THE BOARD: Roy Kelegian. GRADE LEVELS: Pre-school to sixth grade. ENROLLMENT: 58 girls, 59 boys, total: 117. PUBLICATION: Holy Martyr's Armenian Day School Newsletter. SCHOLARSHIPS, LOANS, GRANTS: Available. CONTACT PERSON: Beatrice Kassapian, Secretary.

(470)
SAINT ILLUMINATOR'S ARMENIAN DAY SCHOOL
WOODSIDE ARMENIAN CENTER
69-23 47th AVENUE
WOODSIDE, NEW YORK 11377   (718) 478-4073 (212) 786-0562

PRINCIPAL: Garen Yegparian. CHAIRMAN OF THE BOARD: Ohannes Bezdikian. GRADE LEVELS: Pre-school to sixth grade.

Pennsylvania

(471)
ARMENIAN CATHOLIC SISTERS' ACADEMY
440 UPPER GULPH ROAD
RADNOR, PENNSYLVANIA 19087   (215) 687-4100

PRINCIPAL: Sister Arousiag Sadjonian.

Saturday or One Day Schools
California

(472)
ARMENIAN APOSTOLIC CHURCH OF SANTA CLARA VALLEY SATURDAY SCHOOL
11370 SOUTH STELLING
CUPERTINO, CALIFORNIA 95014   (408) 257-6743

DATE FOUNDED: 1964. SPONSORING ORGANIZATION: Armenian Apostolic Church of Santa Clara Valley. SUBJECTS OFFERED: Armenian language, culture, and history. GRADE LEVELS: Beginning, intermediate, advanced, and adult. ENROLLMENT: 25 girls, 15 boys, total: 40. CONTACT PERSON: Anahid Nalvarian, Armenian Language School Director, and Susan Movsesian, Church School Superintendent.

(473)
ARMENIAN CHURCH OF THE NAZARENE SATURDAY SCHOOL
411 EAST ACACIA AVENUE
GLENDALE, CALIFORNIA 91205   (818) 244-9920

DATE FOUNDED: 1980. **SPONSORING ORGANIZATION:** Armenian Church of the Nazarene. **SUBJECTS OFFERED:** Armenian language. **GRADE LEVELS:** Beginning. **ENROLLMENT:** Total: 45. **CONTACT:** Church Office.

(474)
ARMENIAN EVANGELICAL BRETHREN CHURCH SATURDAY SCHOOL
1576 EAST WASHINGTON BLVD.
PASADENA, CALIFORNIA 91104   **(818) 794-9834**
DATE FOUNDED: 1965. **SPONSORING ORGANIZATION:** Armenian Evangelical Brethren Church. **SUBJECTS OFFERED:** Armenian language, culture, and history. **GRADE LEVELS:** Beginning, intermediate, advanced, and adult. **ENROLLMENT:** 46 girls, 43 boys, total: 89. **CONTACT PERSON:** Ashken Aroyan, Principal.

(475)
ARMENIAN SOCIETY OF LOS ANGELES SATURDAY SCHOOL
221 SOUTH BRAND BLVD.
GLENDALE, CALIFORNIA 91204   **(818) 241-1073**
DATE FOUNDED: 1956. **SPONSORING ORGANIZATION:** Armenian Society of Los Angeles. **SUBJECTS OFFERED:** Armenian language, culture and history. **GRADE LEVELS:** Beginning, intermediate, and advanced. **ENROLLMENT:** 180 girls, 120 boys, total: 300. **CONTACT PERSON:** Alice Avanessian, Executive Secretary.

(476)
HOLY CROSS ARMENIAN APOSTOLIC CATHEDRAL SATURDAY SCHOOL
900 WEST LINCOLN AVENUE
MONTEBELLO, CALIFORNIA 90640   **(213) 727-1114**
DATE FOUNDED: 1979. **SPONSORING ORGANIZATION:** Holy Cross Armenian Cathedral. **SUBJECTS OFFERED:** Armenian language and history. **GRADE LEVELS:** Beginning, intermediate, and advanced. **ENROLLMENT:** 60 girls, 55 boys, total: 115. **CONTACT PERSON:** Rev. Papken Manuelian.

(477)
SAINT GREGORY ARMENIAN APOSTOLIC CHURCH SATURDAY SCHOOL
51 COMMONWEALTH AVENUE
SAN FRANCISCO, CALIFORNIA 94118   **(415) 586-8686**

DATE FOUNDED: 1960. SPONSORING ORGANIZATION: Saint Gregory Armenian Apostolic Church. SUBJECTS OFFERED: Armenian language, culture, and history. GRADE LEVELS: Beginning, intermediate, and advanced. ENROLLMENT: 61 girls, 57 boys, total: 118. CONTACT PERSON: Rostom Aintablian, Principal.

(478)
SAINT GREGORY ARMENIAN APOSTOLIC CHURCH SATURDAY SCHOOL
2215 EAST COLORADO BLVD.
PASADENA, CALIFORNIA 91107   (818) 449-1523
SPONSORING ORGANIZATION: Saint Gregory Armenian Apostolic Church. SUBJECTS OFFERED: Armenian language, culture, history, folk dance, and songs. GRADE LEVELS: Beginning and intermediate. ENROLLMENT: Total: 80. CONTACT PERSON: Fr. Moushegh Tashjian, Parish Priest.

(479)
SAINT PETER ARMENIAN APOSTOLIC CHURCH SATURDAY SCHOOL
17231 SHERMAN WAY
VAN NUYS, CALIFORNIA 91406   (818) 344-4860
DATE FOUNDED: 1958. SPONSORING ORGANIZATION: Saint Peter Armenian Apostolic Church. SUBJECTS OFFERED: Armenian language, culture, history, religious education, and English. GRADE LEVELS: Beginning and intermediate. ENROLLMENT: Total: 90. CONTACT PERSON: Fr. Shahe Semerdjian, Pastor.

Connecticut

(480)
SAINT STEPHEN'S ARMENIAN APOSTOLIC CHURCH SATURDAY SCHOOL
167 TREMONT STREET
NEW BRITAIN, CONNECTICUT 06051   (203) 229-8322
CONTACT PERSON: Rev. Sahak Andekian.

District of Columbia
Washington D.C.

(481)
SAINT MARY'S ARMENIAN APOSTOLIC CHURCH SATURDAY SCHOOL
4125 FESSENDEN STREET, N.W.
WASHINGTON, D.C. 20016   (202) 363-1923 (301) 942-2434

DATE FOUNDED: 1960. **SPONSORING ORGANIZATION:** Saint Mary's Armenian Apostolic Church. **SUBJECTS OFFERED:** Armenian language, culture, history, songs, and dance. **GRADE LEVELS:** Beginning, intermediate, and advanced. **ENROLLMENT.** Total: 75. **CONTACT PERSON:** Rev. Vartanes Kalayjian, Pastor.

Florida

(482)
ARMENIAN SCHOOL OF LONGWOOD
1151 ORIOLE STREET
LONGWOOD, FLORIDA 32750   **(305) 834-5918**
CONTACT PERSON: Varso Nakutis

Illinois

(483)
DANIEL VAROUJAN ARMENIAN SCHOOL
1701 NORTH GREENWOOD
GLENVIEW, ILLINOIS 60025   **(312) 262-8634**
CONTACT PERSON: Arpy Killian.

(484)
MESROBIAN SCHOOL NO. 1
1732 MAPLE STREET
GRANITE CITY, ILLINOIS 62040   **(618) 451-7508**
CONTACT PERSON: Rev. Zaven Poladian.

(485)
SAINT PAUL ARMENIAN APOSTOLIC CHURCH SATURDAY SCHOOL
645 SOUTH LEWIS AVENUE
WAUKEGAN, ILLINOIS 60085   **(312) 234-4026**
CONTACT PERSON: Katherine Mikaelian.

Maryland

(486)
HAMASDEGH ARMENIAN SATURDAY SCHOOL
SOORP KHATCH ARMENIAN APOSTOLIC CHURCH
4906 FLINT DRIVE
CHEVY CHASE, MARYLAND 20816   **(301) 227-6880**

DATE FOUNDED: 1969. **SPONSORING ORGANIZATION:** Soorp Khatch Armenian Apostolic Church. **SUBJECTS OFFERED:** Armenian language, culture, history, English language, and dance. **GRADE LEVELS:** Beginning and intermediate. **ENROLLMENT:** 55 girls, 45 boys, total: 100. **CONTACT PERSON:** Aram Belekjian.

Massachusetts

(487)
HOLY TRINITY ARMENIAN APOSTOLIC CHURCH SATURDAY SCHOOL
886 MAIN STREET
WORCESTER, MASSACHUSETTS 01610   **(617) 752-0782**
CONTACT PERSON: Rev. Vasken Bekiarian.

(488)
SAHAG-MESROB ARMENIAN SCHOOL
SAINT JAMES ARMENIAN APOSTOLIC CHURCH
465 MOUNT AUBURN STREET
WATERTOWN, MASSACHUSETTS 02172   **(617) 923-8860**
DATE FOUNDED: 1932. **SPONSORING ORGANIZATION:** Saint James Armenian Apostolic Church. **SUBJECTS OFFERED:** Armenian language, culture, history, and religious education. **GRADE LEVELS:** Beginning, intermediate, advanced, and adult. **ENROLLMENT:** 158 girls, 143 boys, total: (Saturday & Sunday-Schools combined) 301. **CONTACT PERSON:** Rev. Dajad A. Davidian, Pastor.

(489)
SAINT ASDVADZADZIN ARMENIAN APOSTOLIC CHURCH SATURDAY SCHOOL
211 CHURCH STREET
WHITINSVILLE, MASSACHUSETTS 01588   **(617) 234-3677**
CONTACT PERSON: Rev. Gomidas Der Torossian.

(490)
SAINT GREGORY ARMENIAN APOSTOLIC CHURCH SATURDAY SCHOOL
135 GOODWIN STREET
INDIAN ORCHARD, MASSACHUSETTS 01151   **(413) 543-1845**
CONTACT PERSON: Antranig Baljian.

(491)
SAINT GREGORY ARMENIAN APOSTOLIC CHURCH OF MERRI-MACK VALLEY SATURDAY SCHOOL
158 MAIN STREET
NORTH ANDOVER, MASSACHUSETTS 01845 (617) 685-5038
DATE FOUNDED: 1970. **SPONSORING ORGANIZATION:** Board of Trustees of Armenian Relief Society. **SUBJECTS OFFERED:** Armenian language, culture, and history. **GRADE LEVELS:** Beginning and intermediate. **ENROLLMENT:** 20 girls, 10 boys, total: 30. **CONTACT PERSON:** Tom Vartabedian and Nora Daghlian.

(492)
SAINT STEPHEN'S ARMENIAN APOSTOLIC CHURCH SATURDAY SCHOOL
ARMENIAN CULTURAL & EDUCATIONAL CENTER
47 NICHOLS AVENUE
WATERTOWN, MASSACHUSETTS 02172 (617) 924-7562
CONTACT PERSON: Agnes Ourfalian.

Michigan

(493)
A.R.S. ZAVARIAN SCHOOL NO. 1
19310 FORD ROAD
DEARBORN, MICHIGAN 48128 (313) 336-6840
CONTACT PERSON: Haroutiun Manoogian.

(494)
A.R.S. ZAVARIAN SCHOOL NO. 2
5548 EDINBOROUGH DRIVE
WEST BLOOMFIELD, MICHIGAN 48933 (313) 626-7384
CONTACT PERSON: Hermine Manoogian.

(495)
ARMENIAN CONGREGATIONAL CHURCH OF GREATER DETROIT SATURDAY SCHOOL
26210 WEST 12 MILE ROAD
SOUTHFIELD, MICHIGAN 48034 (313) 352-0680
DATE FOUNDED: 1976. **SPONSORING ORGANIZATION:** Armenian Congregational Church of Greater Detroit. **SUBJECTS OFFERED:** Armenian language, culture, and history. **GRADE LEVELS:** Beginning, intermediate, advanced, and adult. **ENROLLMENT:** 40 girls, 45 boys, total: (Saturday & Sunday-Schools combined) 85. **CONTACT PERSON:** Rev. Dr. Vahan H. Tootikian, Minister.

(496)
SAINT SARKIS ARMENIAN APOSTOLIC CHURCH SATURDAY
SCHOOL
19300 FORD ROAD
DEARBORN, MICHIGAN 48128   (313) 336-6200

Missouri

(497)
MESROBIAN SCHOOL NO. 2
471 WOODSMILL ROAD
SAINT LOUIS, MISSOURI 63141   (314) 991-5070
CONTACT PERSON: Dr. Vatche Ayvazian.

New Jersey

(498)
ARARAT ARMENIAN SCHOOL
ARMENIAN CULTURAL ASSOCIATION OF NEW JERSEY
P.O. BOX 185
MIDDLETOWN, NEW JERSEY 07748   (201) 229-2568
CONTACT PERSON: Armen Bulbulian.

(499)
ARARATIAN ARMENIAN SATURDAY SCHOOL
200 WEST MT. PLEASANT AVENUE
LIVINGSTON, NEW JERSEY 07039   (201) 533-9794
DATE FOUNDED: 1929. SPONSORING ORGANIZATION: Saint Mary
Armenian Apostolic Church. SUBJECTS OFFERED: Armenian lan-
guage, culture, and history. GRADE LEVELS: Beginning, intermediate,
advanced, and adult. ENROLLMENT: 26 girls, 22 boys, total: 48. CON-
TACT PERSON: Vartan Abdo, Superintendent.

(500)
NAREG ARMENIAN SATURDAY SCHOOL
461 BERGEN BLVD.
RIDGEFIELD, NEW JERSEY 07657   (201) 943-2950 (201) 943-9650
DATE FOUNDED: 1959. SPONSORING ORGANIZATION: Saints Var-
tanantz Armenian Apostolic Church of New Jersey. SUBJECTS
OFFERED: Armenian language, culture, history, and English language.
GRADE LEVELS: Beginning and intermediate. ENROLLMENT: 40 girls,
35 boys, total: 75. CONTACT PERSON: Archpriest Vahrich Shirinian.

(501)
SAINT LEON ARMENIAN APOSTOLIC CHURCH WEDNESDAY SCHOOL
12-61 SADDLE RIVER ROAD
FAIR LAWN, NEW JERSEY 07410   (201) 791-2862
DATE FOUNDED: 1953. SPONSORING ORGANIZATION: Saint Leon Armenian Apostolic Church. SUBJECTS OFFERED: Armenian language, culture, and history. GRADE LEVELS: Beginning, intermediate, and advanced. ENROLLMENT: 45 girls, 55 boys, total: 100. CONTACT PERSON: Hermine Menakian, Principal.

(502)
SAINT THOMAS ARMENIAN APOSTOLIC CHURCH SATURDAY SCHOOL
P.O. BOX 53
TENAFLY, NEW JERSEY 07670   (201) 567-5446
DATE FOUNDED: 1960. SPONSORING ORGANIZATION: Saint Thomas Armenian Church. SUBJECTS OFFERED: Armenian language, culture, history, and dance. GRADE LEVELS: Beginning, intermediate, and advanced. ENROLLMENT: Total: 80. CONTACT PERSON: Sylva Der Stepanian.

New York

(504)
SAINT ILLUMINATOR'S SATURDAY SCHOOL
WOODSIDE ARMENIAN CENTER
69-23 47th AVENUE
WOODSIDE, NEW YORK 11377   (718) 361-2426
CONTACT PERSON: Sona Shekookian.

(505)
SAINT MESROB SCHOOL OF ROCKLAND COUNTY
P.O. BOX 118
CONGERS, NEW YORK 10920   (914) 965-6432
CONTACT PERSON: Karabet Tiratsouyan.

(506)
SAINT SARKIS ARMENIAN APOSTOLIC CHURCH SATURDAY SCHOOL
42nd AVENUE & 213th STREET
BAYSIDE, NEW YORK 11361   (718) 229-6790
CONTACT PERSON: Sirpuhi Mark.

Ohio

(507)
HOLY CROSS ARMENIAN APOSTOLIC CHURCH SATURDAY SCHOOL
4402 WALLINGS ROAD
NORTH ROYALTON, OHIO 44133   **(216) 237-4380**
CONTACT PERSON: Anoush Marashlian.

Pennsylvania

(508)
HAIGAZIAN ARMENIAN SCHOOL
SAINT GREGORY ARMENIAN CHURCH
8701 RIDGE AVENUE   **(215) 482-9200**
PHILADELPHIA, PENNSYLVANIA 19128   **(215) 482-3344**

DATE FOUNDED: 1927. **SPONSORING ORGANIZATION:** Armenian Relief Society. **SUBJECTS OFFERED:** Armenian language, culture, history, and English language. **GRADE LEVELS:** Beginning and intermediate. **ENROLLMENT:** 25 girls, 40 boys, total: 65. **CONTACT PERSON:** Archpriest Arsen Hagopian.

Rhode Island

(509)
MOURAD ARMENIAN SCHOOL
402 BROADWAY
PROVIDENCE, RHODE ISLAND 02909   **(401) 831-6399**

SPONSORING ORGANIZATION: Saints Vartanantz Armenian Apostolic Church. **SUBJECTS OFFERED:** Armenian language, culture, history, and religious education. **GRADE LEVELS:** Beginning, intermediate, and advanced. **CONTACT PERSON:** Archpriest Dr. Mesrob Tashjian.

Texas

(509-A)
SAINT KEVORK ARMENIAN APOSTOLIC CHURCH SATURDAY-SCHOOL
3211 SYNOTT ROAD
HOUSTON, TEXAS 77082   **(713) 558-2722**

DATE FOUNDED: 1981. **SUBJECTS OFFERED:** Armenian language, culture, and history. **GRADE LEVELS:** Beginning, intermediate, advanced and adult. **ENROLLMENT:** 30 girls, 40 boys, total: 70. **CONTACT PERSON:** Fr. Nersess Jebejian, Pastor and Superintendent.

Wisconsin

(510)
A.R.S. MARZABED SCHOOL
4100 NORTH NEWMAN ROAD
RACINE, WISCONSIN 53406   **(414) 639-8983**
CONTACT PERSON: Sara Mikaelian, Chairperson

(511)
SAINT MESROB ARMENIAN APOSTOLIC CHURCH SATURDAY SCHOOL
4605 ERIE STREET
RACINE, WISCONSIN 53402   **(414) 639-0531**
DATE FOUNDED: 1935. **SPONSORING ORGANIZATION:** Diocese of the Armenian Church, Department of Religious Education. **SUBJECTS OFFERED:** Armenian language, culture, history, and English language. **GRADE LEVELS:** Beginning, intermediate, and advanced. **ENROLLMENT:** 28 girls, 27 boys, total: 55. **CONTACT PERSON:** Mary Katerdjian, Superintendent.

Section Five

<u>FOUNDATIONS</u>

Foundations
California

(512)
ARAKELIAN K. FOUNDATION
56372 ROAD 200
NORTH FORK, CALIFORNIA 93643   **(209) 877-2252**
CONTACT PERSON: Aram Arakelian.

(513)
ARMENIAN EDUCATIONAL FOUNDATION, INC.
517 EAST WILSON AVENUE, SUITE 103 B
GLENDALE, CALIFORNIA 91206   **(818) 240-3257**
DATE FOUNDED: 1950. **PURPOSE AND ACTIVITIES:** Renders finan-
cial assistance to Armenian schools and students irrespective of their
religious affiliation or denomination in the U.S.A. Assists in establishing
Armenian schools and centers all over the world. **DIRECTORS AND
OFFICERS:** Mardik Hovsepian, Chairman; Hacop Shirvanian, President;
Viken Hovsepian, Vice President; Hrand Simonian, Secretary; Other:
Vahe Karapetian, Nora Sahakian, Arshag Dickranian, Lutvig Mardiro-
sian. **TYPE OF FUNDS:** Fellowships, grants and scholarships. **FUNDS
AVAILABLE TO:** Organizations only. **CONTACT:** A.E.F. Office.

(514)
CHARLES PATEGIAN FOUNDATION
C/O S. M. SAROYAN
160 SANSOME STREET 9th FLOOR
SAN FRANCISCO, CALIFORNIA 94104   **(415) 433-0440**
DONOR: Charles Pategian. **PURPOSE AND ACTIVITIES:** Donates up to
$200 to penniless Armenian refugees who arrive in the port of New York
to be able to pay for the first month's housing. **DIRECTORS AND OFFI-
CERS:** S. M. Saroyan, President; Robert E. Cartwright, Vice President;
Fr. Datev Kaloustian, Director. **TYPE OF FUNDS:** Loans. **CONTACT
PERSON:** S. M. Saroyan.

(515)
KAZANJIAN FOUNDATION
332 NORTH RODEO DRIVE
BEVERLY HILLS, CALIFORNIA 90210   **(213) 272-0616**
DONOR: Kazanjian family. **PURPOSE AND ACTIVITIES:** Scholarships
directed exclusively to private colleges and universities. **TYPE OF
FUNDS:** Grants and loans. **CONTACT PERSON:** Michael Kazanjian.

(516)
THE STEPHEN PHILIBOSIAN FOUNDATION
46-930 WEST ELDORADO DRIVE
INDIAN WELLS, CALIFORNIA 92210   **(619) 568-3920**
DATE FOUNDED: 1969. **DONOR:** Stephen Phillbosian. **PURPOSE AND ACTIVITIES:** Philanthropy; provides scholarships for needy Armenians, especially of Middle Eastern origin. **DIRECTORS AND OFFICERS:** Joseph H. Stein Jr., Chairman.; Louise Danelian, Nazar Daghlian, Albert Momjian, and Richard Aijian, Trustees. **TYPE OF FUNDS:** Scholarships through the Armenian Missionary Association. **FUNDS AVAILABLE TO:** Organizations only. **CONTACT PERSON:** Joseph H. Stein, Jr.

Connecticut

(517)
THE CALVIN K. KAZANJIAN ECONOMICS FOUNDATION
P.O. BOX 1110
WATERBURY, CONNECTICUT 06720 (203) 938-3308 (203) 573-1200
DATE FOUNDED: 1947. **DONOR:** Calvin K. Kazanjian. **PURPOSE AND ACTIVITIES:** Uses any effective and legitimate method to increase knowledge in the area of economics; encourages more rational and intelligent voting in the marketplace and in the polls. **DIRECTORS AND OFFICERS:** Dorothea K. Elston, President; William A. Forbes, Vice President; Guerin B. Carmody, Secretary; Lloyd W. Elston, Treasurer; John C. Schramm, Managing Director. **CONTACT PERSON:** John C. Schramm.

Michigan

(518)
ALEX AND MARIE MANOOGIAN FOUNDATION
3001 WEST BIG BEAVER, SUITE 520
TROY, MICHIGAN 48084   **(313) 588-2000**

(519)
MARDIGIAN FOUNDATION
1525 TOTTENHAM
BIRMINGHAM, MICHIGAN 48009   **(313) 939-9410**

New York

(520)
KEVORKIAN (HAGOP) FOUNDATION
1411 THIRD AVENUE
NEW YORK, NEW YORK 10028   **(212) 988-9304**

Rhode Island

(521)
GEORGE ABRAHAMIAN FOUNDATION
945 ADMIRAL STREET
PROVIDENCE, RHODE ISLAND 02904   **(401) 831-0008**

DATE FOUNDED: 1969. **DONORS:** Abraham G. Abraham and Hurans Abrahamian. **PURPOSE AND ACTIVITIES:** Supports local Armenians financially via scholarships and assists in Armenian church functions, locally. **DIRECTORS AND OFFICERS:** Hurans Abrahamian, President; Abraham G. Abraham, Treasurer; Walter Johnsin, Secretary; and June Masterson, Trustee. **TYPE OF FUNDS:** Grants and scholarships. **CONTACT PERSON:** Abraham G. Abraham.

Section Six

ARMENIAN STUDIES PROGRAMS

Graduate

Under-graduate

Single Courses

Armenian Studies
Graduate Programs
California

(522)
UNIVERSITY OF CALIFORNIA LOS ANGELES (U.C.L.A.)
DEPARTMENT OF NEAR EASTERN LANGUAGES AND CULTURES
LOS ANGELES, CALIFORNIA 90024   **(213) 825-1307**

PROGRAM NAME: Narekatsi Program of Armenian Studies. **DATE FOUNDED:** 1960. **DIRECTOR OF PROGRAM:** Prof. Avedis K. Sanjian. **DEGREES OFFERED:** Graduate program (Ph.D.) and Graduate program (M.A.). **CURRICULUMS:** Upper division: Elementary Modern Armenian; Intermediate Modern Armenian; Advanced Modern Armenian, Elementary Classical Armenian; Intermediate Classical Armenian; Advanced Classical Armenian; Survey of Armenian Literature; Armenian Literature of the 19th and 20th Centuries; Special Studies in Armenian Language and Literature. Graduate Courses: Armenian Intellectual History; History of the Armenian Language; Armenian Literature of the Golden Age (5th Century A.D.), Seminar in Armenian Literature; Seminar in Armenian Paleography; Directed Individual Study (1/2 to 2 courses); Examination Preparation (1/2 to 2 courses); Ph.D. Dissertation Research and Preparation (1/2 to 2 courses). Related Courses in other departments: Armenian History; Introduction to Armenian Oral History; The Caucasus Under Russian and Soviet Rule; Advanced Historiography: Armenia and the Caucasus; Topics in History; Armenia and the Caucasus; Seminar in Armenian History; Introduction to Indo-European Linguistics. **INSTRUCTORS:** Prof. Avedis K. Sanjian and Prof. Richard Hovannisian. **SCHOLARSHIPS, GRANTS, LOANS:** Available. **PUBLICATION:** Armenian Horizon. **CONTACT PERSON:** Narekatsi, Prof. of Armenian Studies.

Massachusetts

(523)
HARVARD UNIVERSITY
DEPARTMENT OF NEAR EASTERN LANGUAGES
6 DIVINITY AVENUE, # 103
CAMBRIDGE, MASSACHUSETTS 02138   **(617) 495-5757**

DATE FOUNDED: 1960. **DIRECTOR OF PROGRAM:** Prof. R. W. Thomson. **DEGREES OFFERED:** Graduate program (Ph.D.), Undergraduate program (B.A.), and Single courses. **CURRICULUMS:** Courses in Armenian language (Classical and Modern), Armenian History and Literature.

INSTRUCTORS: Prof. R. W. Thomson and Dr. K. B. Bardakjian. SCHOLARSHIPS, GRANTS, LOANS: Available. CONTACT PERSON: R. W. Thomson, Chairman.

New York

(524)
COLUMBIA UNIVERSITY
PROGRAM IN ARMENIAN STUDIES
500 KENT HALL, BOX A
NEW YORK, NEW YORK 10027   (718) 520-6951 (212) 280-2013

DATE FOUNDED: 1979. DIRECTOR OF PROGRAM: Prof. Nina G. Garsoian. DEGREES OFFERED: Graduate program (Ph.D.), Graduate program (M.A.), Undergraduate program (B.A.), and Single courses. CURRICULUMS: First Year Modern Armenian, Second Year Modern Armenian, History and Structure of the Armenian Language, Nineteenth and Twentieth Century Armenian Literature, Armenian History and Civilization, Seminar in Armenian and Byzantine Studies. Course offerings and instructors change from year to year. SCHOLARSHIPS, GRANTS, LOANS: Available. PUBLICATION: Columbia University, Program in Armenian Studies Newsletter. CONTACT PERSON: Prof. Nina G. Garsoian.

Undergraduate Programs
California

(526)
AMERICAN ARMENIAN INTERNATIONAL COLLEGE
1950 THIRD STREET
LA VERNE, CALIFORNIA 91750   (714) 593-2594 (714) 593-2595

PROGRAM NAME: Armenian Studies Program. DATE FOUNDED: 1976. DIRECTOR OF PROGRAM: Dr. Garbis Der Yeghiayan. DEGREES OFFERED: Undergraduate program (B.A.), Single courses, and Off-campus courses. CURRICULUMS: Armenian language, literature, culture, history, music, art, and journalism. INSTRUCTORS: Rouben Adalian; Dr. Karnig Kalsdian; Assadour Devletian; Stepan Asdourian; Osheen Keshishian; Dr. Garbis Der Yeghiayan. SCHOLARSHIPS, GRANTS, LOANS: Available. PUBLICATION: Mashtots. CONTACT PERSON: Dr. Garbis Der Yeghiayan, College Dean and Chairman.

(527)
CALIFORNIA STATE UNIVESITY, FRESNO
ARMENIAN STUDIES PROGRAM
FRESNO, CALIFORNIA 93740   **(209) 294-2669 (209) 294-2832**
PROGRAM NAME: Armenian Studies Program. **COURSES OFFERED:**
Undergraduate (B.S.), Minor in Armenian Studies, and Extention
courses. **CURRICULUMS:** Armenian Language, Armenian History I,
Ancient and Medieval; Armenian History II, Modern and Soviet Armenia;
Armenian Miniature Painting; Armenian Architecture; Introduction to
Armenian Studies; Writings of William Saroyan; Armenian Film; Arme-
nian Political Violence; World of Richard Hagopian; Armenian Poetry.
INSTRUCTORS: Dr. Dickran Kouymjian and Hagop Karamanlian. **CON-
TACT PERSON:** Prof. Dickran Kouymjian, Director of Armenian Studies
Program.

Single Courses
California

(528)
CALIFORNIA STATE UNIVERSITY, NORTHRIDGE
18111 NORDHOFF STREET
NORTHRIDGE, CALIFORNIA 91330   **(818) 885-2000**
COURSES OFFERED: Single courses. **CONTACT:** Admissions Office.

(529)
GLENDALE COMMUNITY COLLEGE
1500 NORTH VERDUGO ROAD
GLENDALE, CALIFORNIA 91208   **(818) 240-1000**
COURSES OFFERED: Single courses. **CURRICULUMS:** Armenian Lan-
guage; Armenian History and Culture; Armenians in Diaspora. **CON-
TACT PERSON:** Levon Marashlian or Admissions Office.

(530)
LOS ANGELES CITY COLLEGE
OFFICE OF COMMUNITY SERVICES
855 NORTH VERMONT AVENUE
LOS ANGELES, CALIFORNIA 90029   **(213) 666-1018**
COURSES OFFERED: Single courses. **CURRICULUM:** Armenian
Dance. **INSTRUCTOR:** Richard Unciano. **CONTACT:** Community Serv-
ices Office.

(531)
LOS ANGELES VALLEY COLLEGE
5800 FULTON AVENUE
VAN NUYS, CALIFORNIA 91401   **(818) 781-1200**
COURSES OFFERED: Single courses. **CURRICULUMS:** Elementary Armenian I, Elementary Armenian II. **CONTACT:** Admissions Office.

(532)
PASADENA CITY COLLEGE
SOCIAL SCIENCE DEPARTMENT
1570 EAST COLORADO BLVD.
PASADENA, CALIFORNIA 91106   **(818) 587-7248**
COURSES OFFERED: Single courses. **CONTACT:** Admissions Office.

(533)
UNIVERSITY OF CALIFORNIA, BERKELEY
ADMISSIONS OFFICE
BERKELEY, CALIFORNIA 94720   **(415) 642-6000**
COURSES OFFERED: Single courses. **CURRICULUMS:** History and language courses. **CONTACT:** Admissions Office.

(534)
UNIVERSITY OF SOUTHERN CALIFORNIA SCHOOL OF MUSIC
ARMENIAN MUSIC STUDIES PROGRAM
UNIVERSITY PARK   **(213) 743-6935**
LOS ANGELES, CALIFORNIA 90089-0851   **(213) 743-8901**
COURSES OFFERED: Undergraduate degree (B.A.), one graduate course toward M.A. and Ph.D. **CURRICULUMS:** Under U.S.C.'s Music History and Literature Department, Armenian music courses are offered each academic semester on a specific topic such as: Armenian Folk Music and its Different Genres; The Sacred and Secular Music of Armenia; The Advent of Professional Music in Armenia and others. **CONTACT PERSON:** Dr. Ohannes Salibian, Coordinator.

Massachusetts

(535)
BOSTON UNIVERSITY
ADMISSIONS OFFICE
121 BAY STATE ROAD
BOSTON, MASSACHUSETTS 02215   **(617) 353-2300**

COURSES OFFERED: Single courses. **CURRICULUMS:** Beginning and Continuing Armenian; Armenian Civilization; Armenian Literature. **CONTACT:** Admissions Office.

(536)
TUFTS UNIVERSITY
EXPERIMENTAL COLLEGE ADMISSIONS OFFICE
MEDFORD, MASSACHUSETTS 02155　　　　　　**(617) 381-3170**
CURRICULUM: Occasionally Conversational Armenian. **CONTACT:** Admissions Office.

(537)
UNIVERSITY OF LOWELL
ADMISSIONS OFFICE
LOWELL, MASSACHUSETTS 01854　　　　　　**(617) 452-5000**
COURSES OFFERED: Single courses. **CURRICULUMS:** Basic Armenian Language I and II. **CONTACT:** Admissions Office.

Michigan

(538)
LAWRENCE INSTITUTE OF TECHNOLOGY
SCHOOL OF ART AND SCIENCES
21000 WEST TEN MILE ROAD
SOUTHFIELD, MICHIGAN 48075　　　　　　**(313) 356-0200**
CURRICULUMS: Elementary Armenian, Reading and Writing. **INSTRUCTOR:** Dr. Vahan Tootikian. **CONTACT PERSON:** Zaven Margosian, Dean of School of Art and Sciences or Admissions Office.

(539)
UNIVERSITY OF MICHIGAN, ANN ARBOR
DEPARTMENT OF HISTORY & MODERN LANGUAGES
ANN ARBOR, MICHIGAN 48109　　　　　　**(313) 764-6381**
COURSES OFFERED: Undergraduate degree (B.A.). **CURRICULUMS:** History of the Armenian People from Pre-historic to Modern Times; Armenia in the Nineteenth and Twentieth Centuries; and some Armenian language and literature courses. **INSTRUCTOR:** Ronald Grigor Suny. **CONTACT PERSON:** Ronald Grigor Suny, Professor of Modern Armenian History.

(540)
THE UNIVERSITY OF MICHIGAN, DEARBORN
DEPARTMENT OF HISTORY
4901 EVERGREEN ROAD
DEARBORN, MICHIGAN 48128   **(313) 593-5545 (313) 593-5096**

COURSES OFFERED: Undergraduate degree (B.A.), Undergraduate degree (B.S.). **CURRICULUMS:** Armenia and the Middle East; Modern Soviet Society; Armenian I and II; Advanced Grammar; Writing and Conversation. **CONTACT PERSON:** Dennis R. Papazian, Prof. of History.

(541)
WAYNE STATE UNIVERSITY
5950 CASS AVENUE
DETROIT, MICHIGAN 48202   **(313) 577-2424**
COURSES OFFERED: Single courses. **CURRICULUMS:** Armenian history, culture, and language courses. **CONTACT:** Admissions Office.

New Jersey

(542)
BROOKDALE COMMUNITY COLLEGE
ADMISSIONS OFFICE
LINCROFT, NEW JERSEY 07738   **(201) 842-1900**
CONTACT: Admissions Office.

New York

(543)
A.N.E.C. SIAMANTO ACADEMY
138 EAST 39th STREET
NEW YORK, NEW YORK 10016   **(212) 689-7231**
DATE FOUNDED: 1981. **DIRECTOR OF PROGRAM:** Dr. Steven Checkosky. Albert Bacian, Chairman. **CONTACT PERSON:** Hourig Papazian-Sahagian, Administrator.

Pennsylvania

(544)
UNIVERSITY OF PENNSYLVANIA
ADMISSIONS OFFICE
PHILADELPHIA, PENNSYLVANIA 19104   **(215) 898-8452**

COURSES OFFERED: Undergraduate degree (B.A.), and (B.S.). **CUR-RICULUMS:** History of Caucasus Since 1801; 19th and 20th Century Armenia; First year Armenian; and Elementary Classical Armenian. **INSTRUCTORS:** Robert Hewsen; J. Libaridian, T. Samuelian. **CONTACT PERSON:** T. Samuelian, Instructor.

Rhode Island

(545)
BROWN UNIVERSITY
ADMISSIONS OFFICE
PROVIDENCE, RHODE ISLAND 02912   **(401) 863-1000**
COURSES OFFERED: Single courses. **CONTACT:** Admissions Office.

Section Seven

<u>LIBRARY COLLECTIONS</u>

College and University Libraries

Organization and Research Libraries

Public Libraries

School Libraries

College and University Libraries
California

(546)
AMERICAN ARMENIAN INTERNATIONAL COLLEGE
LIBRARY
1950 THIRD STREET
LA VERNE, CALIFORNIA 91750   **(714) 593-2594 (714) 593-0432**
PERSON IN CHARGE: Dr. Winston L. Sarafian. **LIBARY HOLDINGS:** Books; 10,000 vol. **NEWSPAPER & PERIODICAL SUBSCRIPTIONS:** 297 titles. **DESCRIPTION OF COLLECTION:** A major Armenian library book collection containing history, literature and art books in Armenian and English languages. **CONTACT PERSON:** Dr. Winston L. Sarafian.

(547)
CALIFORNIA STATE UNIVERSITY, FRESNO
HENRY MADDEN LIBRARY
FRESNO, CALIFORNIA 93740   **(209) 294-2174**
LIBRARY HOLDINGS (In Armenian or other languages about Armenian subjects.): Books: 400 titles. **NEWSPAPER & PERIODICAL SUBSCRIP-TIONS** (In Armenian or other languages about Armenian subjects): 3 titles. **DESCRIPTION OF COLLECTION:** A general collection on Armenian art, literature, religion, history, etc. **CONTACT PERSON:** W. F. Heinlen, Head, Reference Dept.

(548)
CALIFORNIA STATE UNIVERSITY, FRESNO
HENRY MADDEN LIBRARY, SPECIAL COLLECTIONS
MAPLE & SHAW AVENUES
FRESNO, CALIFORNIA 93740   **(209) 294-2595**
PERSON IN CHARGE: Ronald J. Mahoney, Head, Dept. of Special Collections. **DESCRIPTION OF COLLECTION:** Approximately 500 books, periodicals, and clippings by and about William Saroyan. **CONTACT PERSON:** Ronald J. Mahoney, Head, Dept. of Special Collections.

(549)
UNIVERSITY OF CALIFORNIA, BERKELEY
GENERAL LIBRARY
SLAVIC COLLECTION #346
BERKELEY, CALIFORNIA 94720   **(415) 642-3773**
LIBRARY HOLDINGS (In Armenian or other languages about Armenian subjects): Books; 3,000 Volumes. **CONTACT PERSON:** Edward Kasinec, Collection Development.

(550)
UNIVERSITY OF CALIFORNIA, LOS ANGELES
RESEARCH LIBRARY
405 HILGARD AVENUE
LOS ANGELES, CALIFORNIA 90024 (213) 825-7893 (213) 825-3942
PERSON IN CHARGE: Gia Aivazian, Librarian for Armenian and Greek.
LIBRARY HOLDINGS (In Armenian or other languages about Armenian subjects): Books: Approximately 17,000 volumes, including manuscripts, and rare early printed books. Audio Visual Materials: Microfilms, microfiches and photographs. Other: Vertical files (archival files). **NO. OF NEWSPAPER & PERIODICAL SUBSCRIPTIONS** (In Armenian or other languages about Armenian subjects): 15 periodicals. (Collection of over 200 current and non-current periodicals and newspapers). **DESCRIPTION OF COLLECTION:** One of the largest collections in the U.S.A. Covers Armenian language, literature, history, church history, arts, folklore, etc. Also strong reference collection books like dictionaries, bibliographies, indexes. **CONTACT PERSON:** Gia Aivazian, Librarian for Armenian and Greek.

Connecticut

(551)
YALE UNIVERSITY LIBRARY
SLAVIC & EAST EUROPEAN COLLECTION
NEW HAVEN, CONNECTICUT 06520   **(203) 436-0230**
LIBRARY HOLDINGS (In Armenian or other languages about Armenian subjects): Approximately 1,000 titles. **CONTACT PERSON:** Titiana Rannit.

Massachusetts

(552)
HARVARD COLLEGE LIBRARY, ARMENIAN COLLECTION
MIDDLE EASTERN DIVISION
CAMBRIDGE, MASSACHUSETTS 02138   **(617) 495-2437**
CONTACT PERSON: Dr. Kevork B. Bardakjian.

Michigan

(553)
MICHIGAN STATE UNIVERSITY
UNIVERSITY LIBRARY, INTERNATIONAL DIVISION
EAST LANSING, MICHIGAN 48824-1048   **(517) 355-2366**

PERSON IN CHARGE: Dr. Eugene De Benko, Head. **LIBRARY HOLD-INGS** (In Armenian or other languages about Armenian subjects): Books: 490 titles, 540 volumes. **NO. OF NEWSPAPER & PERIODICAL SUB-SCRIPTIONS:** One title. **DESCRIPTION OF COLLECTION:** General works on Armenian history and civilization, bibliographies, ethnography, anthropology, sociology, geography, language and literature, mostly in English language, and a few in Russian and French. **CONTACT PER-SON:** Dr. Eugene De Benko, Prof. of Social Science, Head, International Division.

(554)
WAYNE STATE UNIVERSITY
FOLKLORE ARCHIVE
448 PURDY LIBRARY, W.S.U.
DETROIT, MICHIGAN 48202   (313) 577-4053

PERSON IN CHARGE: Janet L. Langlois, Director. **LIBRARY HOLD-INGS:** Books: two titles, Other: 36 field collections (interview/observation) on Armenian and Armenian American folk traditions. **BIBLIOGRAPHIC AIDS:** Annotated holdings list "Armenian and Armenian American Folklore Collections" in process. **DESCRIPTION OF COLLECTION:** 36 field collections (interview/observation) on Armenian American folk traditions have been conducted by supervised students in the Greater Detroit area from the 1940's to the present. They include information on family traditions and customs, folktales, folksongs, narratives about the Armenian massacre, and coming to Detroit. Field materials of Hoogasian-Villas' 100 Armenian Tales included. **CONTACT PER-SON:** Janet Langlois, Director.

Minnesota

(555)
UNIVERSITY OF MINNESOTA
IMMIGRATION HISTORY RESEARCH CENTER
826 BERRY STREET
SAINT PAUL, MINNESOTA 55114   (612) 373-5581

PERSON IN CHARGE: Prof. Rudolph J. Vecoli, Director. **LIBRARY HOLDINGS:** Books: Approximately 150 titles. **NO. OF NEWSPAPER AND PERIODICAL SUBSCRIPTIONS:** 45 titles. **BIBLIOGRAPHIC AIDS:** Guide to Armenian American collection will be prepared in the next couple of years. **DESCRIPTION OF COLLECTION:** The Immigration History Research Center constitutes a unique research facility for the study of American immigration and ethnicity of the last century. The Center's resources fall within two broad areas: voluntary agencies concerned with immigration and ethnicity, and ethnic groups, particularly those originating in Eastern, Central, and Southern Europe and the Middle East. **CONTACT PERSON:** Prof. Rudolph J. Vecoli, Director.

New York

(556)
COLUMBIA UNIVERSITY LIBRARIES
COLUMBIA UNIVERSITY
535 WEST 114th STREET
NEW YORK, NEW YORK 10027   (212) 280-2241 (212) 280-3995

PERSON IN CHARGE: Patricia Battin, Vice President & University Librarian. **LIBRARY HOLDINGS:** Books: Approximately 6,000 titles in the Armenian language. Figures for other languages not available. **NO. OF NEWSPAPER & PERIODICAL SUBSCRIPTIONS** (In Armenian or other languages about Armenian subjects): 15 titles. **DESCRIPTION OF COLLECTION:** Although the bulk of Armenian collection consists of books published in Soviet Armenia, it includes publications from all countries, from the earliest times to the present. This collection is supported by extensive holdings in all Western languages, Russian, Turkish, etc. **CONTACT PERSON:** Frank H. Unlandherm, Middle East Bibliographer.

(557)
CORNELL UNIVERSITY LIBRARIES
OLIN LIBRARY COLLECTION
ITHACA, NEW YORK 14853   (607) 256-3525

LIBRARY HOLDINGS (In Armenian or other languages about Armenian subjects): Books: 800 titles. **CONTACT PERSON:** Marilyn B Kann, Slavic Studies Librarian.

Pennsylvania

(558)
UNIVERSITY OF PENNSYLVANIA LIBRARY
UNIVERSITY OF PENNSYLVANIA
3420 WALNUT STREET   (215) 898-7555
PHILADELPHIA, PENNSYLVANIA 19104   (215) 898-7556

LIBRARY HOLDINGS (In Armenian or other languages about Armenian subjects): Books: 800 titles, 1,000 volumes. **NO. OF NEWSPAPER & PERIODICAL SUBSCRIPTIONS:** 3 titles. **DESCRIPTION OF COLLECTION:** Developed in late 1970's, it consists of literature and some Armenian history. **CONTACT PERSON:** J. Dennis Hyde, Collection Development.

Virigina

(559)
UNIVERSITY OF VIRGINIA
ALDERMAN LIBRARY
SLAVIC BIBLIOGRAPHY
CHARLOTTESVILLE, VIRGINIA 22901   **(804) 924-4979**
PERSON IN CHARGE: Angelika S. Powell. **LIBRARY HOLDINGS** (In Armenian or other languages about Armenian subjects)**:** Books: 337 titles. **DESCRIPTION OF COLLECTION:** Covers general history from early times to present, Armenian question, language, foreign relations, literature, Armenians in the world, religion, antiquities, travel, society and immigration. **CONTACT PERSON:** Angelika S. Powell, Slavic and East European Bibliographer.

Washington State

(560)
UNIVERSITY OF WASHINGTON LIBRARIES
UNIVERSITY OF WASHINGTON
SEATTLE, WASHINGTON 98195   **(206) 543-5588**
PERSON IN CHARGE: Barbara A. Galik, Head, Slavic and East European Section. **LIBRARY HOLDINGS** (In Armenian or other languages about Armenian subjects)**:** Books: 575 titles, approximately 600 volumes. **AUDIO-VISUAL MATERIALS:** In Music Listening Center, there are 18 records on Armenian music, church music, traditional, folk, classic, and jazz music. Other: Atlas in Map Center: Atlas Armianskoi Sovetskoi Sotsialisticheskoi Respublik. **NO. OF NEWSPAPER & PERIODICAL SUBSCRIPTIONS** (In Armenian or other languages about Armenian subjects)**:** 13 periodicals, no newspapers. **DESCRIPTION OF COLLECTION:** Two thirds in English language, the rest is divided equally between Armenian, Russian, French and German. Strong reference collection includes: Bibliographies, dictionaries, specialized atlases and scholarly journals. Largest group of materials covers history (120 titles of which 50 titles are on the Armenian Question). The collection also includes language and linguistics (100 titles) and literature (70 titles). Other subjects covered are: Church history, art, architecture, population trends, and economics. Scope of the collection: from antiquity through contemporary period with emphasis on the 20th century. **CONTACT PERSON:** Barbara A. Galik, Head, Slavic and East European Section.

Organization and Research Libraries
California

(561)
ARMENAK & NUNIA HAROUTUNIAN LIBRARY
ARMENIAN SOCIETY OF LOS ANGELES
221 SOUTH BRAND BLVD.
GLENDALE, CALIFORNIA 91204   (818) 240-0619 (818) 241-1073
PERSON IN CHARGE: Sooren Khachatourian. **LIBRARY HOLDINGS:** Books: over 7,000 volumes. **DESCRIPTION OF COLLECTION:** Books are mainly in the Armenian language, by famous authors such as Raffi, Rouben, Demerjian etc. The collection also covers Armenian history and culture. **CONTACT PERSON:** Sooren Khachatourian, Librarian.

(562)
ARMENOLOGICAL STUDIES RESEARCH AND EXHIBITS
P.O. BOX 742
ENCINO, CALIFORNIA 91316

PERSON IN CHARGE: Melkon Armen Khandjian, Director. **LIBRARY HOLDINGS:** Books: Over 5,000 volumes. **AUDIO-VISUAL MATERIALS:** One on Armenian genocide. Other: Maps, Stamps, coins, etc. **NO. OF NEWSPAPER AND PERIODICAL SUBSCRIPTIONS:** 17 titles. **DESCRIPTION OF COLLECTION:** The collection consists of over 5,000 volumes of books, a great number of which is related to Armenological studies. It also includes ancient maps on Armenia, as well as stamps and coins. **CONTACT PERSON:** Melkon Armen Khandjian.

Maryland

(563)
REFERENCE COLLECTION OF THE MAMIGONIAN FOUNDATION
MAMIGONIAN FOUNDATION
14513 WOODCREST DRIVE
ROCKVILLE, MARYLAND 20853   (301) 460-0353
PERSON IN CHARGE: John L. Gueriguian, M.D., Executive Director. **LIBRARY HOLDINGS:** Books: approximately 1,500 volumes. Other: Very small seed collection of rugs, paintings, records and coins. **DESCRIPTION OF COLLECTION:** A small but balanced collection of books in Armenian, as well as in foreign languages on Armenian topics in history, geography, arts, crafts, literature, plus dictionaries, textbooks, Armenian fauna and flora and scholarly journals, etc. **CONTACT PERSON:** John L. Gueriguian, M.D., Executive Director.

Massachusets

(564)
ARMENIAN CULTURAL FOUNDATION LIBRARY
441 MYSTIC STREET
ARLINGTON, MASSACHUSETTS 02174   **(617) 646-3090**
PERSON IN CHARGE: John Mirak. **DESCRIPTION OF COLLECTION:**
The A.C.F. is a non-profit, independent library and museum with an
extensive collection of Armenian, English, and European language
works, often in first editions. Especially valuable among the Armenian
language works are 19th and 20th century periodicals. The library is
open to the public and qualified scholars through appointment, by writing, or calling. **CONTACT PERSON:** Hagop Atamian, Curator.

(565)
ARMENIAN LIBRARY AND MUSEUM OF AMERICA
THE MESROP BOYAJIAN LIBRARY OF ARMENIAN BOOKS
380 CONCORD AVENUE
BELMONT, MASSACHUSETTS 02178   **(617) 484-4780**

PERSON IN CHARGE: Paul C. Barsam, M.D., President; Vartan Hartunian, Treasurer. **LIBRARY HOLDINGS:** Books: 8,000 titles, 10,000 volumes. Other: includes rugs, coins, oil paintings, prints, paper money and
Armenian stamps. **NO. OF NEWSPAPER & PERIODICAL SUBSCRIP-
TIONS:** 8 titles. **DESCRIPTION OF COLLECTION:** Books, objects and
materials related to the Armenian people, and their history and civilization. Library has periodicals, manuscripts, theses, indexes of resource
materials, microfilms, tapes of oral interviews, and audio-visual materials. The goal is to establish a museum of artifacts, relics, stamps, coins
and currency, costumes, works of art, memorabilia, photographic and
other visual exhibits which illustrate Armenian life, history and culture.
CONTACT PERSON: Angele Hovsepian, Secretary.

(566)
ARMENIAN NATIONAL ARCHIVES
38 ELTON AVENUE
WATERTOWN, MASSACHUSETTS 02172   **(617) 926-4037**

(567)
**NATIONAL ASSOCIATION FOR ARMENIAN STUDIES AND
RESEARCH**
NAASR-LIBRARY
175 MOUNT AUBURN STREET
CAMBRIDGE, MASSACHUSETTS 02138   **(617) 876-7630**

(568)
ZORYAN INSTITUTE LIBRARY
85 FAYERWEATHER STREET
CAMBRIDGE, MASSACHUSETTS 02138   **(617) 497-6713**
LIBRARY HOLDINGS: Books, sound tapes, video tapes, photos and maps. **NO. OF NEWSPAPER AND PERIODICAL SUBSCRIPTIONS:** 48 titles. **PUBLICATION:** The Zoryan Bulletin. **DESCRIPTION OF COLLECTION:** Focuses on contemporary and modern Armenian society, including diaspora. Particular attention is given to audio-visual materials which are at stage of development. **CONTACT PERSON:** Laura Yardumian, Administrative Assistant.

New Jersey

(569)
ARMENIAN GENERAL BENEVOLENT UNION, LIBRARY
A.G.B.U.
585 SADDLE RIVER ROAD
SADDLE BROOK, NEW JERSEY 07662   **(201) 797-7600**
PERSON IN CHARGE: Rima Keushgerian. **LIBRARY HOLDINGS:** Books: 10,000 volumes. **NO. OF NEWSPAPER & PERIODICAL SUBSCRIPTIONS:** 25 titles. **DESCRIPTION OF COLLECTION:** Collection has many books on Armenian literature, history, culture and religion. **CONTACT PERSON:** Rima Keushgerian.

(570)
ARMENIAN MISSIONARY ASSOCIATION OF AMERICA
LIBRARY
140 FOREST AVENUE
PARAMUS, NEW JERSEY 07652   **(201) 265-2607 (201) 265-2608**
LIBRARY HOLDINGS: Books: 2,000 volumes.

New York

(571)
ARMENIAN APOSTOLIC CHURCH OF NORTH AMERICA
EASTERN DIOCESE, LIBRARY
630 SECOND AVENUE
NEW YORK, NEW YORK 10016   **(212) 686-0710**
LIBRARY HOLDINGS: Books: 10,000 volumes.

Pennsylvania

(572)
BALCH INSTITUTE FOR ETHNIC STUDIES LIBRARY
18 SOUTH 7th STREET
PHILADELPHIA, PENNSYLVANIA 19106   **(215) 925-8090**
PERSON IN CHARGE: M. Mark Stolarick, Executive Director. **LIBRARY HOLDINGS** (In Armenian or other languages about Armenian subjects): Books: Approximately 400 books. **NO. OF NEWSPAPER & PERIODICAL SUBSCRIPTIONS: 2 newspapers and several church publications.** **DESCRIPTION OF COLLECTION:** Library has a collection of books on Armenian immigration to North America and Armenian American history and culture. The Balch Institute's research library and museum solicit printed materials, manuscripts and archival records, and artificats which document Armenian immigration to North America. **CONTACT PERSON:** R. Joseph Anderson, Library Director.

Public Libraries
California

(573)
FRESNO COUNTY FREE LIBRARY
2420 MARIPOSA STREET
FRESNO, CALIFORNIA 93721   **(209) 488-3209 (209) 488-3195**
PERSON IN CHARGE: John K. Kallenberg, County Librarian. **LIBRARY HOLDINGS** (In Armenian or other languages about Armenian subjects): Books: 220 titles in Armenian and 300 titles in English language, 260 volumes in Armenian. **AUDIO-VISUAL MATERIALS:** 1 film, 12 phono records, and William Saroyan Collection. **NO. OF NEWSPAPER AND PERIODICAL SUBSCRIPTIONS:** (In Armenian or other languages about Armenian subjects): 9 titles. **DESCRIPTION OF COLLECTION:** The William Saroyan Collection is nearly an exhaustive collection of the published works of Fresno author, William Saroyan. It contains both items by and about Fresno's best-known citizen. English language materials in all formats are included among some foreign language items. Effort is made to obtain first editions, autographed copies, and personal holographic materials that may add to the study of Saroyan's life and work. The collection is available to serious researchers by appointment. A unique classification system further delineates Saroyan's works. In spring of 1984 the William Saroyan Collection increased from 800 items to approximately 1,300 items through the acquisition of the Abromson Collection.

Over $19,000 was raised by the Friends of the Library to purchase this private collection which contained letters, playbills, scripts, manuscripts and many first editions of Saroyan. **CONTACT PERSON:** Marie Stanley, Principal Librarian (General Collection), and Linda Goff, Local History Librarian (Saroyan).

(574)
LOS ANGELES PUBLIC LIBRARY
FOREIGN LANGUAGE DEPT.
630 WEST FIFTH STREET
LOS ANGELES, CALIFORNIA 90071   **(213) 612-3291**
CONTACT PERSON: Sylva Manoogian, Librarian.

District of Columbia
Washington D.C.

(575)
LIBRARY OF CONGRESS
NEAR EAST SECTION
WASHINGTON, D.C. 20540   **(202) 287-5421**
PERSON IN CHARGE: George N. Atiyeh, Section Head. **LIBRARY HOLDINGS:** Books: 5,000. **NO. OF NEWSPAPER AND PERIODICAL SUBSCRIPTIONS:** 13 newspapers and 20 periodicals. **DESCRIPTION OF COLLECTION:** About 5,000 cataloged books in Armenian language dealing with Armenian language, literature, history, social sciences, bibliographies, manuscripts etc., recorded in card files by author, title and subject. **CONTACT PERSON:** Abraham Bodurgil, Area Specialist, Near East Section.

Massachusetts

(576)
BOSTON PUBLIC LIBRARY
666 BOYLSTON STREET
P.O. BOX 286
BOSTON, MASSACHUSETTS 02117   **(617) 536-5400**
PERSON IN CHARGE: Liam M. Kelly, Acting Director, **DESCRIPTION OF COLLECTION:** A small collection of books in Armenian language is available on various topics in the circulating library. In the research library, there are books in various languages, including Armenian, about Armenia and Armenians. Among the serial holdings there are two local newspapers in Armenian, Baikar and Hairenik, with microfilm files dating back to 1939.

(577)
WATERTOWN FREE PUBLIC LIBRARY
EAST BRANCH LIBRARY
481 MOUNT AUBURN STREET
WATERTOWN, MASSACHUSETTS 02172   (617) 924-3728
LIBRARY HOLDINGS (In Armenian or other languages about Armenian subjects): Books: 850 titles. **AUDIO VISUAL MATERIALS:** 245 records.

Michigan

(578)
DETROIT PUBLIC LIBRARY
FOREIGN LANGUAGE COLLECTION
121 GRATIOT AVENUE
DETROIT, MICHIGAN 48226   (313) 224-0580

PERSON IN CHARGE: Celeste Chin, Foreign Language Specialist. **LIBRARY HOLDINGS** (In Armenian or other languages about Armenian subjects): Books: 425 titles, 475 volumes. **NO. OF NEWSPAPER & PERIODICAL SUBSCRIPTIONS:** 2 titles. **DESCRIPTION OF COLLECTION:** The Armenian collection is one of the fifty-six collections in the Foreign Language Department. Over the years books of quality as well as books in demand have been continuously added to this collection. Starting out with only handful of titles in the 1920's, the collection has grown to approximately 475 volumes today, covering just about every subject area. **CONTACT PERSON:** Celeste Chin, Head, Foreign Language Collection.

New York

(579)
THE NEW YORK PUBLIC LIBRARY
THE RESEARCH LIBRARIES, ORIENTAL DIVISION
5th AVENUE & 42nd STREET
NEW YORK, NEW YORK 10018   (212) 930-0716 (212) 930-0721

PERSON IN CHARGE: E. Christian Filstrup, Chief, Oriental Division. **LIBRARY HOLDINGS** (In Armenian or other languages about Armenian subjects): Books: Approximately 3,000 titles, 3,600 volumes. **NO. OF NEWSPAPER & PERIODICAL SUBSCRIPTIONS** (In Armenian or other languages about Armenian subjects): 20 titles. **DESCRIPTION OF COLLECTION:** Contains Soviet and diaspora publications, Bible translations, and significant runs of periodicals such as Gotchang, Hairenik. **CONTACT PERSON:** Satenik Kechejian, Armenian Specialist.

Ohio

(580)
CLEVELAND PUBLIC LIBRARY
FINE ARTS AND SPECIAL COLLECTIONS DEPARTMENT
325 SUPERIOR AVENUE
CLEVELAND, OHIO 44114-1271　　　　　　　　(216) 623-2818
PERSON IN CHARGE: Alice N. Loranth, Head. **LIBRARY HOLDINGS** (In Armenian or other languages about Armenian subjects): Books: 310 titles. **CONTACT PERSON:** Alice N. Loranth, Head of Fine Arts and Special Collections.

(581)
CLEVELAND PUBLIC LIBRARY
FOREIGN LITERATURE DEPARTMENT
325 SUPERIOR AVENUE
CLEVELAND, OHIO 44114-1271　　　　　　　　(216) 623-2895

PERSON IN CHARGE: Natalia Bezugloff, Head. **LIBRARY HOLDINGS** (In Armenian or other languages about Armenian subjects): Books: 800 titles, 960 volumes. **AUDIO VISUAL MATERIALS:** 3 phonodiscs. **DESCRIPTION OF COLLECTION:** A circulating collection containing Armenian literature, history, biography and dictionaries. **CONTACT PERSON:** Natalia Bezugloff, Head of Foreign Literature.

School Libraries
California

(582)
CHARLOTTE & ELISE MERDINIAN ARMENIAN
EVANGELICAL SCHOOL, LIBRARY
5000 COLFAX AVENUE
NORTH HOLLYWOOD, CALIFORNIA 91601　　　　(818) 762-1022
LIBRARY HOLDINGS: Books: 3,000 volumes. **NO. OF NEWSPAPER & PERIODICAL SUBSCRIPTIONS:** 5 titles.

(583)
ROSE AND ALEX PILIBOS ARMENIAN SCHOOL
PUZANT AND ZABEL GRANIAN LIBRARY
1615 NORTH ALEXANDRIA AVENUE
LOS ANGELES, CALIFORNIA 90027　　　　　　(213) 668-2661

PERSON IN CHARGE: Salpi H. Ghazarian. **LIBRARY HOLDINGS:** Books: 7,000 volumes. **AUDIO VISUAL MATERIALS:** 7 filmstrips. **NO. OF NEWSPAPER & PERIODICAL SUBSCRIPTIONS:** 55 titles. **DESCRIPTION OF COLLECTION:** Covers Armenian literature, history, biography, focusing on the modern times. **CONTACT PERSON:** Salpi H. Ghazarian and Ouri Henry.

(584)
VAHAN AND ANOUSH CHAMLIAN ARMENIAN SCHOOL
LIBRARY
4444 LOWELL AVENUE
GLENDALE, CALIFORNIA 91214   **(818) 957-3399**
PERSON IN CHARGE: Caroline Beniasian. **CONTACT PERSON:** Vartkes Ghazarian, Principal.

Michigan

(585)
A.G.B.U. ALEX MANOOGIAN SCHOOL
LIBRARY
22001 NORTHWESTERN HWY.
SOUTHFIELD, MICHIGAN 48075   **(313) 569-2988**
PERSON IN CHARGE: Cynthia Welc, Librarian, Media Specialist. **LIBRARY HOLDINGS:** Books: 3,580 titles. **AUDIO VISUAL MATERIALS:** 16 mm films and slides. Other: Vertical file (pamphlet file) and maps. **NO. OF NEWSPAPER & PERIODICAL SUBSCRIPTIONS:** 40 titles. **DESCRIPTION OF COLLECTION:** An extensive collection of books and magazines written in Armenian or other languages about Armenian subjects. **CONTACT PERSON:** Cynthia Welc, Librarian/Media Specialist or Antranig Chalabian, Public Relations.

Section Eight

BOOKSELLERS AND BOOK PUBLISHERS

Bookstores and Book Publishers

Book Dealers and Vendors

Church Bookstores and Book Selling Services

Bookstores and Book Publishers
California

(586)
ABRIL BOOKSTORE
5450 SANTA MONICA BLVD.
LOS ANGELES, CALIFORNIA 90029   (213) 467-9483

(586-A)
ARAX BOOKSTORE
ARAX PUBLISHING HOUSE AND PRINTING
1768 EAST WASHINGTON BLVD.
PASADENA, CALIFORNIA 91104   (818) 798-5542 (213) 684-2729
DATE FOUNDED: 1980. **MATERIALS AVAILABLE:** Books, periodicals, and audio visuals. **CONTACT PERSON:** Albert Minassian or Nazareth Atchabahian.

(587)
ARMENIAN REFERENCE BOOKS CO.
P.O. BOX 7106
GLENDALE, CALIFORNIA 91205   (818) 507-1525
DATE FOUNDED: 1983. **ADDITIONAL INFORMATION:** Publisher of Armenian American Almanac. **CONTACT PERSON:** Hamo Vassilian.

(588)
EREBOUNI EDITION
5825 SUNSET BLVD., SUITE 203
LOS ANGELES, CALIFORNIA 90028   (213) 465-6168
CONTACT PERSON: Haroutoun Yeretzian.

(588-A)
FALL BOOKSTORE
1200 SOUTH BRAND BLVD., # 7
GLENDALE, CALIFORNIA 91204   (818) 956-1783
CONTACT PERSON: Karl Gregorian.

(589)
MESHAG PRINTING AND PUBLISHING CO.
1302 WISHON
FRESNO, CALIFORNIA 93728   (209) 229-7866
DATE FOUNDED: 1975. **MATERIALS AVAILABLE:** Books. **CATALOG:** Available. **CONTACT PERSON:** Yervant Chaderjian.

(590)
SAKO BOOKSTORE
131-A SOUTH BRAND BLVD.
GLENDALE, CALIFORNIA 91204   **(818) 247-6783**
DATE FOUNDED: 1979. **MATERIALS AVAILABLE:** Books, periodicals, and audio-visuals including Armenian and Iranian cassettes and video cassettes. **CONTACT PERSON:** Vrej Hovsepian.

(591)
SARDARABAD BOOK SERVICE
ARMENIAN YOUTH FEDERATION
108 NORTH BRAND BLVD.
GLENDALE, CALIFORNIA 91203   **(818) 500-0790**
DATE FOUNDED: 1975. **MATERIALS AVAILABLE:** Books, periodicals, and audio visuals. **CATALOG:** Available. **ADDITIONAL INFORMATION:** Special orders accepted. **CONTACT PERSON:** Maral Israbian or Sako Berberian.

(591-A)
SHIRAK BOOKSTORE
4960 HOLLYWOOD BLVD.
LOS ANGELES, CALIFORNIA 90027   **(213) 667-1128**
CONTACT PERSON: Ohannes Hannessian.

Illinois

(592)
GILGAMESH PRESS LTD.
1059 WEST ARDMORE AVENUE
CHICAGO, ILLINOIS 60660   **(312) 334-0327**
DATE FOUNDED: 1978. **MATERIALS AVAILABLE:** Books. **CONTACT PERSON:** Karlen Mooradian.

Massachusetts

(593)
ARMENIAN BOOK CLEARING HOUSE
NATIONAL ASSOCIATION FOR ARMENIAN STUDIES AND RESEARCH
175 MOUNT AUBURN STREET
CAMBRIDGE, MASSACHUSETTS 02138   **(617) 876-7630**

(593-A)
HAIRENIK BOOKSTORE
80 BIGELOW AVENUE
WATERTOWN, MASSACHUSETTS 02172   **(617) 926-3974**

(594)
MEKHITARIST PRESS
98 MOUNT AUBURN STREET
CAMBRIDGE, MASSACHUSETTS 02138   **(617) 547-2132**

New Jersey

(595)
A.G.B.U. ARARAT PRESS
585 SADDLE RIVER ROAD
SADDLE BROOK, NEW JERSEY 07662   **(201) 797-7600**
CATALOG: Available. **CONTACT PERSON:** Terry Chisnolm, Director of Publications.

(596)
A.G.B.U. BOOKSTORE
585 SADDLE RIVER ROAD
SADDLE BROOK, NEW JERSEY 07662   **(201) 797-7600**
DATE FOUNDED: 1959. **MATERIALS AVAILABLE:** Books, records and tapes. **CATALOG:** Available. **CONTACT PERSON:** Bedros Kaye, Manager, or Terry Chisnolm, Director of Publications.

New York

(596-A)
ARMENIAN DIOCESE BOOKSTORE
ARMENIAN APOSTOLIC CHURCH OF NORTH AMERICA EASTERN DIOCESE
630 SECOND AVENUE
NEW YORK, NEW YORK 10016   **(212) 686-0710**

(596-B)
ARMENIAN PRELACY BOOKSTORE
ARMENIAN APOSTOLIC CHURCH OF AMERICA EASTERN PRELACY
138 39th STREET
NEW YORK, NEW YORK 10016   **(212) 689-7810**

(597)
ASHOD PRESS
P.O. BOX 1147
MADISON SQUARE STATION
NEW YORK, NEW YORK, 10159   **(212) 475-0711**
DATE FOUNDED: 1979. **MATERIALS AVAILABLE:** Books. **CATALOG:**
Available. **CONTACT PERSON:** Jack Antressian, Editor.

(598)
CARAVAN BOOKS
P.O. BOX 344
DELMAR, NEW YORK 12054-0344   **(518) 439-5978**
DATE FOUNDED: 1972. **MATERIALS AVAILABLE:** Books. **CATALOG:**
Available.

(599)
MASHDOTS BOOK CORPORATION
198-21 30th AVENUE
FLUSHING, NEW YORK 11358   **(212) 352-3883**

(600)
MASIS BOOKSTORE
231 EAST 24th STREET
NEW YORK, NEW YORK 10010   **(212) 889-3828**

(601)
NEW AGE PUBLISHERS
P.O. BOX 883
PLANDOME, NEW YORK 11030

DATE FOUNDED: 1975. **MATERIALS AVAILABLE:** Books and booklets
on the genocide. **ADDITIONAL INFORMATION:** Publishes original
books and reprints on the general subject of the Genocide, as documentary materials. Has reprinted ''Ambassador Morgenthau's Story'', and an
original book, the recollections of an Armenian girl, ''Rebirth'', in hard
cover. Both books are heavily illustrated. Has also reprinted two supple-
mentary booklets. **CONTACT PERSON:** E. Aprahamian, Editor.

(602)
VOSGEDAR PUBLISHING CO.
198-21 30th Avenue
FLUSHING, NEW YORK 11358

Book Dealers and Vendors
California

(603)
ARMENIAN GENERAL BENEVOLENT UNION
BOOK SERVICE
589 NORTH LARCHMONT BLVD.
LOS ANGELES, CALIFORNIA 90004   **(213) 467-2428**

(604)
ARMENIAN NUMISMATIC SOCIETY
8511 BEVERLY PARK PLACE
PICO RIVERA, CALIFORNIA 90660   **(213) 695-0380**

DATE FOUNDED: 1972. **MATERIALS AVAILABLE:** Books, periodicals, and coins. **CATALOG:** Available. **ADDITIONAL INFORMATION:** Armenological and numismatic books, as well as Armenian coins, medals, bank notes and other collectable items. **CONTACT PERSON:** Y. T. Nercessian.

(605)
ARMENIAN OBSERVER
6646 HOLLYWOOD BLVD., SUITE 207
LOS ANGELES, CALIFORNIA 90028   **(213) 467-6767**

(606)
MAHAKIAN BOOKS
P.O. BOX 1806
BURBANK, CALIFORNIA 91507

DATE FOUNDED: 1965. **MATERIALS AVAILABLE:** Books and periodicals. **CATALOG:** Available. **ADDITIONAL INFORMATION:** Formerly called Hayastan Books. **CONTACT PERSON:** Karnig Mahakian.

(607)
NAVASART FOUNDATION
515 WEST BROADWAY, SUITE D
GLENDALE, CALIFORNIA 91204   **(818) 241-5933**

DATE FOUNDED: 1982. **MATERIALS AVAILABLE:** Books. **CONTACT PERSON:** Armen Donoyan.

Massachusetts

(608)
ARMENIAN WEEKLY
80 BIGELOW AVENUE
WATERTOWN, MASSACHUSETTS 02172   **(617) 926-3974**

(609)
ARMENIAN MIRROR-SPECTATOR
468 MOUNT AUBURN STREET
WATERTOWN, MASSACHUSETTS 02172   (617) 924-4420

New Jersey

(610)
ARMENIAN MISSIONARY ASSOCIATION OF AMERICA
140 FOREST AVENUE
PARAMUS, NEW JERSEY 07652   (201) 256-2607

New York

(611)
ARMENIAN LITERARY SOCIETY, INC.
114 FIRST STREET
YONKERS, NEW YORK 10704   (914) 237-5751 (914) 761-2127
DATE FOUNDED: 1956. MATERIALS AVAILABLE: Books and periodicals. CATALOG: Available. CONTACT PERSON: K. Magarian, Executive Secretary.

(612)
ARMENIAN REPORTER BOOKSTORE
P.O. BOX 600
FRESH MEADOWS, NEW YORK 11365   (718) 380-3636
DATE FOUNDED: 1975. MATERIALS AVAILABLE: Books. CATALOG:
Available.

Church Bookstores
and Book Selling Services
California

(612-A)
ARMENIAN MEKHITARIST FATHERS SCHOOL
4900 MARYLAND AVENUE
GLENDALE, CALIFORNIA 91214   (818) 249-6121
CONTACT PERSON: Fr. Dajad Yardemian, Vice Principal.

(613)
HOLY CROSS ARMENIAN APOSTOLIC CATHEDRAL
900 WEST LINCOLN
MONTEBELLO, CALIFORNIA 90640   **(213) 727-1113**
DATE FOUNDED: 1982. **MATERIALS AVAILABLE:** Books and periodicals. **CONTACT PERSON:** Rev. Papken Manuelian.

(614)
SAINT MARY ARMENIAN CHURCH OF YETTEM
14395 AVENUE 384
YETTEM, CALIFORNIA 93670   **(209) 528-6892 (209) 591-9996**
DATE FOUNDED: 1976. **MATERIALS AVAILABLE:** Books. **CONTACT PERSON:** Rev. Fr. Vartan Kasparian, Parish Priest.

(615)
SAINT PAUL ARMENIAN CHURCH
3767 NORTH FIRST STREET
FRESNO, CALIFORNIA 93726   **(209) 226-6343**
DATE FOUNDED: 1970. **MATERIALS AVAILABLE:** Books. **CONTACT PERSON:** Parish Priest.

District of Columbia
Washington D.C.

(616)
SAINT MARY'S BOOKSTORE
4125 FESSENDEN STREET N.W.
WASHINGTON, D.C. 20016   **(202) 363-1923**
DATE FOUNDED: 1970. **MATERIALS AVAILABLE:** Books. **CONTACT PERSON:** Gary Avedikian, Manager.

Massachusetts

(617)
FIRST ARMENIAN CHURCH OF BELMONT
380 CONCORD AVENUE
BELMONT, MASSACHUSETTS 02178   **(617) 484-4779**
DATE FOUNDED: 1960. **MATERIALS AVAILABLE:** Books, periodicals, and pamphlets. **ADDITIONAL INFORMATION:** Mostly Bibles sold in English and Armenian. **CONTACT PERSON:** Rev. Vartan Hartunian.

(618)
SAINT GREGORY CHURCH BOOKSTORE
110 MAIN STREET
HAVERHILL, MASSACHUSETTS 01830   (617) 372-9227
DATE FOUNDED: 1979. **MATERIALS AVAILABLE:** Books. **CATALOG:** Available. **CONTACT PERSON:** Zarty Chilingirian, Secretary.

Michigan

(619)
SAINT SARKIS ARMENIAN APOSTOLIC CHURCH
19300 FORD ROAD
DEARBORN, MICHIGAN 48128   (313) 336-6200
DATE FOUNDED: 1970. **MATERIALS AVAILABLE:** Books. **CONTACT PERSON:** Geno Sarkisian, Secretary.

New Hampshire

(620)
ARARAT ARMENIAN CONGREGATIONAL CHURCH
4 SALEM STREET
SALEM, NEW HAMPSHIRE 03079   (603) 898-7042

New Jersey

(621)
SAINT LEON BOOKSTORE
12-16 SADDLE RIVER ROAD
FAIR LAWN, NEW JERSEY 07410   (201) 791-2862
DATE FOUNDED: 1982. **MATERIALS AVAILABLE:** Books and periodicals. **ADDITIONAL INFORMATION:** Serves the needs of the parish community. **CONTACT PERSON:** Barbara Hovsepian.

(622)
SAINT THOMAS ARMENIAN APOSTOLIC CHURCH
BOOKSTORE
P.O. BOX 53
TENAFLY, NEW JERSEY 07670   (201) 567-5446
MATERIALS AVAILABLE: Books. **CONTACT PERSON:** Sona Doudoukjian, Bookstore Manager.

(623)
SAINTS VARTANANTZ ARMENIAN APOSTOLIC CHURCH OF NEW JERSEY
461 BERGEN BLVD.
RIDGEFIELD, NEW JERSEY 07657   **(201) 943-2950**
MATERIALS AVAILABLE: Books. CONTACT PERSON: Rev. Vahrich Shirinian, Pastor.

New York

(624)
ARMENIAN DIOCESE BOOKSTORE
ARMENIAN APOSTOLIC CHURCH OF NORTH AMERICA EASTERN DIOCESE
630 SECOND AVENUE
NEW YORK, NEW YORK 10016   **(212) 686-0710**

(625)
ARMENIAN PRELACY BOOKSTORE
ARMENIAN APOSTOLIC CHURCH OF AMERICA EASTERN PRELACY
138 39th STREET
NEW YORK, NEW YORK 10016   **(212) 689-7810**
DATE FOUNDED: 1978. MATERIALS AVAILABLE: Books, periodicals, audio visuals, records, cassettes, mementos and gift items. ADDI-TIONAL INFORMATION: Serves the U.S., Canada, the Middle East, Europe, South America, and Australia. Also provides textbooks for day schools and Sunday schools. Books are on history, politics, language, culture, religion, cookery, poetry, etc. CONTACT PERSON: Hovhannes Doghramadjian, Bookstore Manager.

(626)
PAGOUMAIN BOOKSTORE
SAINT SARKIS ARMENIAN APOSTOLIC CHURCH
42nd AVENUE AND 213th STREET
BAYSIDE, NEW YORK 11361   **(212) 224-2275**

Texas

(626-A)
SAINT KEVORK ARMENIAN APOSTOLIC CHURCH BOOKSTORE
3211 SYNOTT ROAD
HOUSTON, TEXAS 77082   **(713) 558-2722**
DATE FOUNDED: 1984. MATERIALS AVAILABLE: Books, tapes and records. CONTACT PERSON: Rev. Fr. Nersess Jebejian, Pastor.

Section Nine

SPECIAL COLLECTIONS

Special Collections
California

(627)
ARMENOLOGICAL STUDIES RESEARCH AND EXHIBITS
P.O. BOX 742
ENCINO, CALIFORNIA 91316
PERSON IN CHARGE: Melkon Armen Khandjian, Director. **NATURE OF ORGANIZATION:** Archive and library. **DESCRIPTION OF COLLECTION:** Consists of over 5,000 volume books in both Armenian and English. Over 2,000 volumes are related to Armenian studies. The library is in possession of a very unique collection of ancient maps on Armenia, as well as stamps and coins. **CONTACT PERSON:** Melkon Armen Khandjian.

District of Columbia
Washington D.C.

(628)
FREER GALLERY OF ART
SMITHSONIAN INSTITUTION
12th AND JEFFERSON DRIVE, S.W.
WASHINGTON, D.C. 20560   (202) 357-2104 (202) 357-2091
PERSON IN CHARGE: Thomas Lawton, Director. **NATURE OF ORGANIZATION:** Museum and library. **DESCRIPTION OF COLLECTION:** Primarily arts of the Far and Middle East, and a large collection of works by American artists, the largest represented by the works of James McNeill Whistler. The Armenian collection consists of eight manuscripts, including six gospels, a hymnal, and a psalter. The manuscripts represent 700 years of book illumination, from the 11th through the 17th century. For full details on the manuscripts, see Armenian Manuscripts in the Freer Gallery of Arts by Sirarpie Der Nersessian (Freer Gallery of Art Oriental Studies, no. 6, 1963). **CONTACT PERSON:** Ellen Nollman, Head Librarian.

Maryland

(629)
THE WALTERS ART GALLERY, BALTIMORE
600 NORTH CHARLES STREET
BALTIMORE, MARYLAND 21201   (301) 547-9000
PERSON IN CHARGE: Lilian M.C. Randall, Curator. **NATURE OF**

ORGANIZATION: Museum. **DESCRIPTION OF COLLECTION:** Illuminated manuscripts, forming part of a collection of 801 European and non-Western examples. **PUBLICATION ABOUT ARMENIAN COLLECTION:** Available. **CONTACT PERSON:** Lilian M. C. Randall, Curator.

Massachusetts

(630)
PROJECT SAVE
11 CHESTNUT STREET
MELROSE, MASSACHUSETTS 02176   **(617) 662-7806**
PERSON IN CHARGE: Ruth Thomasian, Director. **NATURE OF ORGANIZATION:** Archive. **DESCRIPTION OF COLLECTION:** Project SAVE is an archive devoted to the collection and documentation of photographs of Armenian people, whoever they are, wherever they live, and whatever they do, from the inception of phototgraphy to the present day. **CONTACT PERSON:** Ruth Thomasian, Director.

Michigan

(631)
WAYNE STATE UNIVERSITY
FOLKLORE ARCHIVE
448 PURDY LIBRARY, W.S.U.
DETROIT, MICHIGAN 48202   **(313) 577-4053**
PERSON IN CHRAGE: Janet Langlois, Director. **NATURE OF ORGANIZATION:** Archive. **DESCRIPTION OF COLLECTION:** General collection of field-recorded folk traditions, with urban, ethnic and occupational materials stressed. The Armenian section has 36 field collections on family traditions and customs, folktales, folksongs, narratives about the massacre and coming to Detroit. Susie Hoogasian-Villa's 100 Armenian Tales is also included in the collection. **PUBLICATION ABOUT ARMENIAN COLLECTION:** In process. **CONTACT PERSON:** Janet Langlois, Director.

Minnesota

(632)
IMMIGRATION HISTORY RESEARCH CENTER
UNIVERSITY OF MINNESOTA
826 BERRY STREET
SAINT PAUL, MINNESOTA 55114   **(612) 373-5581**
PERSON IN CHARGE: Prof. Rudolph J. Vecoli, Director. **NATURE OF**

ORGANIZATION: Archive, library and research center. **DESCRIPTION OF COLLECTION:** The Immigration History Research Center constitutes a unique research facility for the study of American immigration and ethnicity of the last century. The center's resources fall within two broad areas of voluntary agencies concerned with immigration, and ethnicity and ethnic groups, particularly those originating in eastern, central, southern Europe, and the Middle East. **CONTACT PERSON:** Prof. Rudolph J. Vecoli, Director.

New York

(633)
AMERICAN MUSEUM OF NATURAL HISTORY
CENTRAL PARK WEST AT 79th STREET
NEW YORK, NEW YORK 10024   **(212) 873-1300 Ext. 522**

PERSON IN CHARGE: Lisa Whittall, Curatorial Assistant. **NATURE OF ORGANIZATION:** Museum. **DESCRIPTION OF COLLECTION:** 89 examples of embroidery, needle lace, costumes and costume pieces, and various other objects made of textile. This collection is held in the Ethnographic Textile Storage and Study Room, and is open, by appointment, to students of textile art and costume history (not open to the general public). **CONTACT PERSON:** Lisa Whittall, Dept. of Anthropology.

Section Ten

NON-PRINT MEDIA

Television Programs

Radio Programs

Television Programs
California

(635)
ARMENIAN TELETIME
13645 VANOWEN STREET
VAN NUYS, CALIFORNIA 91405   **(818) 782-4944 (818) 782-2949**

DATE FOUNDED: 1979. **COMPANY NAME:** Armenian Television Productions, Inc. **DIRECTOR:** Sarky Mouradian. **PRODUCER:** Bouchakian Bros. and Vahan Jansezian. **TELECASTING STATION:** KSCI T.V. 18 in Los Angeles and channel 48 in San Diego. In Fresno, KAIL T.V. channel 53. **TELECASTING LANGUAGE:** Armenian and English. **TELECASTING DAY AND TIME:** Saturdays and Sundays 10:00 to 11:00 A.M. (Pacific time). **CONTACT PERSON:** Vahan Jansezian.

(637)
THE HYE LIGHT
P.O. BOX 1967
GLENDALE, CALIFORNIA 91209   **(818) 249-5556**

DATE FOUNDED: 1982. **COMPANY NAME:** Fidanian Broadcast Services Corp. **DIRECTOR & PRODUCER:** Alek Fidanian. **TELECASTING LANGUAGE:** Armenian and English. **CONTACT PERSON:** Christine Fidanian, Director of Public Relations, or Alek Fidanian, Director.

Radio Programs
California

(638)
ARMENIAN AMERICAN RADIO
14610 COHASSET STREET
VAN NUYS, CALIFORNIA 91405   **(213) 463-4545**   **(818) 781-4444**

DATE FOUNDED: 1957. **COMPANY NAME:** Armenian American Advertising Agency. **DIRECTOR & PRODUCER:** Harry Hadigian (Happy Harry). **BORADCASTING STATION:** KTYM 1460 A.M. **BROADCASTING LANGUAGE:** Armenian and English. **BROADCASTING DAY & TIME:** Saturdays 3 to 5:00 P.M., and Sundays 10:00 to 11:00 A.M. **CONTACT PERSON:** Harry Hadigian, Director.

(639)
ARMENIAN CULTURAL RADIO PROGRAM
2115 15th AVENUE   **(415) 665-8329**
SAN FRANCISCO, CALIFORNIA 94116   **(415) 431-2122**

DATE FOUNDED: 1982. DIRECTOR & PRODUCER: Ed Misserlian.
HOST: Ed Misserlian. BROADCASTING STATION: KUSF, FM 90.3.
BROADCASTING LANGUAGE: Armenian and English. BROADCAST-
ING DAY AND TIME: Sundays, 8:00 to 9:00 A.M. (Pacific time).

(640)
ARMENIAN GOSPEL HOUR, INC.
5847 EAST EL MONTE
FRESNO, CALIFORNIA 93727   **(209) 255-2830**

DATE FOUNDED: 1956. COMPANY NAME: Armenian Gospel Hour, Inc.
DIRECTOR & PRODUCER: Rev. A. J. Hovsepian. BROADCASTING
STATION: KRDU, 1130. BROADCASTING LANGUAGE: Armenian.
BROADCASTING DAY AND TIME: Saturdays, 5:00 P.M. (Pacific time).
CONTACT PERSON: A. J. Hovsepian, Director.

(641)
ARMENIAN RADIO HOUR
2400 UNWIN COURT
SOUTH SAN FRANCISCO, CALIFORNIA 94080   **(415) 761-1362**

DATE FOUNDED: 1966. COMPANY NAME: Armenian Radio Hour, Inc.
DIRECTOR & HOST: Arax Sarian. BROADCASTING STATION: KFAX,
1100 A.M.. BROADCASTING LANGUAGE: Armenian and English.
BROADCASTING DAY AND TIME: Saturdays, 11:30 A.M. to 12:30 P.M.
(Pacific time). CONTACT PERSON: Arax Sarian, Director.

(642)
ARMENIAN RADIO HOUR OF GREATER LOS ANGELES
2115 15th AVENUE   **(415) 665-8329**
SAN FRANCISCO, CALIFORNIA 94116   **(818) 249-5433**

DATE FOUNDED: 1981. COMPANY NAME: Armenian Radio Hour of
Greater Los Angeles. DIRECTOR & PRODUCER: Edward Misserlian.
BROADCASTING STATION: KFOX, FM 93.5 BROADCASTING LAN-
GUAGE: Armenian. BROADCASTING DAY AND TIME: Sundays, 9:00
to 10:00 A.M. (Pacific time). CONTACT PERSON: Edward Misserlian.

(643)
FRESNO ARMENIAN RADIO HOUR
5455 NORTH BOND STREET
FRESNO, CALIFORNIA 93710   **(209) 432-7349**

DATE FOUNDED: 1982. DIRECTOR & PRODUCER: Krikor Greg
Kohayan. HOST/ANNOUNCER: Greg Kohayan and Jannet Stoll.
BROADCASTING STATION: KXTC 790 A.M. BROADCASTING DAY

AND TIME: Sundays, 10:00 to 11:00 A.M. (Pacific time). **CONTACT PERSON:** Greg Kohayan.

(644)
HAMAZKAYIN ARMENIAN RADIO HOUR
51 COMMONWEALTH AVENUE (415) 571-5119
SAN FRANCISCO, CALIFORNIA 94118 (415) 564-9066

DATE FOUNDED: 1980. **COMPANY NAME:** Hamazkayin Armenian Cultural Association, Nigol Aghbalian Chapter, San Francisco. **DIRECTOR:** Varant Kasparian. **PRODUCER:** Hamazkayin Armenian Cultural Association. **HOST/ANNOUNCER:** Tamar Farajian, Sylvia Kaprielian, and Varant Kasparian. **BROADCASTING STATION:** KUSF 90.3 F.M. **BROADCASTING LANGUAGE:** Armenian and English. **BROADCASTING DAY AND TIME:** Saturdays, 9:00 to 10:00 A.M. (Pacific time). **CONTACT PERSON:** Varant Kasparian, Director.

(645)
VOICE OF ARMENIANS
P.O. BOX 1967
GLENDALE, CALIFORNIA 91209 (818) 249-5556

DATE FOUNDED: 1982. **COMPANY NAME:** Fidanian Broadcast Services Corp. **DIRECTOR & PRODUCER:** Alek Fidanian. **BROADCASTING STATION:** Cable. **BROADCASTING DAY & TIME:** 24 hours a day, 7 days a week. **CONTACT PERSON:** Christine Fidanian, Director of Public Relations, or Alek Fidanian, President.

Massachusetts

(646)
ARMENIAN CULTURAL HOUR
FRIENDS OF ARMENIAN CULTURAL SOCIETY
750 SOUTH STREET
WALTHAM, MASSACHUSETTS 02154(614) 893-7080 (617) 876-0114

DIRECTOR: Dr. Keran Chobanian. **BROADCASTING STATION:** WCRB 102.5 F.M. MHz. **BROADCASTING DAY AND TIME:** Sundays, 9:30 A.M. (Eastern time).

(647)
ARMENIAN INDEPENDENT BROADCASTING OF BOSTON
P.O. BOX 46 (617) 623-6600
WATERTOWN, MASSACHUSETTS 02172 (617) 926-6268

DATE FOUNDED: 1980. **COMPANY NAME:** Armenian Independent Broadcasting of Boston. **DIRECTOR & PRODUCER:** Jerair H. Gharibian. **BROADCASTING DAY AND TIME:** Saturdays, 2:30 to 4:00 P.M. (Eastern time).

Michigan

(648)
ARMENIAN AMATEUR RADIO AND TRAFFIC NET (ARARAT NET)
7127 BROOKRIDGE DRIVE
WEST BLOOMFIELD, MICHIGAN 48033   (313) 851-1357
DATE FOUNDED: 1980. **DIRECTOR & PRODUCER:** Stefan Karadian.
HOST/ANNOUNCER: Stefan Karadian. **BROADCASTING STATION:** 20
meter band, 14.340 KHz. **BROADCASTING LANGUAGE:** Armenian and
English. **BROADCASTING DAY AND TIME:** Fridays, 0300 GMT (world-
wide). **CONTACT PERSON:** Stefan Karadian, N8BGD, Net Control.

(649)
ARMENIAN RADIO HOUR OF METROPOLITAN DETROIT
45755 BLOOMCREST DRIVE
NORTHVILLE, MICHIGAN 48167   (313) 349-1193
DATE FOUNDED: 1943. **COMPANY NAME:** Armenian Radio Hour of
Metropolitan Detroit. **DIRECTOR & PRODUCER:** Nerses Serkaian.
HOST/ANNOUNCER: Nerses Serkaian. **BROADCASTING STATION:**
WCAR 1090 A.M. **BROADCASTING LANGUAGE:** Armenian and Eng-
lish. **BROADCASTING DAY AND TIME:** Sundays, 9:00 to 10:30 A.M.
CONTACT PERSON: Nerses Serkaian, Director.

(650)
HERITAGE OF ARMENIAN CULTURE
SAINT JOHN'S ARMENIAN APOSTOLIC CHURCH
22001 NORTHWESTERN HIGHWAY
SOUTHFIELD, MICHIGAN 48075   (313) 569-5998 (313) 569-3405
COMPANY NAME: HARC. **DIRECTOR & PRODUCER:** Edmond Y. Aza-
dian. **BROADCASTING STATION:** WDTR F.M. **BROADCASTING LAN-
GUAGE:** English. **BROADCASTING DAY AND TIME:** Saturdays, 5:00 to
6:00 P.M.

New Jersey

(651)
ARMENIAN RADIO HOUR OF NEW JERSEY
400 SOUTH ORANGE AVENUE   (201) 762-8950
SOUTH ORANGE, NEW JERSEY 07079   (201) 761-1544
DATE FOUNDED: 1979. **DIRECTOR & PRODUCER:** Vartan and Adrine
Abdo. **HOST/ANNOUNCER:** Vartan Abdo, Adrine Abdo, Joyce Var-
toukian, and Hourri Partamian. **BROADCASTING STATION:** WSOU
89.5 F.M. **BROADCASTING LANGUAGE:** Armenian and English.
BROADCASTING DAY AND TIME: Sundays, 3:05 to 5:00 P.M. (Eastern
time). **CONTACT PERSON:** Prof. Vartan Abdo.

(652)
SOUND OF ARMENIA
642 ANDERSON AVENUE   **(201) 945-9150**
CLIFFSIDE PARK, NEW JERSEY 07010   **(212) 786-6535**

DATE FOUNDED: 1976. COMPANY NAME: Hrair's Music Center. DIRECTOR & PRODUCER: Hrair Zakarian. HOST/ANNOUNCER: Hrair Zakarian. BROADCASTING STATION: WHBI 105.9 F.M. BROADCASTING LANGUAGE: Armenian. BROADCASTING DAY AND TIME: Wednesdays, 9:30 to 10:30 P.M. (Eastern time). CONTACT PERSON: Hrair Zakarian.

Pennsylvania

(653)
THE ARMENIAN RADIO HOUR OF PHILADELPHIA
215 SOUTH MADISON AVENUE   **(215) 449-8705**
UPPER DARBY, PENNSYLVANIA 19082   **(215) 853-3341**

DATE FOUNDED: 1979. COMPANY NAME: The Armenian Hour of Philadelphia. DIRECTOR & PRODUCER: Hratch K. Panosian. HOST/ANNOUNCER: Hratch K. Panosian. BROADCASTING STATION: WIBF F.M. 103.9. BROADCASTING LANGUAGE: Armenian and English. BROADCASTING DAY AND TIME: Sundays, 8:30 to 9:30 P.M. (Eastern time). CONTACT PERSON: Hratch K. Panosian.

Rhode Island

(654)
ARMENIAN RADIO HOUR
P.O. BOX 414
PROVIDENCE, RHODE ISLAND 02901   **(401) 421-8988**

DATE FOUNDED: 1947. DIRECTOR & PRODUCER: Russell Gasparian. HOST/ANNOUNCER: Russell Gasparian and Albert Arabian. BROADCASTING STATION: WRIB A.M. 1220. BROADCASTING LANGUAGE: Armenian and English. BROADCASTING DAY AND TIME: Sundays, 9:30 to 10:30 A.M. (Eastern time). CONTACT PERSON: Russell Gasparian.

SCHOLARSHIPS, LOANS

GRANTS, FELLOWSHIPS

Scholarships, Loans, Grants, Fellowships
California

(655)
AMERICAN ARMENIAN INTERNATIONAL COLLEGE
SCHOLARSHIPS COMMITTEE
1950 THIRD STREET
LA VERNE, CALIFORNIA 91750   (714) 593-2594 (714) 593-2594
TITLE OF AWARDS: Armenian Studies Grant, Work-Study Program, Grants-in-Aid, Deans Scholarship. **ELIGIBILITY REQUIREMENTS:** 3.0 GPA (80%), letter of reference, and potential for leadership. **DESCRIPTION OF AVAILABLE FUNDS:** The purpose of the finanacial aids program at AAIC is to reduce the importance of college cost as a factor in college choice. **NUMBER OF AWARDS:** Fifty awards per year. **APPLICATION DEADLINE:** June 1. **TYPE OF FUNDS:** Fellowships, grants, loans and scholarships. **FUNDS AVAILABLE TO:** Individuals only. **FOR INFORMATION AND APPLICATION CONTACT:** Dr. Garbis Der Yeghiayan, Dean.

(656)
ARMENIAN ALLIED ARTS ASSOCIATION
552 WOODLAND COURT
DUARTE, CALIFORNIA 91010   (818) 303-2023

(657)
ARMENIAN ALUMNI ASSOCIATION
P.O. BOX 27280
LOS ANGELES, CALIFORNIA 90027   (818) 507-7686

(658)
ARMENIAN AMERICAN CITIZENS' LEAGUE
4121 WEST 60th STREET
LOS ANGELES, CALIFORNIA 90043

(659)
ARMENIAN AMERICAN MIDDLE EAST CLUB
3929 SANTA CARLOTTA
LA CRESCENTA, CALIFORNIA 91214   (818) 248-8399
ELIGIBILITY REQUIREMENTS: Armenian students attending college or university in California, matriculated students, junior or above, enrolled in a minimum of 12 semester units. **NUMBER OF AWARDS:** Varies between 5 to 7 awards. **APPLICATION DEADLINE:** February of each year. **TYPE OF FUNDS:** Scholarships. **FUNDS AVAILABLE TO:** Individ-

uals only. **FOR INFORMATION & APPLICATION CONTACT:** Yervant Nahabedian, President.

(660)
ARMENIAN BIBLE COLLEGE
1605 EAST ELIZABETH STREET
PASADENA, CALIFORNIA 91104   **(818) 791-2575**

ELIGIBILITY REQUIREMENTS: 1) Pledge to work as a minister, evangelist, missionary or youth director after graduation, 2) Good academic standing, 3) Good character. **APPLICATION DEADLINE:** May 31 of each year. **TYPE OF FUNDS:** Grants and scholarships. **FUNDS AVAILABLE TO:** Individuals only. **ADDITIONAL INFORMATION:** Scholarship applies equally to, a) Full-time students, b) Part-time students, c) Correspondence students. **FOR INFORMATION AND APPLICATION CONTACT:** Dr. Yeghia Babikian, Director.

(661)
ARMENIAN PROFESSIONAL SOCIETY OF THE BAY AREA
C/O DR. CHRISTINE POOCHIGIAN
2529 HAYWARD DRIVE
BURLINGAME, CALIFORNIA 94010   **(415) 692-4898**

ELIGIBILITY REQUIREMENTS: Candidates are required to have shown interest in Armenian affairs, must be full-time students or show evidence of having been admitted to a four-year accredited college or university; must have maintained a minimum GPA of 3.25/4.00 during college study; complete application form; send copies of transcripts of all colleges attended; submit two letters of recommendation from current instructors; transfer students should submit letter of acceptance. **NUMBER OF AWARDS:** Two awards. **APPLICATION DEADLINE:** June 30th of each year. **TYPE OF FUNDS:** Scholarships. **FUNDS AVAILABLE TO:** Individuals only. **FOR INFORMATION AND APPLICATION CONTACT:** Aylin Gulbenkian, Scholarship Chairperson, or Dr. Christine Poochigian, Secretary.

(662)
ARMENIAN PROFESSIONAL SOCIETY
215 WEST MARINERS VIEW LANE
LA CANADA, CALIFORNIA 91011   **(818) 500-1918**

(663)
CALIFORNIA STATE UNIVERSITY, FRESNO
COLLEGE UNION, ROOM 301
FRESNO, CALIFORNIA 93740   **(209) 294-2574**

TITLE OF AWARD: Knights of Vartan, Fresno Lodge #9 Scholarship.

ELIGIBILITY REQUIREMENTS: Recipients must be full-time students (12 units per semester) and maintain a 3.0 GPA. **DESCRIPTION OF AVAILABLE FUNDS:** Two scholarships of $325 each, annually, one for entering freshmen and one for continuing students at C.S.U.F. who have completed 24 semester units. **APPLICATION DEADLINE:** Prior to March 15th of the spring semester preceding need for scholarship. **TYPE OF FUNDS:** Scholarships. **ADDITIONAL INFORMATION:** Recipients must enroll in at least one class in Armenian studies, Armenian language or Armenian history. **FOR INFORMATION AND APPLICATION CONTACT:** Financial Aids Office, Administration Building, Room 296, C.S.U.F., Fresno, California 93740.

(664)
CALIFORNIA STATE UNIVERSITY, FRESNO
COLLEGE UNION ROOM 301
FRESNO, CALIFORNIA 93740   **(209) 294-2574**

TITLE OF AWARD: K. Arakelian Foundation Scholarships. **ELIGIBILITY REQUIREMENTS:** San Joaquin Valley High School Graduates. **DESCRIPTION OF AVAILABLE FUNDS:** $250 scholarships awarded annually. **NUMBER OF AWARDS:** 8 awards. **APPLICATION DEADLINE:** Prior to March 15th of the spring semester preceding need for scholarship. **TYPE OF FUNDS:** Scholarships. **FOR INFORMATION AND APPLICATION CONTACT:** Financial Aids Office, C.S.U.F., Administration Building, Room 296, Fresno, California 93740.

(665)
CALIFORNIA STATE UNIVERSITY, FRESNO
COLLEGE UNION ROOM 301
FRESNO, CALIFORNIA 93740   **(209) 294-2574**

TITLE OF AWARD: Thomas Googooian Memorial Scholarship. **ELIGIBILITY REQUIREMENTS:** Must be a student enrolled or planning to enroll in a program leading to a bachelor's degree. **DESCRIPTION OF AVAILABLE FUNDS:** $500 scholarship awarded annually. **APPLICATION DEADLINE:** Prior to March 15th of the spring preceding need for scholarship. **TYPE OF FUNDS:** Scholarships. **FOR INFORMATION AND APPLICATION CONTACT:** Financial Aids Office, C.S.U.F., Administration Building, Room 296, Fresno, Calforvia 93740.

(666)
CALIFORNIA STATE UNIVERSITY, FRESNO
COLLEGE UNION ROOM 301
FRESNO, CALIFORNIA 93740   **(209) 294-2574**

TITLE OF AWARD: Charles Pategian Scholarships. **ELIGIBILITY REQUIREMENTS:** Interest in Armenian culture. **DESCRIPTION OF**

AVAILABLE FUNDS: Endowment, usually generated 10 scholarships of between $500 to $700 each year. **NUMBER OF AWARDS:** 10 awards. **APPLICATION DEADLINE:** March 30. **TYPE OF FUNDS:** Scholarships. **FOR INFORMATION AND APPLICATION CONTACT:** Financial Aids Office, Administration Building, Room 269, Fresno, California 93740, or send your letter to Dickran Kouymjian, Director of Armenian Studies Program.

(667)
COMPATRIOTIC UNION OF HADJIN
C/O HRATCH KRADJIAN
1110 VICTORIA AVENUE
LOS ANGELES, CALFORNIA 90019   **(213) 935-9929**

TITLE OF AWARD: Compatriotic Union of Hadjin Scholarship Grants. **ELIGIBILITY REQUIREMENTS:** 1) Matriculation as a full-time student in a college or university, 2) Carrying 12 or more units per term, 3) Engaging in a course of study with an objective of obtaining a degree, 4) Having Hadjintsi parentage (at least one parent). **NUMBER OF AWARDS:** Two, $500. **APPLICATION DEADLINE:** May 31. **TYPE OF FUNDS:** Grants and scholarships. **FUNDS AVAILABLE TO:** Individuals only. **ADDITIONAL INFORMATION:** The organization 1) Will apply for a status of charitable tax-exempt organization, 2) Is planning to increase the number and/or size of the awards, 3) Is studying the possibility of making the awards available to all Armenian Americans. **FOR INFORMATION AND APPLICATION CONTACT:** Hratch Kradjian, Treasurer of the organization and Chairman of Scholarship Committee.

(668)
GARIKIAN UNIVERSITY SCHOLARSHIP FUND
THE ARMENIAN APOSTOLIC CHURCH OF AMERICA WESTERN PRE-LACY
4401 RUSSELL AVENUE
LOS ANGELES, CALIFORNIA 90027 (213) 663-8273 (213) 663-8274

TITLE OF AWARD: Garikian University Scholarship. **ELIGIBILITY REQUIREMENTS:** 1) Shall attend one of the universities of California, 2) Should have successfully completed their first academic year at their respective university, 3) Shall pursue their higher studies in one of the following specialized courses or subjects specified by the by-laws governing the provisions of the Garikian University Scholarship Fund: a) Armenian Studies, b) Law, c) Sociology and Psychology, d) Political Science, e) History, f) Literature, g) Journalism, h) Education, i) Music. **NUMBER OF AWARDS:** 10 awards. **APPLICATION DEADLINE:** July 31. **TYPE OF FUNDS:** Grants. **FUNDS AVAILABLE TO:** Individuals only. **FOR INFORMATION AND APPLICATION CONTACT:** Berj S. Bagdoyan, Executive Secretary, Western Prelacy.

(669)
GENERAL SOCIETY OF VASBOURAGAN
6071 EAST BUTLER AVENUE
FRESNO, CALIFORNIA 93727 (209) 251-7272

ELIGIBILITY REQUIREMENTS: Applicant must be a Vantzie undergraduate in a four-year college or university; must apply through his/her local chapter of the General Society of Vasbouragan in Boston, Chicago, Detroit, Fresno, Los Angeles, New Jersey, Niagara Falls, Pawtucket in Rhode Island; and must submit transcript of records with application. **DESCRIPTION OF AVAILABLE FUNDS:** Each chapter is allotted a scholarship of $300 per semester. The amount is subject to change at the Biennial National Conventions. **NUMBER OF AWARDS:** 9 awards. **TYPE OF FUNDS:** Scholarships. **FUNDS AVAILABLE TO:** Individuals only. **FOR INFORMATION AND APPLICATION CONTACT:** Chapter Officers.

(670)
TRIPLE X FRATERNITY — SAN DIEGO CHAPTER
3430 CAMINO DEL RIO N. # 300
SAN DIEGO, CALIFORNIA 92108

TYPES OF FUNDS: Scholarships. **FOR INFORMATION AND APPLICATION CONTACT:** John T. Sivas, Scholarship Committee Chairman.

(671)
UNIVERSITY OF CALIFORNIA, BERKELEY
FINANCIAL AIDS OFFICE
201 SPROUL HALL
BERKELEY, CALIFORNIA 94720 (415) 642-6363

TITLE OF AWARDS: Mangasar M. Mangasarian Scholarship Fund. **ELIGIBILITY REQUIREMENTS:** 1) Undergraduate or graduate, 2) Of Armenian descent. **DESCRIPTION OF AVAILABLE FUNDS:** Up to full cost of tuition, fees, books, supplies, maintenance, and all other costs of attendance, not to exceed demonstrated need. Funds are made via endowments from a trust fund. **NUMBER OF AWARDS:** Depending upon availability of funds. **APPLICATION DEADLINE:** Approximately February of each year. **TYPES OF FUNDS:** Scholarships. **FUNDS AVAILABLE TO:** Individuals only. **ADDITIONAL INFORMATION:** Students apply via a general scholarship application and must obtain a minimum GPA (which may vary each year); must be students at U.C. Berkeley (may apply at U.C.L.A. also); applications are available each December, and are due each February of the year preceding the year to which the scholarship would apply. **FOR INFORMATION AND APPLICATION CONTACT:** Emmet T. Scales, Assistant Financial Aid Director.

(672)
UNIVERSITY OF CALIFORNIA, BERKELEY
FINANCIAL AIDS OFFICE
201 SPROUL HALL
BERKELEY, CALIFORNIA 94720   **(415) 642-6363**
TITLE OF AWARDS: Aram Torossian Memorial Scholarship. **ELIGIBIL-
ITY REQUIREMENTS:** 1) student who has attended U.C. Berkeley for at
least one year, 2) has demonstrated need for financial assistance, 3) is of
Armenian parentage. **DESCRIPTION OF AVAILABLE FUNDS:** Funds
are made via endowments and gifts. **NUMBER OF AWARDS:** Depending
upon availability of funds. **APPLICATION DEADLINE:** Approximately
February of each year. **TYPE OF FUNDS:** Scholarships. **FUNDS AVAILA-
BLE TO:** Individuals only. **ADDITIONAL INFORMATION:** Students apply
via a general scholarship application and must obtain a minimum GPA
(which may vary each year); must be attending U.C. Berkeley; applications are available each December, and are due each February of the
year preceding the year to which the scholarship would apply. **FOR
INFORMATION AND APPLICATION CONTACT:** Emmet T. Scales,
Assistant Financial Aid Director.

(673)
UNIVERSITY OF CALIFORNIA, BERKELEY
FINANCIAL AIDS OFFICE
201 SPROUL HALL
BERKELEY, CALIFORNIA 94720   **(415) 642-6363**
TITLE OF AWARDS: Neshan Zovick Scholarship. **ELIGIBILITY
REQUIREMENTS:** 1) Financial need, 2) Armenian descent. **DESCRIP-
TION OF AVAILABLE FUNDS:** Funds are made via an endowment.
NUMBER OF AWARDS: Depending upon availability of funds. **APPLI-
CATION DEADLINE:** Approximately February of each year. **TYPES OF
FUNDS:** Scholarships. **FUNDS AVAILABLE TO:** Individuals only. **ADDI-
TIONAL INFORMATION:** Students apply via a general scholarship appli-
cation and must obtain a minimum GPA (which may vary each year);
students must be attending U.C. Berkeley; applications are available
each December, and are due each February of the year preceding the
year to which the scholarship would apply. **FOR INFORMATION AND
APPLICATION CONTACT:** Emmet T. Scales, Assistant Financial Aid
Director.

(674)
UNIVERSITY OF CALIFORNIA, BERKELEY
ARMENIAN ALUMNI ASSOCIATION
C/O 450 SUTTER STREET, SUITE 1326
SAN FRANCISCO, CALIFORNIA 94108   **(415) 421-0317**

TITLE OF AWARDS: U.C. Berkeley Armenian Alumni Scholarship Award. **ELIGIBILITY REQUIREMENTS:** One high school senior with acceptance to freshman class at Berkeley and one undergraduate student enrolled at U.C. Berkeley. **DESCRIPTION OF AVAILABLE FUNDS:** One $500 cash for entering freshman student and one $500 cash for continuing student. **NUMBER OF AWARDS:** 2 awards. **APPLICATION DEADLINE:** April 15. **TYPES OF FUNDS:** Scholarships. **FOR INFORMATION AND APPLICATION CONTACT:** Dr. Jack M. Saroyan, President or Thelma Tajirian, Scholarship Chairperson.

(675)
UNIVERSITY OF CALIFORNIA, LOS ANGELES
DEPARTMENT OF NEAR EASTERN LANGUAGES & CULTURES
LOS ANGELES, CALIFORNIA 90024　　　　　　**(213) 825-1307**

TITLE OF AWARDS: Kareken Der Avedisian Memorial Endowment Fund. **FOR INFORMATION AND APPLICATION CONTACT:** U.C.L.A. Fellowship & Assistantship Section, 1228 Murphy Hall, Los Angeles, California 90024.

(676)
UNIVERSITY OF CALIFORNIA, LOS ANGELES
DEPARTMENT OF NEAR EASTERN LANGUAGES & CULTURES
LOS ANGELES, CALIFORNIA 90024　　　　　　**(213) 825-1307**

TITLE OF AWARDS: Kaspar Hovannisian Memorial Scholarship For Armenian Studies. **FOR INFORMATION AND APPLICATION CONTACT:** U.C.L.A. Fellowship & Assistantship Section, 1228 Murphy Hall, Los Angeles, California 90024.

(677)
UNIVERSITY OF CALIFORNIA, LOS ANGELES
DEPARTMENT OF NEAR EASTERN LANGUAGES & CULTURES
LOS ANGELES, CALIFORNIA 90024　　　　　　**(213) 825-1307**

TITLE OF AWARDS; Mangasar M. Mangasarian Scholarship. **FOR INFORMATION & APPLICATION CONTACT:** U.C.L.A. Fellowship & Assistantship Section, 1228 Murphy Hall, Los Angeles, California 90024.

(678)
UNIVERSITY OF SOUTHERN CALIFORNIA
U.S.C. FRIENDS OF ARMENIAN MUSIC
UNIVERSITY PARK
LOS ANGELES, CALIFORNIA 90089 (213) 743-6935 (213) 743-8901

TITLE OF AWARD: U.S.C. Friends of Armenian Music Scholarship Award. **ELIGIBILITY REQUIREMENTS:** Armenian music students enrolled at U.S.C. School of Music, taking Armenian music courses offered by Music History and Literature Department. **DESCRIPTION OF AVAILABLE FUNDS:** Toward tuition. **NUMBER OF AWARDS:** 1 to 3 awards. **APPLICATION DEADLINE:** June to July. **TYPES OF FUNDS:** Scholarships. **FUNDS AVAILABLE TO:** Individuals only. **FOR INFOR-MATION AND APPLICATION CONTACT:** Dr. William Thomson, Dean U.S.C. School of Music.

Massachusetts

(679)
ARMENIAN AMERICAN MEDICAL ASSOCIATION
20 CLARENDON ROAD
BELMONT, MASSACHUSETTS 02178   **(617) 489-4070**

ELIGIBILITY REQUIREMENTS: Medical students of Armenian parent-age, who have successfully finished the first year of medicine, in a recognized medical school, and have financial need. **DESCRIPTION OF AVAILABLE FUNDS:** Income from invested funds, donated by the mem-bership. **NUMBER OF AWARDS:** 3 awards. **APPLICATION DEADLINE:** September 15. **TYPE OF FUNDS:** Scholarships. **FUNDS AVAILABLE TO:** Individuals only. **FOR INFORMATION AND APPLICATION CON-TACT:** Edward Karian, M.D., Chairman of Scholarship Committee, 324 Common Street, Watertown, Massachusetts 02172.

(680)
ARMENIAN RELIEF SOCIETY OF NORTH AMERICA, INC.
SCHOLARSHIP COMMITTEE
38 ELTON STREET
WATERTOWN, MASSACHUSETTS 02172   **(617) 926-5892**

(681)
ARMENIAN RENAISSANCE ASSOCIATION, INC.
67 LEONARD STREET
BELMONT, MASSACHUSETTS 02178   **(617) 489-1365**

TITLE OF AWARD: Executive Council Scholarship. **ELIGIBILITY REQUIREMENTS:** 2nd year college student. **NUMBER OF AWARDS:** 1 award. **APPLICATION DEADLINE:** To be announced. **TYPE OF FUNDS:** Scholarships. **FUNDS AVAILABLE TO:** Individuals only. **ADDI-TIONAL INFORMATION:** First scholarship to be given in spring 1985. **FOR INFORMATION AND APPLICATION CONTACT:** Martha Hana-nian, Secretary.

(682)
HAI-GUIN SCHOLARSHIP ASSOCIATION
P.O. BOX 509
BELMONT, MASSACHUSETTS 02178
ELIGIBILITY REQUIREMENTS: The purpose of this club is to provide scholarships to promote the higher educational and vocational development of students of Armenian origin, residing in the state of Massachusetts. **DESCRIPTION OF AVAILABLE FUNDS:** A five hundred dollar scholarship award may be granted to each of one or more Armenian students residing and attending college in Massachusetts. The scholarship will be granted to students who have completed the first semester of the freshman year. The selection will be based on high scholastic achievement and financial need. **APPLICATION DEADLINE:** December 15. **TYPE OF FUNDS:** Scholarships.

(683)
ZORYAN INSTITUTE
85 FAYERWEATHER STREET
CAMBRIDGE, MASSACHUSETTS 02138   **(617) 497-6713**
ELIGIBILITY REQUIREMENTS: 1) Academic standing, 2) Relevance, 3) Intellectual integrity. **TYPE OF FUNDS:** Fellowships, grants, and scholarships. **FUNDS AVAILABLE TO:** Individuals and organizations. **ADDITIONAL INFORMATION:** Pending available funds, grants and research, fellowships will be made available to encourage research and publications in areas of interest of the institute. **FOR INFORMATION AND APPLICATION CONTACT:** Gerard Libaridian, Director.

Michigan

(684)
WAYNE STATE UNIVERSITY
5950 CASS, # 222
DETROIT, MICHIGAN 48202   **(313) 577-2424**
TITLE OF AWARDS: The Michael M. Assarian Scholarship. **ELIGIBILITY REQUIREMENTS:** This fund is established to recognize scholastic achievement, encourage continued progress, and provide assistance to Armenian students in financing their education at Wayne State University. It is to be administered according to the following provision: 1) Applications may be accepted from full-time Armenian students of Wayne State University or from Armenian students accepted for study at Wayne State University. 2) Recipients will be selected on the basis of scholastic achievement, desirable qualities of character and leadership, and financial need. 3) Recipients will be selected by the Office of Schol-

arships and Financial Aids in accordance with the general policies and practices in effect for scholarships at the university. **DESCRIPTION OF AVAILABLE FUNDS:** 1) The amount of the scholarship is $1,000. 2) The Office of Scholarships and Financial Aids will disburse the awards according to regular university procedures. If at any time, the university policies and procedures in effect for the administration of scholarships and funds are changed, these provisions are automatically modified to conform. **NUMBER OF AWARDS:** 1 award. **TYPES OF FUNDS:** Scholarships. **FUNDS AVAILABLE TO:** Individuals only. **FOR INFORMATION AND APPLICATION CONTACT:** Thomas H. Kachadurian, Financial Aid Officer.

New Jersey

(685)
ARMENIAN GENERAL ATHLETIC UNION
ALUMNI ASSOCIATION
211 GRAND BLVD.
EMERSON, NEW JERSEY 07630   **(201) 261-4796**
FOR INFORMATION AND APPLICATION CONTACT: Peter Ajemian, Scholarships Chairman.

(686)
ARMENIAN GENERAL BENEVOLENT UNION OF AMERICA
SCHOLARSHIPS COMMITTEE
585 SADDLE RIVER ROAD
SADDLE BROOK, NEW JERSEY 07662   **(201) 707-7600**
ELIGIBILITY REQUIREMENTS: Financial need, grades, area of study, and Armenian community involvement. **DESCRIPTION OF AVAILABLE FUNDS:** A.G.B.U. Endowment Funds. **APPLICATION DEADLINE:** February 15. **TYPES OF FUNDS:** Fellowships, grants, loans, and scholarships. **FUNDS AVAILABLE TO:** Individuals only. **FOR INFORMATION AND APPLICATION CONTACT:** Mirjan Kirian, Executive Secretary of Education Committee.

(687)
ARMENIAN MISSIONARY ASSOCIATION OF AMERICA
140 FOREST AVENUE
PARAMUS, NEW JERSEY 07652   **(201) 265-2607 (201) 265-2608**
FOR INFORMATION AND APPLICATION CONTACT: Dr. John G. Keuhnelian, Scholarship Chairman.

(688)
DAUGHTERS OF VARTAN SCHOLARSHIP
54 FOSTER ROAD
TENAFLY, NEW JERSEY 07670
FOR INFORMATION AND APPLICATION CONTACT: Shakee B. Kapakjian.

(689)
JOHN M. AZARIAN MEMORIAL ARMENIAN YOUTH
SCHOLARSHIP FUND
352 LAFAYETTE AVENUE
HAWTHORNE, NEW JERSEY 07506   **(201) 423-0001**
TITLE OF AWARD: John M. Azarian Memorial Armenian Youth Scholarship Fund. **ELIGIBILITY REQUIREMENTS:** An Armenian college student with financial need, preferably an accounting or business major scholar. **NUMBER OF AWARDS:** 1 award per year. **APPLICATION DEADLINE:** June 2nd to May 31st. **TYPES OF FUNDS:** Scholarships. **ADDITIONAL INFORMATION:** Scholarship awarded in September for fall semester. **FOR INFORMATION AND APPLICATION CONTACT:** John M. Azarian, Jr.

New York

(690)
COLUMBIA UNIVERSITY
GRADUATE SCHOOL OF ARTS SCIENCES
106 LOW LIBRARY
NEW YORK, NEW YORK 10027   **(212) 280-4737**
TITLE OF AWARDS: Krikor and Clara Zohrab Fellowships. **ELIGIBILITY REQUIREMENTS:** Must be a graduate student in Armenian Studies Program at Columbia University. **APPLICATION DEADLINE:** February 1st. **TYPES OF FUNDS:** Fellowships. **FUNDS AVAILABLE TO:** Individuals only. **FOR INFORMATION AND APPLICATION CONTACT:** Office of Admissions and Financial Aid.

(691)
SAINT NERSESS ARMENIAN SEMINARY
150 STRATTON ROAD
NEW ROCHELLE, NEW YORK 10804   **(914) 636-2003**

(692)
THE STUDENT FUND OF THE UNION OF MARASH ARMENIANS
C/O SIROON P. SHAHINIAN
ONE SUSSEX ROAD
GREAT NECK, NEW YORK 11020   **(516) 829-6837**

TITLE OF AWARDS: Dikran Halajian Memorial Fund. **ELIGIBILITY REQUIREMENTS:** 1) Marashtsi lineage, 2) Good moral character, 3) Financial need, 4) Attending or expecting to attend an accredited college or university for intended course of study, 5) Satisfactory academic achievement evidence by official transcripts of all grades. **DESCRIPTION OF AVAILABLE FUNDS:** Up to three annual awards for outstandiang high school achievement, scholarship awards to undergraduate and graduate students from the student fund and the Dikran Halajian fund. The interest on principal funds is awarded annually from the funds of the student fund and the Dikran Halajian Memorial Fund. **APPLICATION DEADLINE:** October 30. **TYPES OF FUNDS:** Scholarships. **FUNDS AVAILABLE TO:** Individuals only. **ADDITIONAL INFORMATION:** 1) Up to two awards of $500 are made from the Dikran Halajian Memorial Fund, 2) Maximum amount of individual awards from the student fund is $400 annually, 3) Students may receive a maximum of four awards. **FOR INFORMATION AND APPLICATION CONTACT:** Siroon P. Shahinian, Ph.D., Secretary, and John Halajian, President.

Rhode Island

(693)
ARMENIAN STUDENTS' ASSOCIATION OF AMERICA, INC.
P.O. BOX 6947
PROVIDENCE, RHODE ISLAND 02940

ELIGIBILITY REQUIREMENTS: Loans: 2.0 grade point average; Armenian descent enrolled in junior college, college, university or professional school on full-time basis in the U.S. Outright grants: 2.5 grade point average; enrolled in four year college or university and have completed at least one year of graduate school; all on full-time basis; of Armenian descent. **DESCRIPTION OF AVAILABLE FUNDS:** Loans: $500 per semester, maximum $4,000; Grants: $500 to $1,000 on an annual basis, no limit. **NUMBER OF AWARDS:** Grants: approximately 5 awards per year, and Loans: 50 to 60 loans per year. **APPLICATION DEADLINE:** Grants: April 1st, Loans: fall semester, July 15; spring semester, December 1st; summer, April 1st. **TYPES OF FUNDS:** Grants and loans. **FUNDS AVAILABLE TO:** Individuals only. **FOR INFORMATION AND APPLICATION CONTACT:** Scholarship Committee, Armenian Students' Association of America, Inc.

Section Twelve

BIBLIOGRAPHIES
Books About Armenia and Armenians
in English Language 1960-1983

Massacres

History and Culture

Language

Literature

Arts and Related Works

Religion

Cook Books

Biographies

Armenians in Foreign Countries

Armenians in America

Armenia — Description and Travel

Reference Books

Armenian Massacres

(694)
Aintablian, Alexander, 1901- **Clash of Souls**/by Alexander Aintablian. Beirut: United Printers and Traders, 1977. 215p.

(695)
An Anthology of Historical Writings on the Armenian Massacres of 1915/by Viscount James Bryce and others. Beirut: Hamaskaine Armenian Cultural Association, 1970. 243p.

(696)
Arlen, Michael J., 1895-1956. **Passage to Ararat** by Michael J. Arlen. 1st Edition. N.Y.: Farrar, Straus & Girouz, 1975. 293p.

(697)
Armaghanian, Arshalouise. **Arsha's World and Yours**/by Arshalouise Armaghanian. 1st Edition. N.Y.: Vantage Press, 1977. 96p.

(698)
Armenian Apostolic Church of America, Prelacy. **A Heroic Posterity** N.Y.: Armenian Apostolic Church of America, 1976. vii, 151p.

(699)
The Armenian Genocide; First 20th Century Holocaust, 65th Anniversary Memorial 1915-1980/by Richard Diran Kloian. 2nd edition. Fresno, CA: United Armenian Commemorative Committee, Armenian Assembly, Walnut Creek, CA: 1980. 304p.

(700)
Armenian Historical Research Association. **The Turkish Armenicide; The Genocide of the Armenians by Turks:** Newtown Square, PA: 1965.

(701)
Avakian, Lindy V. **The Cross and the Crescent**/by Lindy V. Avakian. Los Angeles: DeVoross, 1965. 309p.

(702)
Barooshian, Stephen M. **My Story**/by Stephen Barooshian. N.Y.: Vantage Press, 1978.

(703)
Bedoukian, Kerop, 1907- **Some of Us Survived: The Story of an Armenian Boy**/by Kerop Bedoukian. 1st American edition. N.Y.: Farrar, Straus Girouz, 1979. 241p. (Juvenile literature)

(704)
Bedoukian, Kerop, 1907- **The Urchin: An Armenian's Escape**/by Kerop Bedoukian. London: J. Murray, 1978. vii, 186p.

(705)
Bonsal, Stephen. **Suitors and Suppliants; The Little Nations at Versailles**/by Stephen Bonsal. Introduction by A. Krock. N.Y.: Prentice-Hall, 1946. (Reprinted, Port Washington, N.Y.: Kennikat Press, 1969.)

(706)
Boyajian, Dickran H. **Armenia: The Case For a Forgotten Genocide**/by Dickran H. Boyajian. Westwood, N.J.: Educational Book Crafters, 1972. xiii, 498p.

(707)
Bryce, James Bryce, Viscount, 1838-1922. **Transcaucasia and Ararat** by James B. Viscount. N.Y.: Arno Press, 1970. xix, 526p.

(708)
Caraman, Elizabeth. **Daughter of the Euphrates**/by Elizabeth Caraman, collaboration with William Lytton Payne. 2nd edition N.Y.: Armenian Missionary Association of America, 1979. xix, 277p.

(709)
Chakalian, Manouk. **Journey For Freedom**/by Manouk Chakalian. N.Y.: Carlton Press, 1976.

(710)
Chaliand, Gerard, 1934-   **Le Genocide Des Armenians, 1915-1917, The Armenians, From Genocide to Resistance**/by Gerard Chaliand and Yves Ternon. Translated by Tony Berrett. London: Zed Press, 1983.

(711)
Dadrian, Vahakn N. **The Methodological Components of Genocide in Recent Studies in Modern Armenian History**/by Vahakn Dadrian. Cambridge, Mass.: Armenian Heritage Press, 1972.

(712)
Daghlian, Levon K. **Under the Gallows**/by Levon Daghlian. Belmont, Mass., 1970.

(713)
Egitkhanoff, Marie Abelian. **Escape: A Sequel to Terror by Night and Day**/by Marie Abelian Egitkhanoff and Ken Wilson. Mountain View, CA: Pacific Press Pub. Association, 1982. 124p.

(714)
Egitkhanoff, Marie Abelian. **Terror by Night and Day: An Armenian Girl's Story**/by Marie Abelian Egitkhanoff and Ken Wilson. Cover illustration and design by Tim Mitoma. Mountain View, CA: Pacific Press Pub. Association, 1980. 144p.

(715)
**The First Holocaust: The Genocide Against the Armenian Nation,
1915-1923**/edited by Hagop Terjimanian. Pasadena, CA: Seran editions, 1982. 104p.

(716)
Al-Ghusayn, Fa'iz. **Martyred Armenia**/by Fa'iz Al-Ghusayn. Translated from the original Arabic. N.Y.: Tankian Publishing Corp, 1975. 64p.

(717)
Gibbons, Herbert Adams, 1880-1934. **The Blackest Page of Modern History: Events in Armenia in 1915, the Facts and the Responsibilities**/by Herbert Adams Gibbons. N.Y.: London: Tankian Publishing Co., 1975. 47p.

(718)
Gidney, James Brock. **A Mandate for Armenia**/by James B. Gidney. Kent, Ohio: Kent State University Press, 1967. x, 270p.

(719)
Glockler, Henry W. **Interned in Turkey, 1914-1918**/by Henry Glockler Beirut: Sevan Press, 1969.

(720)
Guttmann, Josef, 1902-   **The Beginnings of Genocide: An Account of the Armenian Massacres in World War I**/by Josef Guttmann. The memories of Naim Bey compiled by Aram Andonian. Newtown Square, PA: The Armenian Historical Research Association, 1965. A-K, 19, xiv, 84p.

(721)
Hartunian, Abraham H. **Neither to Laugh Nor to Weep: A Memoir of the Armenian Genocide**/by Abraham H. Hartunian. Translated from the original Armenian manuscripts by Vartan Hartunian. Boston: Beacon Press, 1968. 206p. (Reprinted by Armenian Missionary Association of America, 1976.)

(722)
Henry, James Dodds. **Baku; An Eventful History**/by James Dodds Henry. N.Y.: Arno Press, 1977. xviii, 256p. (Reprint of the 1905 edition)

(723)
Housepian, Marjorie, 1923-   **The Smyrna Affair**/by Marjorie Housepian. 1st edition. N.Y.: Harcourt Brace Jovanovich, 1971. xi, 269p.

(724)
Hovannisian, Richard G. **The Armenian Holocaust: A Bibliography Relating to the Deportation, Massacres, and Dispersion of Armenian People, 1915-1918**/by Richard Hovannisian. 2nd revised printing. Cambridge, Mass.: National Association For Armenian Studies and Research; Armenian Heritage Press, 1978, 1980.

(725)
Kash, Sarkis H. **Crime Unlimited**/by Sarkis H. Kash. So. Milwaukee, Wis.: Journal Printing Co., 1965. 101p.

(726)
Kasparian, Alice Odian. **The History of the Armenians of Angora and Stanos; From Pre-Christian & Galatian Periods Up to 1918**/by Alice Odian Kasparian. Beirut: Doniguian Press, 1971. 72p.

(727)
Kasparian, Haigaz K. **Minutes of Secret Meeting Organizing the Turkish Genocide of the Armenian; What Turkish Sources Say on the Subject**/by Haigaz K. Kazarian. Boston: Commemorative committee on the 50th anniversary of the Turkish massacres of Armenians, 1965. 14p.

(728)
Kayaloff, Jacoues. **The Battle of Sardarabad**/by Jacques Kayaloff. The Hague, Mouton, 1973.

(729)
Kerr, Stanley Elphinstone. **The Lions of Marash; Personal Experiences with American Near East Relief, 1919-1922**/by Stanley E. Kerr. Introduction by Richard Hovannisian. 1st edition. Albany: State University of New York Press, 1973. xxv, 318p.

(730)
Lanne, Peter. **Armenia, The First Genocide of the XX Century**/by Peter Lanne. Translated from the German original by Krikor Balekdjian. Munich: Institute for Armenian Studies, 1979. 215p.

(731)
Martyrdom and Rebirth Fateful Events in the Recent History of the Armenian People/by Arshag Sarkisian and others. Preface by G.P. Gooch. Published on the occasion of the 50th anniversary of the massacres of 1915 by the Diocese of the Armenian Church of America. N.Y.: 1965. 105p.

(732)
Morgenthau, Henry, 1856-1946. **The Murder of a Nation**/by Henry Morgenthau, American Ambassador to Turkey 1913-1916. Preface by Prof. W. H. Medlicott. 2nd edition. Los Angeles, CA: A.G.B.U. Ararat Press, 1982. 120p.

(733)
Mukhitarian, Onnig. **An Account of the Glorious Struggle of Van-Vasbouragan**/by Onnig Mukhitarian. Translated by Sammual S. Tarpinian. Detroit, Michigan: Central Executive General Society of Vasbouragan, 1980. 62p.

(734)
Na'im, Bey. **The Memories of Naim Bey: Turkish Official Documents Relating to the Deportations and Massacres of Armenians**/compiled by Aram Andonian with an introduction by Viscount Gladstone. Reprinted with a new preface by the Armenian Historical Research Association. Newtown Square, PA: AHRA, 1964. xiv, 83p.

(735)
Nalbandian, Louise. **The Armenian Revolutionary Movement; the development of Armenian Political Parties Through the Nineteenth Century.** Berkeley: University of California Press, 1963. ix, 247p.

(736)
Nazer, James. **The First Genocide of the 20th Century; the Story of the Armenian Massacres in Text and Pictures**/compiled by James Nazer. N.Y.: T & T Publishing, 1968. 159p.

(737)
Papajian, Sarkis. **Chunkoosh**/by Sarkis Papajian. Fresno, CA: Crown Printing Co., 1976.

(738)
Parsegian, Lawrence V. **Human Rights and Genocide; The Hope, The Reality, and Still The Hope: a Status Report**/Prepared by L. V. Parsegian under auspices of Diocese of the Armenian Church of America. N.Y.: Diocese of the Armenian Church of America, 1975. 45p.

(739)
Rejebian, Ermance. **Pilgrimage to Freedom**/by Ermance Rejebian. 1973. 47p.

(740)
Sarian, Nerses. **I Shall Not Die**/by Nerses Sarian. Introduction by Eric W. Gosden. London: Oliphants, 1967.

(741)
Sarkisian, Ervand Kazarovich. **Vital Issues in Modern Armenian History; A Documented Expose of Misrepresentation in Turkish Histography**/by E. K. Sarkisian and R. G. Sahakian. Translated and edited by Elisha Charkian. Watertown, Mass.: Armenian Studies, 1965. 82p.

(742)
Shiragian, Arshavir. **The Legacy: Memoirs of an Armenian Patriot**/by Arshavir Shiragian. Boston, Mass.: Hairenik Press, 1976.

(743)
Sutherlan, James Kay, 1897- **The Adventures of an Armenian Boy; An Autobiography and Historical Narrative Encompassing**

the Last Thirty Years of the Ottoman Empire. Ann Arbor, Michigan: Ann Arbor Press, 1964.

(744)
Taft, Elise Hagopian, 1906-   **Rebirth: The Story of an Armenian Girl Who Survived the Genocide and Found Rebirth in America**/by Elise Hagopian Taft. 1st edition. Plandome, N.Y.: New Age Publisher, 1981. ix, 142p.

(745)
Tcholakian, Arthur, 1928-   **The Walking Tree**/by Arthur Tcholakian. Flushing, N.Y.: Paradon Publishers, 1975. 68p.

(746)
Ternon, Yves. **The Armenians: History of a Genocide**/by Yves Ternon. Translated from the French by Rouben Cholakian. Delmar, N.Y.: Caravan Books, 1981. 368p.

(747)
Terzian, Aram. **An Armenian Miscellany; Window on History**/by Aram Terzian. Paris: Librairie Oriental H. Samuelian, 1969. 231p.

(748)
Toriguian, Shavarsh. **The Armenian Question and International Law**/by Shavarsh Toriguian. Beirut: Hamaskaine Press, 1973. 330p.

(749)
Toynbee, Arnold Joseph, 1889-1975. **Armenian Atrocities; The Murder of a Nation**/by Arnold Toynbee. With a speech delivered by Lord Bryce in the House of Lords. N.Y.: Tankian Pub. Co., 1975. 125p.

(750)
Toynbee, Arnold Joseph, 1889-1975. **Experiences**/by Joseph A. Toynbee. N.Y.: Oxford University Press, 1969.

(751)
Toynbee, Arnold Joseph, 1889-1975. **The Murderous Tyranny of the Turks**/by Arnold A. Toynbee. With a preface by Viscount Bryce. N.Y.: Tankian Pub. Corp., 1975. 48p. (Reprint)

(752)
Toynbee, Arnold Joseph, 1889-1975. **The Treatment of Armenians in The Ottoman Empire, 1915-1916,** documents presented to Viscount Grey of Fallon, Secretary of State. 2nd edition. Beirut, 1972. xlii, 684, 30p.

(754)
Yeranian, Arthur S. **The Civilized**/by Arthur S. Yeranian. 1st edition. Smithtown, N.Y.: Exposition, 1980. x, 160p.

(755)
Zarewand. **United and Independent Turania, Aims and Designs of the Turks**/by Zareward. Translated from the Armenian by V. N. Darian. Leiden: Brill, 1971. xiii, 174p.

History and Culture

(756)
The A.G.B.U.: A Mission in Service to the Armenian People. Saddle Brook, N.J.: A.G.B.U., 1983.

(757)
Adonts, Nikolari G. (Adontz, Nicholas). **Armenia in the Period of Justinian: The Political Conditions Based on the Naxarar System**/by Nikolari Adonts. Translated from the Russian with partial revisions, added notes, bibliographical notes, and appendices by Nina G. Garsoian. Lisbon: Calouste Gulbenkian Foundation, 1970. 529 + 405p.

(758)
Aftandilian, Gregory L. **Armenia, Vision of a Republic: The Independence Lobby in America, 1918-1927**/by Gregory Aftandilian. Boston, Mass.: Charles River Books, 1981. 79p.

(759)
Agat'angeghos. **History of the Armenians**/by Agathangehos. Translated and commentary by R. W. Thomson. 1st edition. Albany: State University of New York Press, 1976. xcvii, 527p.

(760)
Aharonian, Aharon. **Intermarriage and the Armenian American Community**/by Aharon Aharonian. Shrewsbury, Mass.: Aharonian, 1983.

(761)
Andonian, Hagop. **Modern Armenia**/by Hagop Andonian. N.Y.: A.G.B.U., 1966. 212p.

(762)
Antreassian, Jack Arthur, 1920-   **Ararat: A Decade of Armenian American Writing**/edited by Jack Antreassian. N.Y.: A.G.B.U., 1969. 442p.

(763)
Arlen, Michael J., 1895-1956. **Passage to Ararat**/by Michael J. Arlen. 1st edition. N.Y.: Farrar, Straus & Giroux, 1975. 293p.

(764)
Armaghanian, Arshalouise. **Arsha's World and Yours**/by Arshalouise Armaghanian. 1st edition. N.Y.: Vantage Press, 1977. 96p.

(765)
Armenia: An Abridged Historic Outline of Its Church and People. N.Y.: Diocese of the Armenian Church of America, 1964. 64p.

(766)
The Armenian Academy of Sciences After 25 Years/edited by P. Agaian and et al. Washington: Joint Publications Research Service, 1969. c, 521p.

(767)
Armenian Church of America. **The Armenian Church: A Brief Outline of Her History and Hierarchical Sees.** N.Y.: Diocese of the Armenian Church of America, 1973. 32p.

(768)
Armenian Church of America. **Martyrdom and Rebirth; Fateful Events in the Recent History of the Armenian People.** Preface by G. P. Gooch. N.Y.: Diocese of the Armenian Church of America, 1965.

(769)
The Armenian Image in History and Literature/edited by Richard G. Hovannisian. Malibu, CA: Undena Publications, 1981. vi, 269p.

(770)
Armenian Inscriptions From the Sinai, with Appendixes on the Georgian and Latin Inscription/edited by Michael Stone. Cambridge, Mass.: Harvard University Press, 1982. 250p.

(771)
The Armenian Republic, 50th Anniversary, 1918-1968. Tehran: Alik Press, 1968.

(772)
Bible. O.T. Apocrypha. 2 Esdras. Armenian. **Armenian Version of IV Ezra**/edited by Michael E. Stone. Missoula, Montana: Scholars Press, 1979. xv, 315p.

(773)
Arzoumanian, Zaven. **Bishop Sebeos; Lewond the Priest; Kirakos of Gandzak**/by Zaven Arzoumanian. Wynnewood, PA: St. Sahag and St. Mesrob Armenian Church, 1981. 51p.

(774)
Azarya, Victor. **Urban Life Behind Monastery Walls: Armenian Quarter of Jerusalem**/by Victor Azarya. Berkeley, CA: University of California Press, 1983. 224p.

(775)
Baliozian, Ara. **The Armenians: Their History & Culture**/by Ara Baliozian. 2nd edition. N.Y.: Ararat Press, 1980. xvi, 191p.

(776)
Baliozian, Ara. **Views/Reviews/Interviews**/by Ara Baliozian. Los Angeles, CA: A/G Press, 1982. 110p.

(777)
Baloian, James. **The Ararat Papers**/by James Baloian. N.Y.: Ararat Press, 1979. 56p.

(778)
Barber, Noel. **The Sultans**/by Noel Barber. N.Y.: Simon and Schuster, 1973.

(779)
Bauer, Elizabeth. **Armenia, Past and Present**/by Elizabeth Bauer. N.Y.: Armenian Prelacy, 1981. 181p.

(780)
Bliss, Edwin M. **Turkey and the Armenian Atrocities**/by Edwin Bliss. Fresno, CA: Meshag Pub., 1982. 574p.

(781)
Bournoutian, George A. **Eastern Armenia in the Last Decades of Persian Rule, 1807-1828: A Political and Socioeconomical Study of the Khanate of Erevan on the Eve of the Russian Conquest**/by George Bournoutian. Malibu, CA: Undena Pub., 1982. xxii, 290p.

(782)
Bryce, James Bryce Viscount. **An Anthology of Historical Writings on the Armenian Massacres of 1915**/by James Bryce Viscount Bryce. Beirut: Hamazkain, 1970.

(783)
Bryce, James Bryce Viscount. **The Treatment of Armenians in the Ottoman Empire, 1915-1916**/by James Bryce. Beirut, 1972.

(784)
Burney, Charles Allen. **The Peoples of the Hills; Ancient Ararat and Caucasus**/by Charles Burney and David Marshall Lang. London: Weidenfeld and Nicolson, 1971. xv, 323p.

(785)
Chailiand, Gerard, 1937-   **The Armenians: From Genocide to Resistance**/by Gerard Chailiand & Yves Ternon. Translated by Tony Berrett. London: Zed Press, 1983. 125p.

(786)
Charanis, Peter. **The Armenians in the Byzantine Empire**/by Peter Charanis. Lisbon: Distributors Livraria Bertrand, 1963. 63p.

(787)
The Cilician Kingdom of Armenia/contributors T.S.R. Boase (et-al), edited by T.S.R. Boase. Edinburgh: Scottish Academic Press, 1978. xii, 206p.

(788)
Conference on Modern Armenian History. Harvard, 1970. **Recent Studies in Modern Armenian History: Conference Sponsored by the National Association for Armenian Studies and Research.** Cambridge, Mass.: Armenian Heritage Press, 1972. x, 141p.

(789)
Der Nersessian, Sirarpie, 1896-   **The Armenians**/by Sirarpie Der Nersessian. London: Thames & Hudson, 1969. 216p.

(790)
Dr. H. Markarian Conference on Armenian Culture (1st: 1979: University of Pennsylvania) **Classical Armenian Culture: Influences and Creativity**/by Thomas J. Samuelian. Chico, CA: Scholars Press, 1982. x, 223p.

(791)
East of Byzantium: Syria & Armenia in Formative Period/by Nina G. Garsoian. Thomas F. Mathews, Robert Thomson editors. Washington, D.C., Dumbarton Oaks: Center for Byzantine Studies, Trustees for Harvard University, 1982. xii, 222p.

(792)
Eliseus, Saint, Vardapet, d. 480. **History of Vardan and the Armenian War**/by Elishe; translation and commentary by Robert W. Thomson. Cambridge, Mass.: Harvard University Press, 1982. viii, 353p.

(793)
Etmekjian, James. **The French Influence on the Western Armenian Renaissance, 1843-1915**/by James Etmekjian. N.Y.: Twayne, 1964. 292p.

(794)
Gidney, James Brock. **A Mandate for Armenia**/by James B. Gidney. Kent, Ohio: Kent State University Press, 1967. x, 270p.

(795)
Grigorian, Mesrop K. **Armenians in the Service of the Ottoman Empire, 1860-1908**/by Mesrob K. Krikorian. London; Boston; Routledge and Kegan Paul, 1977, 1978. xii, 148p.

(796)
Gulbekian, Yedvard. **Avarayr in Historical Perspective**/by Yedvard Gulbekian. N.Y.: Diocese of Armenian Church, 1971.

(797)
Hagop-Krikor. **Known and Unknown Armenians (From Noah to Nowadays)** by Hagop-Krikor. Translated from French text by Colin Nicholls. Paris: H. K. Djirdjirian, 1980. 122p.

(798)
Hagopian, John D. **Kiss Me, I'm Armenian**/by John Hagopian. Phoenix, AZ: Jurobian Press, 1982. 140p.

(799)
Hamalian, Leo. **Burn After Reading**/by Leo Hamalian. New York: Ararat Press, 1978. 178p.

(800)
Hintlian, Kevork. **History of the Armenians in the Holy Land**/by Kevork Hintlian. Jerusalem: St. James Press, 1976. 68p.

(801)
Housepian, Marjorie, 1923-   **The Smyrna Affair**/by Majorie Housepian. 1st edition. N.Y.: Harcourt Brace Jovanovich, 1971. xi, 269p.

(802)
Hovannisian, Richard G. **Armenia on the Road to Independence,
1918**/by Richard G. Hovannisian. Berkeley, CA: University of California Press, 1967. viii, 364p.

(803)
Hovannisian, Richard G. **The Republic of Armenia**/by Richard G. Hovannisian. Berkeley, CA: University of California Press, 1971. 547p.
vol. 1.

(804)
Hovannisian, Richard G. **The Republic of Armenia**/by Richard Hovannisian. Berkeley, CA: University of California Press, 1982. 600p. vol. 2.

(805)
Hovhannes V. Draskhanakertts'i. Catholicos of Armenia, d. 925. **History
of the Armenians**/by Hovhannes Draskhanakertts'i. A fascism.
Reproduction of the 1912 tiflis edition with an introduction by Krikor
Maksoudian. Delmar, N.Y.: Caravan Books, 1980. xxix, 427p.

(806)
Karagezian, Ruben A. **Soviet Armenia 50 Years**/by Ruben Karagezian.
Yerevan: Publishing House of the CC of CP of Armenia, 1970. 54p.

(807)
Kasparian, Hovhannes. **Anthology of Quotations on Armenians**/by
Hovhannes Kasparian. Evanston, Ill: Ouzounian House, 1967. 131p.

(808)
Kelekian, Susan. **Retracing the Footsteps of Our Forefathers**/by
Susan Kelekian. N.Y.: Armenian Apostolic Church of America, 1977.
159p.

(809)
Kurkjian, Vahan M. **A History of Armenia**/by Vahan Kurkjian. N.Y.:
A.G.B.U., 1964. 526p.

(810)
Lang, David Marshall, 1924-   **Armenia: Cradle of Civilization**/by
David Marshall Lang. 3rd edition. London: George Allen & Unwin,
1980. 320p. (First edition 1970, second edition 1978).

(811)
Lang, David Marshall, 1924-   **The Armenians**/by David Marshall
Lang and Christopher J. Walker. Rev. 1981 edition. London: Minor-
ity Rights Group, 1981. 24p.

(812)
Lang, David Marshall. **The Armenians: A People in Exile**/by David Marshall Lang. London; Boston: Allen & Unwin, 1981. xi, 203p.

(813)
Manandian, Hakob, 1873-1952. **The Trade and Cities of Armenia in Relation to Ancient World Trade**/by H. A. Manandian. Translated from the 2nd revised edition by Nina G. Garsoian. Lisbon: Armenian Library of the Galouste Gulbenkian, 1965. 248p.

(814)
Martyrdom and Rebirth, Fateful Events in the Recent History of the Armenian People/by Arshag Sarkisian and others. Preface by G. P. Gooch. Published on the occasion of the 50th anniversary of the massacres of 1915 by the Diocese of the Armenian Church of America, N.Y.: 1965. 105p.

(815)
Matossian, Mary Allerton Kilbourne. **The Impact of Soviet Policies in Armenia**/by Mary Matossian. Leiden, Netherlands: E. J. Brill, 1962. x, 239p. (Reprinted in 1981, Westpoint, CT. by Hyperian Press).

(816)
Megerditchian, Ervant, 1889-   **The Treasures of Vasbourgan**/by Ervant Megerditchian. Watertown, MA: 1966. 639p.

(817)
Minasian, Edward. **They Came From Ararat: The Exodus of the Armenian People to the United States**/by Edward Minasian. Berkeley, CA: 1961. viii, 287p.

(818)
Montgomary, John Warwick. **The Guest for Noah's Ark.** A Treasury of Documented Accounts From Ancient Times to the Present Day of Sightings of the Ark and Exploration of Mount Ararat, with a Narration of the Author's Successful Ascent to the Noah's Mountain. 2nd edition revised and expanded. Minneapolis: Dimension Books, 1974, 1972. 384p.

(819)
Mooradian, Karlen, 1935-   **Armenian Journalism: A History and Interpretation**/by Karlen Mooradian. Evanston, Ill: 1963. ix, 631p.

(820)
Morgan, Jacques Jean Marie de, 1857-1924. **The History of the Armenian People; From the Remotest Times to the Present Day**/by Jacques Morgan. Preface by Gustave Schlumberger. Illustrated with 296 maps, plans, and documentary sketches by the author. Translated by Ernest F. Barry. Boston: Hairenik Press, 1965. 430p.

(821)
Morgenthau, Henry, 1856-1946. **Ambassador Morgenthau's Story**/by Henry Morgenthau. Plandome, N.Y.: New Age Publishers, 1975. 408p.

(822)
Morgenthau, Henry, 1856-1946. **The Tragedy of Armenia**/by Henry Morgenthau. Plandome, N.Y.: New Age Publishers, 1975.

(823)
Moses of Khoren, 5th cent. **History of the Armenians**/by Moses Khorenats's; translation and commentary on the literary sources by Robert W. Thomson. Cambridge: Harvard University Press, 1978. viii, 408p.

(824)
Moses of Khoren, 5th cent. **Patmut'iwn Hayots' = History of the Armenians**/by Moses Khorenats'i. A facsim. Reproduction of the 1913 Tiflis edition with an introduction by Robert Thomson. Delmar, N.Y.: Caravan Books, 1981. xxi, 62, 396p.

(825)
Nalbandian, Louise. **The Armenian Revolutionary Movement; The Development of Armenian Political Parties Through the Nineteenth Century**/by Louise Nalbandian. Berkeley: University of California Press, 1963. ix, 247p.

(826)
Nansen, Fridtjof, 1861-1930. **Armenia and the Near East**/by Fridtjof Nanson. N.Y.: Da Capo Press, 1976. 324p. (Reprinted of 1928 Ed.)

(827)
National Association For Armenian Studies and Research. **Recent Studies in Modern Armenian History.** Cambridge, MA: Armenian Heritage Press, 1972.

(828)
Norehad, Bedros. **The Armenian General Benevolent Union**/by Bedros Norehad. N.Y.: A.G.B.U., 1966.

(829)
Papajian, Sarkis. **A Brief History of Armenia**/by Sarkis Papajian. Fresno, CA: Evangelical Union of North America, 1976,1974. viii, 134p.

(830)
Papazian, Kapriel Serope, 1887-   **Merchants From Ararat: A Brief Survey of Armenian Trade Through the Ages**/by K. S. Papazian. Edited and Rev. by P. M. Manuelian. N.Y.: Ararat Press, 1979. vii, 56p.

(831)
Petrosyan, Gavriil. **Armenia: Socialist Republics of Soviet Union**/by Gavriil Petrosyan. Moscow: Novosti Press Agency Pub. House, 1981. 62p.

(832)
Piotrovskii, Boris Borisovich, 1908-   **The Ancient Civilization of Urartu**/by Boris B. Piotrovsky. Translated from the Russian by James Hogarth. N.Y.: Cowles Book Co., 1969. 221p.

(833)
Piotrowski, Thaddeus M. **The Armenian Diaspora in Manchester, N.H.**/ by Thaddeus M. Piotrowski. Manchester, N.H.: Piotrowski, 1977. vi, 69p.

(834)
Poladian, Terenig, Vartabed, 1914-1963. **The Role of Armenia in History**/by Terenig Poladian. 3rd edition. Jerusalem: St. James Press, 1970. 34p.

(835)
Rhowben, 1882-1951. **Armenian Freedom Fighters: The Memoirs of Ruben Der Minasian.** Translated and edited by James G. Mandalian. Boston, MA: Hairenik Association, 1963. 244p.

(836)
Sanjian, Avedis Krikor, 1921-   **The Armenian Communities in Syria Under Ottoman Dominion**/by Avedis K. Sanjian. Cambridge, MA: Harvard University Press, 1965. xi, 390p.

(837)
Sanjian, Avedis Krikor, 1921-   **Colophons of Armenian Manuscripts, 1301-1480; A Source for Middle Eastern History**/ Selected, translated, and annotated by Avedis K. Sanjian. Cambridge, MA: Harvard University Press, 1969. xv, 459p.

(838)
Sarafian, Kevork Avedis, 1889-1975. **History of Education in Armenia**/ by Kevork A. Sarafian, with introductions by Lester B. Rogers and Rev. Bishop Kareki. Revised edition. La Verne, CA: La Verne College, 1978. 356p.

(839)
Sarkisian, Ervand Kazarovich. **Vital Issues in Modern Armenian History; A Documented Expose of Misrepresentation in Turkish Histography**/by E. K. Sarkisian and R. G. Sahakian. Translated and edited by Elisha Charkian. Watertown, Mass.: Armenian Studies, 1965. 82p.

(840)
Sarkisyanz, Emanuel. **A Modern History of Transcaucasian Armenia: Social, Cultural, and Political**/by Manuel Sarkisyanz. Leiden, Netherlands: Distributed by E. J. Brill, 1975. xvi, 413p.

(841)
Seltzer, Carl Coleman. **The Racial Characteristics of Syrians and Armenians.** Based upon data collected/by W. B. Cline, C. S. Coon, J. M. Andrews, and W. C. Dupertuis/by Carl C. Seltzer. Cambridge, MA: The Museum, 1936. N.Y.: Kraus, reprinted 1967. vi, 77p.

(842)
Sevougian, Novritza K. **At the Crossroads of Civilization**/by Novritza Sevougian. Beirut, Sevan Press, 1962. xi, 283p.

(843)
Shirvanzade, 1858-1935. **For the Sake of Honor = Badvi Hamar**/by Alexandre Shirvanzade; translated and with an introduction by Nishan Parlakian. Design and illustration by Paul Sagsoorian. N.Y.: St. Vartan Press, 1976. 117p.

(844)
Soviet Armenia/contributor, A. A. Aslanyan and others. Moscow: Progress Publishers, 1971. 255p.

(845)
Soviet Armenian. Soviet Life Magazine. Special issue. May 1983. No. 5 (320) N.W., Washington, D.C.

(846)
Stone, Frank A. **Armenian Studies for Secondary Students: A Curriculum Guide**/by Frank Stone. Storrs: University of Connecticut, 1974. 55p.

(847)
Suny, Ronald Grigor. **Armenia in the Twentieth Century**/by Ronald Suny. Chico, CA: Scholars Press, 1983. 87p.

(848)
Svajian, Stephen G., 1906-1977. **A Trip Through Historic Armenia**/by Stephen G. Svajian. N.Y.: Greenhill Pub., 1977. xx, 643p.

(849)
Tachat, 1888-   **The End of Davo the Traitor: An Episode of the Armenian Revolution**/by Dajad Terlemezian. Boston, MA: Hairenik Association, 1975. 52p.

(850)
Ter-Ghevondian, A. N. **The Arab Emirates in Bagratid Armenia**/by Aram Ter-Ghewondyan. Translated by Nina G. Garsoian. Lisbon: Calouste Gulbenkian Foundation: Distributors, Livraria Bertland, 1976. xi, 244p.

(851)
Terzian, Aram. **An Armenian Miscellany; Window on History**/by Aram Terzian. Paris: Librairie Oriental H. Samuelian, 1969. 231p.

(852)
Thomas, Don Michael. **Ararat**/by D. M. Thomas, N.Y.: Viking Press, 1983. 192p.

(853)
Totovents, Vahan, 1889-1937. **Scenes From an Armenian Childhood**/ by Vahan Totovents. Translated from the Armenian with a foreword by Mischa Kudian. London: Oxford University Press, 1962. 182p. (Reprinted in 1980 by Mashtots Press, London)

(854)
Tozer, Henry F. **Turkish Armenia & Eastern Asia Minor**/by Henry F. Tozer. AMS Press.

(855)
Toynbee, Arnold Joseph, 1889-1975. The Treatment of Armenians in the Ottoman Empire, 1915-16; documents presented to Viscount Grey of Fallon, Secretary of State. 2nd edition. Beirut, 1972. xlii, 684, 30p.

(856)
Trask, Roger R. **The United States Response to Turkish Nationalism and Reform, 1914-1939**/by Roger R. Trask. Minnesota: University of Minnesota Press, 1971.

(857)
Trumpener, Ulrich. Germany and the Ottoman Empire, 1914-1918/by Ulrich Trumpener. Princeton, New Jersey: Princeton University Press, 1968.

(858)
Varjabedian, Sisag H. **The Armenians; From Prehistoric Times to the Present: A Digest of their History, Religion, Language, Literature, Arts, and Culture in General**/by Sisag Hagop Varjabedian. 2nd edition. Chicago: Varjabedian, 1977. 194p.

(859)
Villa-Hoogasian, Susie. **Armenian Village Life Before 1914**/by Susie Villa Hoogasian and Mary Kilbourne Matossian. Detroit: Wayne State University Press, 1982. 197p.

(860)
Villa-Hoogasian, Susie. **100 Armenian Tales and Their Folkloristic Relevance.** Collected and edited by Susie Hoogasian-Villa. Detroit: Wayne State University Press, 1966. 602p. (Reprinted 1982)

(861)
Walker, Christopher, 1942-   **Armenia, The Survival of a Nation**/by Christopher J. Walker. London: Croom Helm, 1980. 446p.

(862)
Zarian, Gostan, 1885-1969. **Bancoop & the Bones of the Mammoth**/by Gostan Zarian. Selected & translated by Ara Baliozian. N.Y.: Ashod Press, 1982. xxii, 115p.

Language

(863)
Afarian, Krikor. **I Am Learning Armenian**/by Krikor Afarian. Beirut: Shirak Press, 1971. 111p.

(864)
Andonian, Hagop. **Modern Armenian**/by Hagop Andonian. N.Y.: A.G.B.U. 1966. 212p.

(865)
Arakelian, Luke. **ABC of Armenian, A Prep Book, Conversation, Reading, Grammar**/by Luke Arakelian. 9th ed. Vienna: Mekhitarist Press; Cambridge, MA: St. Gregory Mekhitarist Armenian Language School. 1971. 151p.

(866)
Arakelian, Luke. **Armenian Language For Daily Use, Reading and Conversation.** Cambridge, Mass: St. Gregory Mekhitarist Armenian Language School, 1967.

(867)
Avakian, Arra S. **Armenian Book of Chuckles: ABC**/by Arra Avakian. Fresno, CA: Avakian, 1979. 88p.

(868)
Bardakjian, Kevork B. **A Textbook of Modern Western Armenian**/by Kevork B. Bardakjian, and Robert W. Thomson. 1st edition. Delmar, N.Y.: Caravan Books, 1977. viii, 319p.

(869)
Baylerian, George D. **A Practical Armenian and English Book: Learn Armenian in Your Home**/edited, illustrated by George D. Baylerian. Birmingham, Michigan: Baylerian, 1971. 176p.

(870)
Bedrossian, Matthias. **New Dictionary: Armenian-English**/by Matthias Bedrossian. Venice: St. Lazarus Armenian Academy, 1875-79; (reprinted, Beirut: Librairie du Liban) distributed, Troy, MI: International Book Center, 1974. xxx, 786p.

(871)

Boy, Stella Malkasian. **Functional Armenian: Level One**/by Stella Malkasian Boy & Hagop Atamian. N.Y.: A.G.B.U., 1977. xx, 212p. (text in English & Armenian)

(872)

Damme, Dirk Van. **A Short Classical Armenian Grammar**/by Dirk Van Damme. 2nd edition. Fribourge: University Press; Gottingen: Vendenhoeck & Ruprecht, 1978. 60p.

(873)

Etmekjian, James. **A Graded West Armenian Reader; Selections From Armenian Literature**/adopted and edited by James Etmekjian. N.Y.: American Council of Learned Societies & National Association for Armenian Studies and Research, 1963. xv, 187p.

(874)

Fairbanks, Gordon H. **Spoken Eastern Armenian**/by Gordon H. Fairbanks and Earl W. Stevik. Ithaca, N.Y.: Spoken Language Services, 1975. 403p.

(875)

Godel, Robert. **An Introduction to the Study of Classical Armenian**/by Robert Godel. Wiesbaden: Reichert Verlag, 1975. x, 139p.

(876)

Greppin, John A. **Classical and Middle Armenian Bird Names: A Linguistic, Taxonomic, and Mythological Study**/by John A. C. Greppin. Delmar, N.Y.: Caravan Books, 1978. xxi, 290p.

(877)

Greppin, John A. **Classical Armenian Nominal Suffixes: A Historical Study**/by John A. C. Greppin. Wien: Mechitharisten-Buchdruckerei, 1975. 158p.

(878)

Greppin, John A. **Initial Vowel and Aspiration in Classical Armenian**/by John A. C. Greppin. Wien: Mechitharisten-Buchdr., 1973. 70p.

(879)

Gulian, Kevork H. **Elementary Modern Armenian Grammer**/by Kevork H. Gulian. N.Y.: F. Ungor, 1965. vi, 196p.

(880)

International Conference on Armenian Linguistics (1st: 1979: University of Pennsylvania) **First International Conference On Armenian Linguistics: Proceedings, the University of Pennsylvania, Philadelphia, 11-14 July 1979.** Sponsored by the Society for Armenian Studies; edited by John A.C. Greppin. N.Y.: Caravan Books, 1980. 246p.

(881)
Khantrouni, Dicran. **Armenian-English Modern Dictionary**/by Dicran Khantrouni and Madiros Koushakdjian. Koniguian & Sons Pub., 1970. 15, 416p.

(882)
Khoushakdjian, Mardiros. **English-Armenian, Armenian-English Modern Dictionary**/by M. Khoushakdjian and D. Khantrouni. Beirut: G. Doniguian & Sons Pub. House; New York: Distributed by W. S. Heinman, 1976-1978. 949, 416p.

(883)
Khoushakdjian, Mardiros. **English-Armenian Modern Dictionary**/by Mardiros Khoushakdjian and Dicran Khantrouni. Doniguian & Sons Pub., 1970. 16,949p.

(884)
Koudoulian, Kourken. **Armenian Names and Their Meanings**/by Kourken Koudoulian. Los Angeles. 1977. 157p. (text in Armenian & English)

(885)
Kouyoumdjian, Mesrob G., 1897-1983. **A Comprehensive Dictionary, Armenian-English**/by Mesrob G. Kouyoumdjian. Watertown, Mass.: 1970. 1150p.

(886)
Kouyoumdjian, Mesrob G., 1897-1983. **A Comprehensive Dictionary of Idioms, English-Armenian**/by Mesrob Kouyoumdjian. Cairo: Vosguedar Press, 1969. 668p.

(887)
Kouyoumdjian, Mesrob G., 1897-1983. **A Comprehensive Dictionary, English-Armenian**/by Mesrob G. Kouyoumdjian. Le Caire, Journal Arev, 1961. 114p.

(888)
Kouyoumdjian, Mesrob G., 1897-1983. **A Dictionary of Proverbs & Quotations, Armenian-English, English-Armenian**/by Mesrob Kouyoumdjian, 1967. 46,471p.

(889)
Kouyoumdjian, Mesrob G., 1897-1983. **A Practical Dictionary For Adults: Armenian-English, English-Armenian**/by Mesrob Kouyoumdjian. Le Caire: Fonds National Armenien, 1973. 544, 10, 747p.

(890)
Kouyoumdjian, Mesrob G., 1897-1983. **A New Pocket Dictionary, English Armenian, Armenian-English**/by Mesrob Kouyoumdjian. 1970. 352, 318p.

(891)
Krmoyan, Sona Mkrtch. **English-Armenian Dictionary, For Secondary Schools**/by Sona Mkrtch Krmoyan. 1968. 204p.

(892)
Kurkjian, Haroutiun. **Practical Textbook of Western Armenian**/by Haroutiun Kurkjian. Beirut: Armenian Diaspora Series, no. 3., 1980.

(893)
Mann, Stuart Edward, 1905-   **Armenian and Indo-European; Historical Phonology**/by Stuart E. Mann. London: Luzac, 1963. xxxvi, 203p.

(894)
Mann, Stuart Edward, 1905-   **An Armenian Historical Grammar in Latin Characters: Morphology, Etymology, Old Texts**/by Stuart Edward Mann. London: Luzac, 1968. 1,174p.

(895)
Melkonian, Zareh. **Armenian Made Easy**/by Zareh Melkonian. New York: A.G.B.U., 1972. 3 vol.

(896)
Melkonian, Zareh. **Im Girks (My Book)**/by Zareh Melkonian. Detroit, 1979.

(897)
Roszko, Casimir F. **A Classical Armenian Grammar (Morphology, Syntax, Texts, Vocabulary)**/by F. Casimir Roszko. Indianapolis: Catholic Seminary Foundation of Indianapolis, 1970. 146p.

(898)
Thomson, Robert W. 1934-   **An Introduction to Classical Armenian**/by Robert W. Thomson. 1st edition. Delmar, N.Y.: Caravan Books, 1975. iii,253p.

Literature

(899)
Akillian, Michael. **The Eating of Names**/by Michael Akillian. N.Y.: Ashod Press, 1983.

(900)
Ananikian, Mardiros Harootioon, 1875-1934. **Armenian (Mythology)** by Mardiros Ananikian. **African (Mythology)** by Alice Werner. N.Y.: Cooper Square Pub., 1964. viii, 448p.

(901)
Anthology of Armenian Poetry/translated and edited by Diana Der Hovanessian and Marzbed Margossian. N.Y.: Columbia University Press, 1978. xxii, 357p.

(902)
An Anthology of Western Armenian Literature/edited by James Etmekjian. Delmar, N.Y.: Caravan Books, 1980. xx, 477p.

(903)
Antreassian, Andranik. **The Cup of Bitterness, and Other Stories**/by
Antranig Antreasian. Translated from the Armenian by Jack Antrea-
ssian. Illustration by Adrina Zanazanian. 1st edition. N.Y.: Ashod
Press, 1979. 134p.

(904)
Antreassian, Jack Arthur, 1920-   **The Confessions of Kitchoonie**/
by Jack Antreassian. 1st edition. N.Y.: Ashod Press, 1979. 95p.

(905)
Antreassian, Jack Arthur, 1920-   **Unworthy Offspring & Other
Writings**/by Jack Antreassian. N.Y.: St. Vartan Press, Diocese of
the Armenian Church, 1975.

(906)
Armenia: Annual Volume Review of National Literature/edited by
Vahe Oshagan. Griffon House, 1982. 280p.

(907)
Armenian-American Poets: A Bilingual Anthology/compiled and
translated by Garig Basmadjian. Detroit: Alex Manoogian Cultural
Fund of the Armenian General Benevolent Union, 1976. xvii, 141p.

(908)
Armenian Folk-tales and Fables/translated by Charles Downings, illustrated by William Papas. London: Oxford University Press, 1972. xiii,
217p.

(909)
The Armenian Image in History and Literature/edited by Richard
Hovannisian. Malibu, CA: Undena Publications, 1981. vi, 269p.

(910)
Armenian North American Poets: An Anthology/edited by Lorne
Shirinian. St. Jean, Que.: Manna, 1974. iv, 104p.

(911)
Armenian Poetry, Old and New: A Bilingual Anthology/compiled and
translated with an introduction by Aram Tolegian. Detroit: Wayne
State University Press, 1979. 379p.

(912)
Avakian, Sohie. **Armenian Short Stories**/by Sohie Avakian. New Delhi:
NBT, 1981.

(913)
Balakian, Peter, 1951-   **Sad Days of Light: Poems**/by Peter Balakian. New York: Sheep Meadow Press, 1983. 79p.

(914)
Baliozian, Ara. **The Horrible Silence: An Auto-biographical Novel**/by
Ara Baliozian. Pasadena, CA: Maral Quality Printers, 1982. 72p.

(915)
Bedikian, A. **The Golden Age in the Fifth Century, An Introduction to Armenian Literature in Perspective.** N.Y.: Armenian Missionary Association, 1963. 128p.

(916)
Bedrossyan, Mark D. **The First Genocide of the 20th Century**/by Mark Bedrossyan. Manasquan Park, N.J.: Cilicia Foundation, 1983.

(917)
Baronian, Hagop, 1843-1891. **Honourable Baggars: A Satire**/by Hagop Baronian. Translated from the Armenian and edited by Mischa Kudian. London: BMC Mashtots Press, 1978. 95p.

(918)
Baronian, Hagop, 1843-1891. **The Perils of Politeness**/by Hagop Baronian. Translated by Jack Antreassian. N.Y.: Ashod Press, 1983.

(919)
Blackwell, Alice Stone, 1857-1950. **Armenian Poems, Rendered into English Verse**/by Alice Stone Blackwell. Delmar, N.Y.: Caravan Books, 1978. 295p. (Reprint of 1917 edition)

(920)
Carswell, John, 1931-   **Kutahya Tiles and Pottery From the Armenian Cathedral of St. James, Jerusalem**/by John Carswell. C.J.F. Dowsett: Oxford Claremdom Press, 1972. 2 vol.

(921)
Cox, Claude E. **The Armenian Translation of Deuteronomy**/by Claude Cox. Edited by Michael Stone. Chico, CA: Scholars Press, 1981.

(922)
Cretan, Gladys Yessayan. **A Gift From the Bride**/by Gladys Cretan Yessayan. Boston, MA: Little, 1964.

(923)
Cretan, Gladys Yessayan. **Sunday for Sona**/Illustrated by Barbara Flynn. N.Y.: Lothrop, Lee & Shepard, 1973. 32p.

(924)
Daredevils of Sassoun: **The Armenian National Epic**/translated by Leon Surmelian. Denver: Alan Swallow, 1964. 280p.

(925)
David of Sassoun: **The Armenian Folk Epic in Four Cycles**/translated and with an introduction and notes by Artin K. Shalian. Athens, OH: Ohio University Press, 1964. 377p.

(926)
Der Hovanessian, Diana. **How to Choose Your Past**/by Diana Der Hovanessian. A.G.B.U., Ararat Press. 107p.

(928)
Emin, Gevorg, 1918-　　**Seven Songs of Armenia**/by Gevorg Emin. Translated by Isabel Chookaszian. Yerevan: Armenian Society for Friendship and Cultural Relations with Foreign Countries, 1970. 79p.

(929)
Emin, Gevorg, 1918-　　**Seven Songs of Armenia**/by Gevorg Emin. Translated from Armenian by Mkrtich Soghikian. Moscow: Progress Publishers, 1981. 231p.

(930)
Emin, Gevorg, 1918-　　**Songs of Armenia: Selected Poems**/by Gevorg Emin. Translated by Dorian Rottenberg. Moscow: Progress Publishers, 1979. 203p.

(931)
Ephraem Syrus, Saint. **An Exposition of the Gospel**/by Saint Ephraem Syrus, edited by George A. Egan. Louvain, Secretariat du Corpus SCO, 1968. 2 vol.

(932)
Etmekjian, James. **The French Influence on the Western Armenian Renaissance, 1843-1915**/by James Etmekjian. N.Y.: Twayne, 1964. 292p.

(934)
A Graded West Armenian Reader; Selections From Armenian Literature/edited by James Etmekjian. N.Y.: American Council of Learned Societies, National Association of Armenian Studies and Research, 1963. 187p.

(935)
Granian, Puzant. **Selected Poems 1936-1982**/by Puzant Granian. Translated by Ara Baliozian. Flushing, N.Y.: Voskedar Corp. 1983.

(936)
Hacikyan, Agop Jack, 1931-　　**The Battle of the Prophets**/by A. J. Hacikyan. Montreal; New York: Abaka, 1981.

(937)
Haig, H. H. **The First Genocide; A Play in Four Acts.** N.Y.: Vintage Press, 1967. 77p.

(938)
Hamalian, Leo. **As Others See Us: The Armenian Image in Literature**/by Leo Hamalian. 1st edition. New York: Ararat Press, 1980. 146p.

(940)
Hamalian, Leo. **Burn After Reading**/by Leo Hamalian. N.Y.: Ararat Press, 1978. 178p.

(941)

Hamalian, Leo. **The View From Ararat: Another Decade of Armenian American Writing**/by Leo Hamalian. Saddle Brook, N.Y.: Ararat Press, 1983.

(942)

Hashian, Jack. **Mamigon (A Novel)** by Jack Hashian. N.Y.: McCann & Geoghegan, 1982. 318p.

(943)

Hogrogian, Nonny. **The Contest: An Armenian Folktale**/by Nonny Hogrogian. N.Y.: Macmillan, 1976.

(944)

Hogrogian, Nonny. **One Fine Day**/by Nonny Hogrogian. N.Y.: Macmillan, 1971.

(945)

Hogrogian, Nonny. **Pigs Never See the Stars, Proverbs From the Armenian**/by Nonny Hogrogian. Aurora, Oregon: Two Rivers Press, 1982.

(946)

Hogrogian, Nonny. **Rooster Brother**/by Nonny Hogrogian. N.Y.: Macmillan, 1974.

(947)

Isahakian, Avetik, 1875-1957. **Scent, Smile, and Sorrow: Selected Verse (1891-1957) and Jottings from Notebooks**/by Avedick Isahakian. Edited and translated from the Armenian with an introduction, notes, and illustration by E.B. Charakian. Watertown, MA: Library of Armenian Studies, 1975. 80p.

(948)

Isahakian, Avetik, 1875-1957. **Selected Works: Poetry and Prose**/by Avetik Isahakian. Translated from the Armenian by Mischa Kudian. Designed by Georgi Klodt. Moscow: Progress Publishers, 1976. 132p.

(949)

Isahakian, Avetik, 1875-1957. **The Muse of Sheerak: Selected Works of Avetik Isahakian**/compiled and translated from the Armenian by Mischa Kudian. London: Mashtots Press, 1975.

(950)

Khatchadourian, Haig. **Shadows of Time**/by Haig Khatchadourian. N.Y.: Ashod Press, 1983.

(951)

Kherdian, David. **Country Cat, City Cat**/by David Kherdian. N.J.: Four Winds, 1979.

(952)
Kherdian, David. **Finding Home**/by David Kherdian. N.Y.: Greenwillow, 1981. x, 242p.

(953)
Kherdian, David. **Homage to Adana**/by David Kherdian. Fresno: Giligia Press, 1971.

(954)
Kherdian, David. **On the Death of My Father and Other Poems**/by David Kherdian. Fresno, CA: Giligia Press, 1970.

(955)
Kherdian, David. **Place of Birth**/by David Kherdian. Portland, Oregon: Breitexbush Books, 1983p.

(956)
Kherdian, David. **The Road From Home: The Story of An Armenian Girl**/by David Kherdian. 1st edition. N.Y.: Greenwillow Books, 1979. xi, 238p. (Juvenile literature)

(957)
Kudian, Mischa. **The Bard of Loree. The Great Armenian Writers' Selected Works**/compiled and translated by Mischa Kudian. London: Mashtots Press, 1970. 120p.

(958)
Kudian, Mischa. **More Apples Fell From Heaven**/by Mischa Kudian. London: Mashtots Press, 1983.

(959)
Kudian, Mischa. **Tell Me, Bella: A Selection of Stories**/compiled and translated from the Armenian by Mischa Kudian. London: Mashtots Press, 1972. 127p.

(960)
Kudian, Mischa. **The Saga of Sassoun: The Armenian Folk Epic**/retold by Micha Kudian; illustrated by Victor Amhurs. London: Kaye & Ward, 1970. 175p.

(961)
Kudian, Mischa. **Soviet Armenian Poetry**/compiled and translated from the Armenian by Mischa Kudian. London: Mashtots Press, 1974. viii, 88p.

(962)
Manoukian, Mourad. **101 Rubaiyat: In Armenian and English**/by Mourad Manoukian. Jerusalem: St. James Press, 1973. 109p.

(963)
Manuelian, P.M. **Proverbs From the Armenian**/by P.M. Manuelian. Translated by David Kherdian. Aurora, Oregon: Two Rivers Press, 1982.

(964)
Melikian, Lucik. **Forbidden Days of Ramazan**/by Lucik Melikian. Saddle
Brook, N.J.: Ararat Press, 1980. 318p.

(965)
Najarian, Peter. **Voyages**/by Peter Najarian. N.Y.: Ararat Press, 1979.
150p

(966)
Pilibosian, Helene. **Carvings From an Heirloom, Oral History Poems**/
by Helene Pilibosian. Watertown, MA: Ohan Press, 1983. 73p.

(967)
Pilikian, Hovhannes, I. 1915-   **An Armenian Symphony and Other
Poems**/by Hovhanness Pilikians. London: Counter-Point Publica-
tions, 1980.

(968)
Saroyan, William, 1908-1981. **Births**/by William Saroyan. Introduction by
David Kheridian. Berkeley, CA: Creative Arts Book Co., 1983.

(969)
Saroyan, William, 1908-1981. **Hairenik, 1934-39.** An anthology of short
stories and poems by young Armenian writers in the United States,
and translations of selected short stories from the original Armenian,
collected from issues of the Hairenik Weekly. 1934-39 inclusive, with
an introduction by William Saroyan. Freeport, N.Y.: Books for Libraries Press, 1971. xvii, 305p.

(970)
Saroyan, William, 1908-1981. **My Name is Saroyan**/by James H. Tashjian. N.Y.: Coward McCann, 1983. 391p.

(971)
Saryan, Sarkis. **Language Connections: Kinship of Armenian with
Sister Indo-European Languages**/by Sarkis Saryan. Cape Cod,
MA: Sarmen Book Co., 1983.

(972)
Sasowntsi Davit. **Daredevils of Sassoun: The Armenian National Epic**/
translated by Leon Surmelian. Illustrated by Paul Sagsoorian. London: Allen & Unwin, 1966. 251p.

(973)
Sasowntsi Davit. **Daredevils of Sassoun: The Armenian National Epic**/
translated by Leon Surmelian. Illustrated by Paul Sagsoorian. Denver: A. Swallow, 1964. 279p.

(974)
Sasowntsi Davit. **David of Sassoun, Armenian Folk Epic**/translation
with introduction and notes by Aram Tolegian. N.Y.: Bookman Associates, 1961. 140p.

(975)
Sasowntsi Davit. **David of Sassoun: The Armenian Folk Epic in Four Cycles.** The original text translated with an introduction and notes by Artin K. Shalian. Athens, Ohio: Ohio University Press, 1964. 377p.

(976)
Sewak, Parowyr, 1924-1971. **Selected Poems**/by Paruir Sevak, translated with an introduction by Garig Basmadjian. Jerusalem: Saint James Press, 1973. 71p.

(977)
Shahnour, Shahan. **Retreat Without Songs**/by Shahan Shahnour. London: Mashtots Press, 1982.

(979)
Sheohmelian, Ohannes, 1909-   **Three Apples From Heaven: Armenian Folktales**/by Ohannes Sheohmelian. Illustrated by Adrina Zanazanian. Saddle Brook, N.J.: Ararat Press, 1983.

(980)
Shipley, Alice M. **We Walked, Then Ran**/by Alice Shipley. Edited by Mary Hawkins. A.M. Shipley, 1983. 300p.

(981)
Shirvanzade, 1858-1935. **For the Sake of Honor = Badvi Hamar**/by Alexandre Shirvanzade; translated and with an introduction by Nishan Parlakian. Design and illustration by Paul Sagsoorian. N.Y.: St. Vartan Press, 1976. 117p.

(983)
Stephen Calonne, David. **William Saroyan: My Real Work is Being**/by David Stephen Calonne. Chapel Hill, N. Carolina: University of N.C. Press, 1983.

(984)
Surmelian, Leon Z., 1905-   **Apples of Immortality: Folktales of Armenia**/by Leon Surmelian. UNESCO collection of representative works. Series of translations from the literatures of the USSR. London: George Allen & Unwin; Berkeley, CA: University of California Press, 1968. 319p. (Reprinted by Greenwood Press, 1983)

(985)
Tashjian, Virginia A. **Once There Was and Was Not**/by Virginia Tashjian. Boston, MA: Little Brown, 1966. 83p.

(986)
Tashjian, Virginia A. **Three Apples Fell From Heaven**/by Virginia Tashjian. Boston, MA: Little Brown, 1964.

(987)
Tcholakian, Arthur, 1928-   **The Walking Tree**/by Arthur Tcholakian Flushing, N.Y.: Paradon Publisher, 1975. 63p.

(988)
Tekeyan, Vahan. **Sacred Wrath: The Selected Poems of Vahan Tekeyan**/translated by Diana Der Hovanessian & Marzbed Margossian. Flushing, N.Y.: Ashod Press, 1983.

(989)
Towmanian, Hovhannes, 1869-1923. **Hovannes Toumanian Selected Works**/by Hovhannes Towmanian. Poetry edited by Dorian Rottenberg. Prose works edited by Brian Bean, designed by V. Dober. Moscow: Progress Publishers, 1969. 180p.

(990)
Towmanian, Hovhannes, 1869-1923. **Hovhannes Toumanian; a Selection of Stories, Lyrics, and Epic Poems**/translated by Dorian Rottenberg and Brian Bean. Edited by Arra M. Garab. N.Y.: T & T Pub., 1971.

(991)
We of the Mountains; Armenian Short Stories/translated from Russian by Fainna Glogoeva. Moscow: Progress Publishers, 1972. 245p.

(992)
Yessayan, Zabel. **The Gardens of Silihdar and Other Writings**/by Zabel Yessayan. Translated by Ara Baliozian. N.Y.: Ashod Press, 1982. 104p.

(993)
Zahrat, 1924-   **Selected Poems**/by Zahrat. Translated from the Armenian by Ralph Setian-Huall. Canada: Manna Publishing, 1974.

(994)
Zarian, Gostan, 1885-1960. **Bancoop and the Bones of the Mammoth**/by Gostan Zarian. Selected and translated by Ara Baliozian. N.Y.: Ashod Press, 1982. xxii, 115p.

Arts and Related Works

(995)
Aprahamian, Valentina. **Jewelry Art of Armenia**/by Valentina Aprahamian. Yerevan: Central Pub. House, 1983.

(996)
Armenian Art Treasures of Jerusalem/edited by Bezalel Narkiss, in collaboration with Michael E. Stone; historical survey by Avedis Sanjian; managing editor, Alexander Peli; photography by David Harris. Jerusalem: Massada Press, 1979. 174p.

(997)
Armenian Cienema: A Source Book/by Pilikian. London: Counter Point
   Publications. 100p.

(998)
Armenian Folk Festival at the New York World's Fair, 1964-1965.
   N.Y.: Armenian Folk Festival Committee, 1964.

(999)
Arutiunian, V. **The Art of Soviet Armenia**/by V. Arutiunian. Leningrad:
   Aurora Art Publishers, 1972.

(1000)
Azanvour, Charles. **Yesterday When I Was Young**/by Charles Azna-
   vour. W.H. Allen, 1979.

(1001)
Bedoukian, Paul Z. **Coinage of the Artaxiads of Armenia**/by Paul Z.
   Bedoukian. London: Royal Numismatic Society, 1978. x, 81p.

(1002)
Bedoukian, Paul Z. **Coinage of Cilician Armenia**/by Paul Bedoukian.
   N.Y.: American Numismatic Society, 1962. xxxi, 494p.

(1003)
Bedoukian, Paul Z. **Coinage of Cilician Armenia**/by Paul Z. Bedoukian.
   Rev. edition. Danbury, Conn.: Bedoukian, 1979. xxxi, 494p.

(1004)
Bedoukian, Paul Z. **Selected Numismatic Studies of Paul Z.
   Bedoukian.** Los Angeles: Armenian Numismatic Society, 1981.
   xxxvi, 570p.

(1005)
Chanashian, Mesrop. **Armenian Miniature Paintings of the Monastic
   Library at San Lazaro**/by Mesrop Jahashian. English version of the
   text by Bernard Grebanier. Venice, Casa Edibrice Armena, 1966.

(1006)
Carswell, John, 1931-   **New Julfa, The Armenian Churches and
   Other Buildings**/by John Carswell. Oxford, Clarendon Press, 1968.
   xv, 103p.

(1007)
Cone, Lawrence. **Armenian Church Architecture**/by Lawrence K.
   Cone. New York: Heath Cote Pub. Co., 1974. 159p.

(1008)
Contributions to the Archaeology of Armenia/by V. P. Alekseev and
   others. Translated by Arlene Krimgold. Edited by Henry Field. Cambridge, Mass: Peabody Museum, 1968. xi, 232p.

(1009)
Der Nersessian, Sirarpie, 1896-   **Aghtamar, Church of the Holy Cross**/by Sirarpie Der Nersessian. Cambridge, Mass: Harvard University, 1965. 60p.

(1010)
Der Nersessian, Sirarpie, 1896-   **Armenian Art**/by Sirarpie Der Nersessian. Translated by Shelia Bourne and Angela O'Shea. London: Thames & Hudson; distributer, New York: Norton, 1978. 270p.

(1011)
Der Nersessian, Sirarpie, 1896-   **Armenian Manuscripts in the Walters Art Gallery**/by Sirarpie Der Nersessian. Baltimore, Maryland: The Trustees, 1973. x, 111, 243p.

(1012)
Documents of Armenian Architecture Series, An exhaustive Collection of photos and essays in English, Armenian and Italian. Milan: University and Architecture of the Academy of Science of Armenia. 1974-

(1013)
Dournovo, Lydia A. **Armenian Miniatures**/by Lydia Dournovo. Preface by Sirarpie Der Nersessian. Text translated from French by Irene J. Underwood. New York: H. N. Abrams, 1961. 181p.

(1014)
Essays on Armenian Music/edited by Vrej Nersessian. London: Published by Kahn & Averill for the Institute of Armenian Music, 1978. 222p. (text in English, French, and German)

(1015)
Etmekjian, James. **The French Influence of the Western Armenian Renaissance, 1843-1915**/by James Etmekjian. N.Y.: Twayne Publisher, 1964. 292p.

(1016)
Gink, Karoly. **Armenia: Landscape and Architecture**/photos by Karloy Gink; text by Karoly Gombos; translated by Rudolph Fischer. N.Y.: Corvina Press, 1974. 63p.

(1017)
Goekjian, Valeria. **The Christian Literature and Fine Arts of the Armenians**/by Valeria Goekjian. N.Y.: Diocese of the Armenian Church, 1973.

(1018)
Hye Guin, The Costumes of Armenian Women. Tehran: Armenian Society, 1976.

(1019)
Kasparian, Alice Odian. **Armenian Needlelace and Embroidery**/by Alice Odian Kasparian. Virginia, EPM Publications of McLean, 1983. 128p.

(1020)
Keusseyan, Krikor. **Carzou: Painter of a Magic World**/by Krikor Keusseyan. Translated by Ara Kalaykjian. Southfield, MI: A.G.B.U., Alex Manoogian Cultural Foundation, 1982. 200, 70p.

(1021)
Khatchatrian, A. **Monuments of Armenian Architecture With Analytical Essay on Armenian Architecture**/by A. Khatchatrian. Beirut: Hamazkain, 1973.

(1022)
MacDonald, William. **Early Christian and Byzantine Architecture**/by William MacDonald, George Braziller, 1965.

(1023)
Mandakounian, Armen. **World's Favorite Classics & Armenian Piano Studies**/arranged, compiled & edited by Armen Mandakounian. Hollywood, CA: Armen Mandakounian, 1982. 95p.

(1024)
Mazmanian, Nazel M. **The Art Gallery of Armenia (Yerevan)**/edited by H. Igitian, 1975. 179p.

(1025)
Monuments of Armenian Architecture/by Garo Kourken Kassabian. English texts by Antoine Kehyaian. Beirut: Hamazkain, 1972. xiv, 78p.

(1026)
Piotrovski, Boris. **Urartu: The Kingdom of Van and Its Art**/by Boris Piotrovski. N.Y.: Frederick A. Praeger, 1967.

(1027)
Raphaelian, Harry M. **Rugs of Armenia; Their History and Art**/by Harry Raphaelian with introduction by Felix Marti-Ibanez. New Rochelle, N.Y.: An A-atol Silvas Pub., 1960. 87p.

(1028)
Rosenberg, Harold. **Arshile Gorky: The Man, The Time, The Idea**/by Harold Rosenberg. N.Y.: Horizon, 1962.

(1029)
Samsonian, Simon. **Simon Samsonian: His World Through Paintings**/edited by M. Haigents. 112p. (text in English, Armenian, French and Russian).

(1030)
Sanjian, Avedis Krikor, 1921-   **Colophons of Armenian Manuscripts, 1301-1480; A Source For Middle Eastern History**/selected, translated and annotated by Avedis K. Sanjian. Cambridge, MA: Harvard University Press, 1969. xv, 459p.

(1031)
Sarian, John M. **Record Guide, Armenian Musicians and Composers/** by John Sarian. N.Y.: Ararat Press, 1979. 56p.

(1032)
Seven Bites From a Raisin, Proverbs From the Armenian/selected and translated by P. M. Manuelian, illustrated by Suzanne Anoushian Froundjian. Saddle Brook, MI: A.G.B.U., Ararat Press. 110p.

(1033)
Utudjian, Edouard. **Armenian Architecture, 4th to 17th Century/** translated by Geoffery Capner. Paris: Editions Albert Morance, 1968. 181p. (text in English and Armenian)

Religion

(1034)
Armenia: An Abridged Historic Outline of Its Church and People. N.Y.: Diocese of the Armenian Church of America, 1964. 64p.

(1035)
Armenian and Biblical Studies/edited by Michael E. Stone. Jerusalem: St. James Press, 1976. 300p.

(1036)
Armenian Church. Liturgy and Ritual. Pataragamatoyts. English & Armenian. Selections, **Divine Liturgy of The Armenian Church.** 2nd edition. N.Y.: Armenian Church Diocese, 1971. xii, 82, 131p.

(1037)
Armenian Church of America. Liturgy and Ritual. **The Blessing of Marriage According to the Canon of the Armenian Church**/music by Wardan Sarxian; translation by Archbishop Tiran. Philadelphia: Torkom Manoogian, 1960. 4, 63p.

(1038)
Armenian Church of America. Liturgy and Ritual. **The Book of Hours; or the Order of Common Prayers of the Armenian Apostolic Orthodox Church.** Matins, prime, vespers and occasional offices. Evanston, Ill.: 1964. 104, xxivp.

(1039)
Armenian Church of America. **The Consecration of a Cathedral**/editor and designer, Walter Kaprielian. N.Y.: Diocese of the Armenian Church of America, 1969. 76, 28p.

(1040)
Arzoumanian, Zaven. **The Origins of the Armenian Christianity; Armenians in America**/by Zaven Arzoumanian. Wynnewood, PA: St. Sahag and St. Mesrob Armenian Church, 1978. 39p.

(1041)
Ashjian, Arten. **Mesrob Mashdots, The Great Vartabed**/by Arten Ashjian. N.Y.: Armenian Church Youth Organization, 1962.

(1042)
Athanasius, Saint. **The Armenian Version of the Letters of Athanasiusto Bishop Seropian Concerning the Holy Spirit**/by George A. Egan. Salt Lake City: University of Utah Press, 1968. xvii, 214p.

(1043)
Bedikian, A. **The Golden Age in the Fifth Century, An Introduction to Armenian Literature in Perspective.** N.Y.: Armenian Missionary Association, 1963. 128p.

(1044)
Chakmakjian, Hagop A. **Armenian Christology and Evangelization of Islam, A Survey of the Relevance of the Christology of the Armenian Apostolic Church to Armenian Relations With Its Muslem Environment**/by Hagop A. Chakmakjian. Leiden, E. J. Brill, 1965. xiii, 146p.

(1045)
Chopourian, Giragos H. **Our Armenian Christian Heritage; A Course For the Junior High Age**/by Giragos Chopourian. 2nd edition. Armenian Evangelical Union of America, 1974. 122, T1-T15p.

(1046)
Chopourian, Giragos H. **The Armenian Evangelical Reformation: Causes and Effects**/by Giragos H. Chopourian. N.Y.: Armenian Missionary Association of America, 1972. xvi, 170p.

(1047)
Der Nersessian, Sirarpie. **Aghtámar. Church of the Holy Cross**/by Sirarpie Der Nersessian. Cambridge: University of Harvard, 1965.

(1048)
Dowling, Theodore Edward, 1837-1921. **The Armenian Church**/by Theodore Edward Dowling, with an introduction by the Lord Bishop of Salisbury. N.Y.: AMS Press, 1970. 160p. (reprint of the 1910 edition)

(1049)
East of Byzantium: Syria and Armenia in Formative Period/by Nina G. Garsoian, Thomas F. Mathews, Robert Thomson editors. Washington, D.C., Dumbarton Oaks: Center For Byzantine Studies, Trustees for Harvard University, 1982. xii, 222p.

(1050)
Fortescue, Edward Francis Knottesford. **The Armenian Church, Founded by St. Gregory the Illuminator; Liturgy, Doctrine and Ceremonies of This Ancient National Church**/by E.F.K. Fortescue, with an appendix by S. C. Malan. AMS Press. 1970. 336p.

(1051)
Frivold, Leif. **The Incarnation; A Study of the Doctrine of the Incarnation in the Armenian Church in the 5th & 6th Centuries According to the Book of Letters**/by Frivold. Oslo: Universitets Forlaget; N.Y.: Distributed by Columbia University Press, 1981. 236p.

(1052)
Garsoian, Nina G., 1923-   **The Paulician Heresy, A Study of the Origin and Development of Paulicianism in Armenia and the Eastern Provinces of the Byzantine Empire**/by Nina Garsoian. The Hague and Paris: Mouton, 1967. 293p.

(1053)
History of St. Mary Armenian Apostolic Church, 1911-76, Yettem. California. Yettem, CA: St. Mary, 1977. 168p.

(1054)
Kiwleserian, Babgen, 1868-1936. **The Armenian Church**/by Papken Catholicos Gulesserian. Translated by Terenig Vartabed Poladian. 2nd edition. N.Y.: AMS Press, 1970. xii, 61p. (reprint of 1939 edition)

(1055)
Megerdichian, Robert. **The Armenian Churches in North America: Apostolic, Protestant and Catholic. A Geographical and Historical Survey**/by Robert Megerdichian. N.J.: Society For Armenian Studies, 1983. 134p.

(1056)
Moore, Elinor A. **The Ancient Churches of Old Jerusalem**/by Elinor Moore. Beirut: Khayats, 1961.

(1057)
Nersoyan, Hagop J. **A History of the Armenian Church; With Thirty Five Stories**/by Hagop Nersoyan. N.Y.: Council for Religious Education, Diocese of the Armenian Church of North America, 1963. xiv, 287p.

(1058)
Nersoyan, Hagop J. **The Faith of the Armenian Church, the Teacher's Book**/by Hagop Nersoyan. N.Y.: Council For Religious Education, Diocese of Armenian Church of North America, 1960. xvi, 239p.

(1059)
Nersoyan, Hagop J. **Stories From the History of the Armenian Church**/by Hagop Nersoyan. Illustrated by Joseph Kalemkerian. N.Y.: Council For Religious Education, Diocese of the Armenian Church of North America, 1963. vii, 214p.

(1060)
The Pillars of the Armenian Church/compiled and edited by Dickran H. Boyajian. Watertown, MA: Baikar Press, 1962. xviii, 426p.

(1061)
Rycaut, Paul, 1628-1700. **The Present State of the Greek and Armenian Churches, Anno Christi, 1678**/written at the command of His Majesty. London: J. Starkey, 1679. N.Y.: AMS Press, 1970. 452p.

(1062)
Sarkissian, Karekin. **The Armenian Church in Contemporary Times**/by Bishop Karekin Sarkissian. N.Y.: Prelacy of the Armenian Apostolic Church of America, 1970. 44p.

(1063)
Sarkissian, Karekin. **The Council of Chalcedon and the Armenian Church**/by Karekin Sarkissian. 2nd edition. N.Y.: Armenian Church Prelacy, 1975. xvii, 264p.

(1064)
Stone, Michael E., 1938-   **Armenian Apocrypha: Relating to the Pastriorchs and Prophets**/edited with introduction and translation by Michael Stone. Jerusalem: Israel Academy of Sciences and Humanities, 1982.

(1065)
Tootikian, Vahan H. **Reflections of an Armenian**/by Vahan H. Tootikian. Detroit: Armenian Heritage Committee, 1980. 250p.

(1066)
Tootikian, Vahan H. **The Armenian Evangelical Church**/by Vahan H. Tootikian. Southfield, Michigan: Armenian Heritage Committee, 1982. 322p.

(1067)
Toumanoff, Cyrill. **Studies in Christian Caucasian History**/by Cyrill Toumanoff. Washington, D.C.: Georgetown University Press, 1963.

Cookery

(1068)
Antreassian, Alice, 1922-   **Armenian Cooking Today**/by Alice Antreassian. N.Y.: St. Vartan Press, Diocese of the Armenian Church, 1975. 189p.

(1069)
Antreassian, Alice, 1922-   **Classic Armenian Recipes: Cooking Without Meat**/by Alice Antreassian and Marian Jebejian. Designed and illustrated by Adrima Zanazanian. 1st edition. N.Y.: Ashod Press, 1981. ix, 308, xxxip.

(1070)
Armenian General Benevolent Union of America. Detroit Women's Chapter. **Treasured Armenian Recipes.** N.Y.: A.G.B.U., 1947. 126p. (reprinted several times)

(1071)
Baboian, Rose. **Armenian American Cookbook, simplified Armenian Near East Recipes**/by Rose Baboian. Lexington, MA: Rose Baboian. 1964. 208p.

(1072)
Baboian, Rose. **The Art of Armenian Cooking**/by Rose Baboian. 1st edition. Garden City, N.Y.: Doubleday, 1971. xviii, 264p.

(1073)
Bezjian, Alice. **The Complete Armenian Cookbook, Including Favorite International Recipes**/by Alice Bezjian. Fair Lawn. N.J.: Rosekeer Press, 1983. 280p.

(1074)
Getsoian, Anne. **Favorite Armenian and Syrian Recipes of Anne Getsoian; Middle Eastern Recipes of Anne Getsoian**/by Anne Getsoian. San Diego, CA: Getsoian, 1979. 89p.

(1075)
Hogrogian, Rachel. **The Armenian Cookbook**/by Rachel Hogrogian Illustrated by Nonny Hogrogian. 1st edition. N.Y.: Atheneum, 1971. xxi, 152p.

(1076)
McQueen-Williams, Morvyth, 1911-1976. **A Diet For 100 Healthy, Happy Years**/by Morvyth McQueen-Williams and Barbara Apisson. Edited by Norman Ober. Englewood Cliffs, N.J.: Prentice-Hall, 1977. 220p.

(1077)
Naccachian, Kricor. **Armenian and Selected Favorite Recipes**/by Kricor Naccachian. Fresno, CA: Trinity Guild. 156p.

(1078)
Uvezian, Sonia. **The Cuisine of Armenia**/by Sonia Uvezian. Illustrated by Dickran Palulian. 1st edition. N.Y.: Harper & Row, 1974. xiii, 412p.

(1079)
Zane, Eva. **Middle Eastern Cookery**/by Eva Zane. 114p. (includes Armenian recipes)

Biographies

(1080)
Aharonian, Aharon G. **The Ohanian Family: Descendants of Ohan Ohanian of Mezireh, Armenia**/by Aharon G. Aharonian. Shrewsbury, Mass.: Aharonian, 1979. xii, 80p.

(1081)
Aintablian, Alexander, 1901-   **Clash of Souls**/by Alexander Aintblian. Beirut: United Printers and Traders, 1977. viii, 215p.

(1082)
Arlen, Michael J., 1895-1956. **Exiles; Passage to Ararat; Two Works**/by Michael J. Arlen, N.Y.: Penguin Books, 1982.

(1083)
Armaghanian, Arshalouise. **Arsh's World and Yours**/by Arshalouise Armaghanian. 1st edition. N.Y.: Vantage Press, 1977. 96p.

(1084)
Aroian, John H. **Mountains Stand Firm**/by John H. Aroian. N.Y.: Green Hill Pub., 1977. 169p.

(1085)
Asadorian. **Gomidas Vartabed: His Life and Work**/by Asadorian. N.Y.: 1969.

(1086)
Ashjian, Arten. **Mesrob Mashdotz, The Great Vartabed**/by Arten Ashjian. N.Y.: Armenian Church Youth Organization, 1962.

(1087)
Avakian, Asdghig, 1911-   **"Stranger" No More, An Armenian From Lebanon Tells Her Story**/by Asdghig Avakian, New Rev. edition. Antelias, 1968. 266p.

(1088)
Aved, Thomas G. **The Little Armenian Boy: Childhood Reminiscence of Turkish Armenia**/by Thomas G. Aved. Fresno, CA: Pioneer Pub. Co., 1979. 180p.

(1089)
Baliozian, Ara. **The Call of the Crane; the Ambitions of a Pig**/by Ara Baliozian. N.Y.: Voskedar Publishing Corp., 1983.

(1090)
Banker, Oscar H. **Dreams and Wars of an American Inventor**/by Oscar H. Banker (Asadoor Sarafian). Bay Village, Ohio: Bob Hull Books, 1982. 252p.

(1091)
Baromian, Haig. **Barefoot Boy From Anatolic**/by Haig Baromian. Granada Hills, CA: Baromian, 1983. 130p.

(1092)
Bedoukian, Kerop, 1907-   **Some of Us Survived; the Story of an Armenian Boy**/by Kerop Bedoukian. 1st edition. N.Y.: Farrar Straus Giroux, 1979. 241p. (Juvenile literature)

(1093)
Bedoukian, Kerop, 1907-   **The Urchin; An Armenian's Escape**/by Kerop Bedoukian. London: John Murray, 1978. vii, 186p.

(1094)
Chakalian, Manouk, **Journey For Freedom**/by Manouk Chakalian. N.Y.: Carlton Press, 1976.

(1095)
Davidian, Nectar. **The Seropians: First Armenian Settlers in Fresno County, California. Recollections of George Seropian (1868-1947)** as related to Nectar Davidian during two interviews on April 23 and May 2, 1945 at his residence in San Francisco. Berkeley, CA. 1965. iv, 35p.

(1096)
Der Megerditchian, Ervant. **The Life of the Armenian Emigrant**/by Ervant Der Megerditchian. North Quincy, Mass: Christopher Publishing House, 1970.

(1097)
Dyer, Donita. **Pearl, Her Love Touched Two Worlds**/by Donita Dyer. Whearon, Ill.: Tyndale House, 1977. 254p.

(1098)
Egitkhanoff, Marie Abelian. **Escape: A Sequel to Terror by Night and Day**/by Marie Abelian Egitkhanoff with Ken Wilson. Mountain View, CA: Pacific Press Pub. Association, 1982. 124p.

(1099)
Floan, Howard R. **William Saroyan**/by Howard Floan. N.Y.: Twayne Publisher, 1966.

(1100)
Granian, Puzant. **My Land, My People**/by Puzant Granian. Translated by Ara Baliozian. Los Angeles: Narek Publishing Co., 1978. 146p.

(1101)
Hartunian, Abraham H. **Neither to Laugh Nor to Weep; A Memoir of the Armenian Genocide**/by Abraham H. Hartunian. Translated from the original Armenian manuscripts by Vartan Hartunian. Boston: Beacon Press, 1968. 206p. (reprinted by Armenian Missionary Association of America, 1976)

(1102)
Kalfaian, Aris. **Chomaklou the History of an Armenian Village**/by Aris Kalfaian. N.Y.: Chomaklou Compatriotic Society, 1982. 217p.

(1103)
Kandarian, Bella A. **Fifty Years in Fresno; the Life Story of Bella A. Kandarian**/by Bella Kandarian. N.Y.: Exposition Press, 1963. 87p.

(1104)
Keyan, Haykas. **No Choice But One**/by Haykas Keyan. N.Y.: Armen House, 1978. 320p.

(1105)
Keyishian, Harry. **Michael Arlen**/by Harry Keyishian. 150p.

(1106)
Kherdian, David. **The Road From Home; the Story of an Armenian Girl**/by David Kherdian. 1st edition. N.Y.: Greenwillow Books, 1979. xi, 238p.

(1107)
Mooradian, Karlen. **Arshil Gorky Adoian**/by Karlen Mooradian. Chicago: Gilgamesh Press Limited, 1978. 314p.

(1108)
Mooradian, Karlen. **The Many Worlds of Arshile Gorky**/by Karlen Mooradian. Chicago: Gilgamesh Press, 1982. 327p.

(1109)
Nazarian, Kaloost, 1863-1942. **The Autobiography of Kaloost Nazarian, an Armenian Immigrant**/translated from the Armenian by Prapione Nazarian Sivaslian; edited by Lelan E. Bibb. Owensboro, KY: Cook-McDowell Publications, 1980. 134p.

(1110)
Rejebian, Ermance. **Pilgrimage to Freedom**/by Ermance Rejebian. Rejebian, 1973. 47p.

(1110-A)
Rhowben, 1882-1951. **Armenian Freedom Fighters;** The Memoirs of Ruben Der Minasian. Translated and edited by James G. Mandalian. Boston, MA: Hairenik Association, 1963. 244p.

(1111)
Sanjian, Avedis. **Private Letters of Vahan Tekeyan**/compiled, edited and annotated by Avedis Sanjian. N.Y.: Tekeyan Cultural Association, 1983.

(1112)
Sarafian, Kevork A. **From Immigrant to Educator**/by Kevork Sarafian. N.Y.: Vantage Press, 1963.

(1113)
Sarian, Nerses. **I Shall Not Die**/by Nerses Sarian. Introduction by Eric W. Gosden. London: Oliphants, 1967.

(1114)
Saroyan, Aram. **William Saroyan**/by Aram Saroyan. N.Y.: Harcourt Brace Jovanovich, 1983. 192p.

(1115)
Shahverdian, A. **A. Spendiaryan, Biography of the Composer**/by A. Shahverdian. Erevan, 1971.

(1116)
Sharian, Bedros M. **I Love America: Missionery Address and My Experiences Here and There**/by Bedros M. Sharian, Sr. 1st edition. N.Y.: Vantage Press, 1974. 64p.

(1117)
Shiragian, Arshavir. **The Legacy. Memoirs of an Armenian Patriot**/by Arshavir Shiragian. Translated by Sonia Shiragian. Boston, MA: Hairenik Press, 1980. xvi, 217p.

(1118)
Sutherland, James Kay, 1897-   **The Adventures of an Armenian Boy, an Autobiography and Historical Narrative Encompassing the Last Thirty Years of the Ottoman Empire**/by James Sutherland. Ann Arbor, Michigan: Ann Arbor Press, 1964.

(1119)
Taft, Elise Hagopian, 1906-   **Rebirth: The Story of an Armenian Girl Who Survived the Genocide and Found Rebirth in America**/by Elise Hagopian Taft. 1st edition. Plandome, N.Y.: New Age Publishers, 1981. ix, 142p.

(1121)
Torgerson, Dial, 1928-   **Kerkorian: An American Success Story**/by Dial Torgerson. N.Y.: Dial Press, 1974. 306p.

(1122)
Totovents, Vahan, 1889-1937. **Scenes From an Armenian Childhood/** by Vahan Totovents. Translated from the Armenian with a foreword by Mischa Kudian. London: Oxford University Press, 1962. 182p. (Reprinted in 1980 by Mashtots Press, London)

(1123)
Varjabedian, Hermine D. **The Great 4: Mesrob, Komidas, Antranik, Toramanian**/by Hermine Varjabedian. Beirut, 1969.

(1124)
Zarian, Gostan, 1885-1969. **Bancoop and the Bones of the Mammoth/** by Gostan Zarian. Selected and translated by Ara Baliozian. 1st edition. N.Y.: Ashod Press, 1982. xxii, 115p.

(1125)
Zarian, Gostan, 1885-1969. **Traveller and His Road**/by Gostan Zarian. Translated by Ara Baliozian. N.Y.: Ashod Press, 1981. xviii, 161p.

(1126)
World Who's Who of Armenians/edited by Anne Avakian Bishop. Los Angeles. First edition, 1977-

Armenians In Foreign Countries

(1127)
Armenians in Ontario. Issue editor, Isabel Kapreilian. Polyphony Vol. 4 no. 2 Fall/Winter. Ontario, Toronto: Multicultural History Society, 1982. 136p.

(1128)
Azarya, Victor. **Urban Life Behind Monastery Walls: The Armenian Quarter of Jerusalem**/by Victor Azarya. Berkeley, CA: University of California Press, 1983. 224p.

(1129)
Bazil, Anne. **Armenian Settlements in India, From the Earliest Times to the Present Day**/by Anne Bazil. Calcutta: Armenian College, 1969. 6, 282, 23, 3p.

(1130)
Darpasian, Hrach B., 1904-   **Erzurum (Garin), Its Armenian History and Traditions**/by Hratch A. Tarpassian. Translated from the Armenian by Nigol Schaghaldian. N.Y.: Garin Compatriotic Union of United States, 1975. V, 270p.

(1131)
Grigorian, Mesrob K. **Armenians in the Service of the Ottoman Empire, 1860-1908**/by Mesrob K. Grigorian. London, Boston: Routlede and Kegan Paul, 1978. xii, 148p.

(1132)
Hintlian, Kevork. **History of the Armenians in the Holy Land**/by Kevork Hintlian. Jerusalem: St. James Press, 1976. 68p.

(1133)
Kerr, Stanley Elphinstone. **The Lions of Marash; Personal Experiences with American Near East Relief, 1919-1922**/by Stanley E. Kerr. Introduction by Richard Hovannisian. 1st edition. Alabany: State University of New York Press, 1973. xxv, 318p.

(1134)
Mirzaian, Aramais. **Armenians, A Pilgrim People in "Tierra Australia"**/compiled and arranged by Father Aramais Mirzaian. Sydney: Aramais Mirzaian, 1975. 204p.

(1135)
Mirzaian, Aramais. **Armenians in Australia and New Zealand**/by A. Mirzaian. Sydney: Father A. Mirzaian, 1966. 258p.

(1136)
Mirzaian, Aramais. **The Wandering Armenians**/compiled and arranged by Father Aramais Mirzaian and Dr. Charles Price. Sydney: Fr. A. Mirzaian, 1980. 116p.

(1137)
Sanjian, Avedis Krikor, 1921-   **The Armenian Communities in Syria Under Ottoman Dominion**/by Avedis K. Sanjian. Cambridge: Harvard University Press, 1965. xi, 390p.

(1138)
Seth, Mesrovb. **Armenians in India, From the Earliest Times to the Present Day**/by Mesrovb Jacob Seth. New Delhi: Oxford & IBH Co., 1983.

(1139)
Soviet Asian Ethnic Frontiers/edited by William C. McCogg, Jr. and Brian D. Silver. N.Y.: Pergamon Press, 1979. xx, 280p.

Armenians In America

(1140)
Ararat Quarterly. Vol. xviii no. 1 Winter 1977. Special Issue. **Armenians in America**/edited by Jack Antreassian. N.Y.: A.G.B.U., 1977. 146p.

(1141)
Arzoumanian, Zaven. **The Origins of the Armenian Christianity; Armenians in America**/by Zaven Arzoumanian. Wynnewood, PA: St. Sahag and St. Mesrob Armenian Church, 1978. 39p.

(1142)
Avakian, Arra S. **The Armenians in America**/by Arra Avakian. Minneapolis: Lerner Publications Co., 1977. 87p. (juvenile literature)

(1143)
Davidian, Nectar. **The Seropians; First Armenian Settlers in Fresno County, California.** Recollections of George Seropian (1868-1947) as related to Nectar Davidian during two interviews on April 23 and May 2, 1945 at his residence in San Francisco. Berkeley, CA, 1965. iv, 35p.

(1144)
Federal Writers' Project. Massachusetts. **The Armenians in Massachusetts**/written and compiled by the Federal Writers' Project of the Works Progress Administration for the State of Massachusetts, Boston; Armenian Historical Society, N.Y.: AMS Press, 1975. 148p.

(1145)
Henry, Sheila Eileen, 1933-   **Cultural Persistence and Socio-Economic Mobility: A Comparative Study of Assimilation Among**

Armenians and Japanese in Los Angeles/by Sheila E. Henry. San Francisco: R & E Research Associates, 1978. x, 128p.

(1146)
Kulhanjian, Gary A. **The Historical and Sociological Aspects of Armenian Immigration to the United States 1890-1930**/by Gary Kulhanjian. San Francisco: R & E Research Associates, 1975. vi, 83p.

(1147)
Mahakian, Charles. **History of the Armenians in California**/by Charles Mahakian. San Francisco: R & E Research Associates, 1974. vii, 92p. (reprinted from author's thesis, 1935)

(1148)
Malcom, Vartan M., 1883-   **The Armenians in America**/by Vartan Malcom, with an introduction by James W. Gerard. Preface by Leon Dominian. Boston, Mass: The Pilgrim Press, 1919; San Francisco: R & E Research Associates, 1969. xxiv, 142p.

(1149)
Minasian, Edward. **They Came From Ararat: The Exodus of the Armenian People to the United States**/by Edward Minasian. Berkeley, CA: 1961. viii, 287p.

(1150)
Mirak, Robert. **Torn Between Two Lands, Armenians in America 1890 to World War I**/by Robert Mirak. Combridge, Mass: Harvard University Press, 1983. 370p.

(1151)
Piotrowski, Thaddeus M. **The Armenian Diaspora in Manchester, New Hampshire**/by Thaddeus M. Piotrowski. Manchester, NH: Piotrowski, 1977. vi, 69p.

(1152)
Tashjian, James H. **The Armenians of the United States and Canada: a Brief Study**/by James Tashjian. Boston, Mass: Armenian Youth Federation, 1947. 62p. (reprinted in San Francisco by R & E Research Associates, 1970)

(1153)
Wallis, Wilson Dallam, 1886-   **Fresno Armenians, to 1919**/by Wilson D. Wallis. Introduction by Nectar Davidian. Lawrence, KA: Coronado Press, 1965. 80p.

(1154)
Wertsman, Vladimir, 1929-   **The Armenians in America, 1618-1976: A Chronology & Fact Book**/compiled and edited by Vladimir Wertsman. Dobbs Ferry, N.Y.: Oceana Publications, 1978. viii, 138p.

(1155)
Yeretzian, Aram Serkis. **A History of Armenian Immigration to America with Special Reference to Conditions in Los Angeles**/by Aram Serkis Yeretzian. San Francisco: R & E Research Associates, 1974. viii, 78p. (reprinted from author's thesis, 1923)

Armenia — Description and Travel

(1156)
Arlen, Michael J. 1895-1956. **Passage to Ararat**/by Michael Arlen. New York: Farrar, Straus & Giroux, 1975: Valantine Books, 1976. 293p.

(1157)
Armenia Observed/edited by Ara Baliozian. An Introduction by Jack Vartoogian. N.Y.: Ararat Press, 1979. xl, 225p.

(1158)
Khandoyan, Constantine. **Soviet Armenia**/by Constantine Khandoyan. Translated by Hratch Boudjiganian. Edited by Tinatin Belousova. Yerevan: Armenian Society For Friendship and Cultural Relations with Foreign Countries, 1976. 45p.

(1159)
Lynch, Harry Finnis Blosse, 1862-1913. **Armenia, Travels and Studies.** Vol. 1: The Russian Provinces. vol 2: The Turkish Provinces. Beirut: Khayats, 1965. 2 vol. (Reprinted edition)

(1160)
Mandel 'shtam, Osip Ymil' evich, 1891-1923. **Journey to Armenia**/by Osip Mandelshtam; revised translation by Clarence Brown, with an introduction by Bruce Chatwin; drawings by Hiang Kee. London: Next editions in association with Faber & Faber, 1980. 66p.

(1161)
Mirzaian, Aramais. **Sydney, Armenian Guide Book**/compiled and arranged by Aramais Mirzaian. Cammeray, Armenian Parsonage, 1970.

(1162)
Moses of Khoren, 5th cent. **History of the Armenians**/by Moses Khorenats'i, translation and commentary on the literary sources by Robert W. Thomson. Cambridge: Harvard University Press, 1978. viii, 408p.

(1163)
Moses, of Khoren, 5th cent. **Patmut'iwn Hayots' = History of the Armenians**/by Moses Khorenats'i. A facsim. Reproduction of the 1913 Tiflis edition, with an introduction by Robert Thomson. Delmar, N.Y.: Caravan Books, 1981. xxi, 62, 396p.

(1164)
Nansen, Fridtjof, 1861-1930. **Armenia and the Near East**/by Fridtjof
  Nansen. N.Y.: Da Capo Press, 1976. 324p.

(1165)
Soviet Armenia/contributors, A.A. Aslanyan and others. Moscow:
  Progress Publishers, 1971. 255p.

(1166)
Svajian, Stephen G., 1906-1977. **A Trip Through Historic Armenia**/by
  Stephen G. Svajian. N.Y.: Greenhill Pub., 1977. xx, 643p.

(1167)
Tcholakian, Arthur, 1928-   **Armenia: State, People, Life**/photo-
  graphed and written by Arthur Tcholakian. 1st edition. N.Y.: Paradon
  Pub. Co., 1975. 320p.

Reference Books
(Dictionaries, Directories, Bibliographies, Etc.)

(1168)
Ananikian, R.G. **Yerevan: A Guide**/translation from the Russian by Sh.
  Wakefield. Moscow: Progress Publishers, 1982. 94, 48p.

(1169)
Anessian, H.S. **The Armenian Question & the Genocide of the Arme-
  nians in Turkey, a Brief Bibliography of Russian Materials.** La
  Verne, CA: American Armenian International College, 1983. (text in
  Russian & English)

(1170)
Armenia: A Collection of Pamphlets, (in the Oriental Division). New
  York: New York Public Library, 1979. 1 reel 35mm. (Microfilm of
  pamphlets published in various places before 1957).

(1171)
Armenia. Special Research Department of Restoration of Armenian Cultural Historical Monuments. **Illustrated Guide-Map of Historical
  Architectural Monuments of Soviet Armenia**/compiled and drawn
  by Avakian, edited by L. Barseghian; author of the text, A. Kalanta-
  ryan. Yerevan: Special Research Department of Restoration of
  Armenian Cultural Historical Monuments, 1968.

(1172)
Armenian Assembly. **Directory of Armenian Scholars in American and
  Canadian Academic Institutions.** 2nd edition. Washington, D.C.:
  The Armenian Assembly, 1976. 48p.

(1173)
Armenian Directory/Yellow Pages, 1980-   Glendale, CA: Uniarts,
  4th edition, 1983. 256p. (annual)

(1174)
**The Armenian Genocide; First 20th Century Holocaust, 65th Anni-
versary Memorial 1915-1980**/by Richard Diran Kloian. 2nd edition.
Fresno, CA: United Armenian Commemorative Committee, Armenian Assembly, 1980. 304p.

(1175)
Armenian S.S.R. Dept. of Foreign Tourism. **Yerevan Guide Map**/com-
piled by M.H. Mesropian. Yerevan: Architectural and Planning Dept.
of Yerevan, 1968.

(1176)
Armenian Telephone Directory, 1958-   Toronto, Ontario Canada,
Armenian Holy Trinity Church.

(1177)
Atikian, Martha Bilezikian, **Armenian Names**/by Martha Atikian Bilezikian
and Hagop Atikian, 1973. 71p.

(1178)
Avakian, Anne M. **Armenia and the Armenians in Academic Disserta-
tions: A Bibliography**/compiled by Anne M. Avakian. Berkeley, CA:
Professional Press, 1974. 38p.

(1179)
Bedrossian, Matthias. **New Dictionary: Armenian-English**/by Matthias
Bedrossian. Venice: St. Lazarus Armenian Academy, 1875-79.
(reprinted in Beirut: Librairie Du Liban) distributor, Troy, Michigan:
International Book Center, 1974. xxx, 786p.

(1180)
British Library. Dept. of Oriental Manuscripts and Printed Books. **Catalogue of Early Armenian Books, 1512-1850**/by Vrej Nersessian
(for British Library and Bodleian Library) London: British Library,
1980. 172p.

(1181)
**Catalogue of Twenty-Three Important Armenian Illuminated Manu-
scripts Which Will Be Sold by Auction**/by Messres. Satheby & Co.
London: Satheby, 1967. 58p.

(1182)
Chakmakjian H. H. **A Comprehensive Dictionary, English-Armenian/**
edited by H. H. Chakmakjian. Beirut, 1978. 1326p.

(1183)
Der Nersessian, Sirarpie. **Armenian Manuscripts in the Freer Gallery
of Art**/by Sirarpie Der Nersessian. Washington, D.C.: Smithsonian
Institution, Freer Gallery of Art (Oriental Studies no. 6), 1963. xix,
146p.

(1184)
Der Nersessian, Sirarpie. **Armenian Manuscripts in the Walters Art Gallery**/by Sirarpie Der Nersessian. Baltimore: The Trustees, 1973. x, 111p. 243p. of illus.

(1185)
Documents of Armenian Architecture Series. An Exhaustive Collection of Photos and Essays in English, Armenian and Italian. Milan: Milan University, Academy of Science of Armenian. 1974-

(1186)
English-Armenian, Armenian-English Modern Dictionary/by M. Koushakdjian and D. Khantrouni. Beirut: G. Doniguian & Sons Pub. House; N.Y.: Distributed by W.S. Heinman, 1976-78. 949, 416p.

(1186-A)
Etmekjian, James. **A Graded West Armenian Reader; Selections From Armenian Literature**/adopted and edited by James Etmekjian. N.Y.: American Council of Learned Societies & National Association for Armenian Studies and Research, 1963. xv, 187p.

(1187)
Garsoian, Nina G. **The Paulician Heresy. A Study of the Origin and Development of Paulicianism in Armenia and the Eastern Provinces of the Byzantine Empire**/by Nina G. Garsoian. The Hague and Paris: Mouton, 1967. 293p.

(1189)
Greater Boston Armenian Directory, 1973. Boston Armenian Relief Society, Soseh Chapter, 1973.

(1190)
A Guide Book For the International Symposium on the History and Geology/compiled by B.N. Arakelian . . . et at. Edited by S.S. Mekerchian, translated into English by P.M. Mesrobian. Yerevan: Pub. House of the Armenian Academy of Sciences, 1967. 97p.

(1191)
Gulbenkian, Edward V. **Armenian Press Directory**/by Edward V. Gulbenkian. London: Harq Publications, 1971. 75p.

(1192)
Haykazian College. College Library. **Hayagidakan Gradaran. Armenian Periodical Collection.** Beirut: Armenian College, 1974. 164p. (includes section for titles in languages other than Armenian)

(1193)
Hovannisian, Richard G. **Armenia on the Road to Independence, 1918**/by Richard G. Hovannisian. Berkeley, CA: University of California Press, 1967. viii, 364p.

(1194)
Hovannisian, Richard G. **The Armenian Holocaust: A Bibliography Relating to the Deportation, Massacres, and Dispersion of Armenian People, 1915-1918**/by Richard Hovannisian. 2nd revised printing. Cambridge, Mass: National Association For Armenian Studies and Research; Armenian Heritage Press, 1978. xiv, 41p.

(1195)
Hovannisian, Richard G. **The Republic of Armenia I**/by Richard G. Hovannisian. Berkeley, CA: University of California Press, 1971. 547p. vol. 1.

(1196)
Hovannisian, Richard G. **The Republic of Armenia II**/by Richard Hovannisian. Berkeley, CA: University of California Press, 1982. 600p. vol. 2.

(1197)
Khantrouni, Dicran. **Armenian English Modern Dictionary**/by Dicran Khantrouni and Mardiros Koushakdjian. Koniguian & Sons Pub., 1970. 15,416p.

(1198)
Kherdian, David. **A Bibliography of William Saroyan**/by David Kherdian. Roger Beacham, 1965.

(1199)
Khoushakdjian, Mardiros. **English Armenian Modern Dictionary**/by Mardiros Khoushakdjian and Dicran Khantrouni. Doniguian & Sons Pub., 1970. 16,949p.

(1200)
Koudoulian, Kourken. **Armenian Names and Their Meanings**/by Kourken Koudoulian. Los Angeles, 1977. 157p. (text in Armenian & English)

(1201)
Kouyoumdjian, Mesrob G., 1897-1983. **A Comprehensive Dictionary Armenian English**/by Mesrob G. Kouyoumdjian. Watertown, Mass: 1970. 1150p.

(1202)
Kouyoumdjian, Mesrob G., 1897-1983. **A Comprehensive Dictionary, English Armenian**/by Mesrob G. Kouyoumdjian. Le Caire, Journal Arev, 1961. 114p.

(1203)
Kouyoumdjian, Mesrob G., 1897-1983. **A Comprehensive Dictionary of Idioms, English Armenian**/by Mesrob Kouyoumdjian. Cairo: Vosguedar Press, 1969. 669p.

(1204)
Kouyoumdjian, Mesrob G., 1897-1983. **A Dictionary of Proverbs & Quotations, Armenian English, English Armenian**/by Mesrob Kouyoumdjian. 1967. 46, 471p.

(1205)
Kouyoumdjian, Mesrob G., 1897-1983. **A New Pocket Dictionary, English Armenian, Armenian English**/by Mesrob Kouyoumdjian. 1970. 352, 318p.

(1206)
Kouyoumdjian, Mesrob G., 1897-1983. **A Polyglottic Law Dictionary in English, French, Armenian and Turkish Languages**/by M.G. Kouyoumdjian. Cairo: Vosguedar Press, 1979. 394p.

(1207)
Kouyoumdjian, Mesrob G., 1897-1983. **A Practical Dictionary For Adults: Armenian English, English Armenian**/by Mesrob Kouyoumdjian. Le Caire: Fonds National Armenien, 1973. 544, 10, 747p.

(1208)
Krmoyan, Sona Mkrtch. **English Armenian Dictionary, For Secondary Schools**/by Sona Mkrtch Krmoyan, 1968. 204p.

(1209)
Kulhanjian, Gary A. **A Guide on Armenian Immigrants, Studies, and Institutions**/by Gary A. Kulhanjian, 1977. viii, 720. (thesis M.A. William Paterson College of New Jersey)

(1210)
Lang, David Marshall. **Armenia, Cradle of Civilization**/by David Marshall Lang. 3rd edition. London; Boston: Allen & Unwin, 1980. 320p.

(1211)
Manandian, Hakob, 1873-1952. **The Trade and Cities of Armenia in Relation to Ancient World Trade**/by H.H. Manandian. Translated from the 2nd rev. edition by Nina G. Garsoian. Lisbon, Armenian Library of the Galouste Gulbenkian, 1965. 248p.

(1212)
Mann, Stuart Edward. **Armenian and Indo-European; Historical Phonology**/by Stuart E. Mann. London, Luzac & Co., 1963. xxxvi, 203p.

(1213)
Megerdichain, Robert. **The Armenian Churches in North America, Apostolic, Protestant and Catholic. A Geographical and Historical Survey**/by Robert Megerdichian. New Jersey, Society For Armenian Studies, 1983. 134p.

(1214)
Morgan, Jacques Jean Marie de, 1857-1924. **The History of the Armenian People; From the Remotest Times to the Present Day**/by Jacques Morgan. Preface by Gustave Schlumberger. Illustrated with 296 maps, plans, and documentary sketches by the author. Translated by Ernest F. Barry. Boston: Hairenik Press, 1965. 430p.

(1215)
Nazigian, A. **The Armenian Literature in Foreign Languages: A Bibliography**/by A. Nazigian and A. Tsitsinian. Edited with a forework by R. Ishkhanian. Erevan: Armenian Ministry of Culture, 1971. 376.

(1216)
Nersessian, Vrej, 1948-   **An Index of Articles on Armenian Studies in Western Journals**/by V. Nersessian. London: Luzac & Co., 1976. 95p.

(1217)
Ovena, A Directory of the Armenian Diaspora Personalities & Organizations 1980. First edition. Beirut: Editorial Board of Ovena, Haigazian College, 1980. xviii, 195p.

(1218)
Papajian, Sarkis. **A Brief History of Armenia**/by Sarkis Papajian. Fresno, CA: Evangelical Union of North America, 1976. 134p.

(1219)
Pilikian, Hovhanness I. **Armenian Cienema: A Source Book**/by Hovhanness Pilikian. London: Counter-Point Publications. 104p.

(1220)
Salmaslian, Armenag. **Bibliographie de l'Armenie**/by Armenag Salmaslian. 2nd edition. Erevan: Izd-vo Akademii Nauk Armianskoi SSR, 1969. 468p. (a bibliography in English & other languages)

(1221)
Sanjian, Avedis Krikor. **A Catalogue of Medieval Armenian Manuscripts in the United States**/by Avedis Sanjian. Berkeley, CA: University of California Press, 1976. 863p.

(1222)
Sarian, John M. **Record Guide, Armenian Musicians and Composers**/ by John Sarian. N.Y.: Ararat Press, 1979. 56p.

(1223)
Surmelian, Leon. **Apples of Immortality: Folktales of Armenia.** UNESCO Collection of representative works. Series of translation from the literatures of the U.S.S.R./by Leon Surmelian. London: George Allen & Unwin; Berkeley, CA: University of California Press, 1968. 319p.

(1224)
United States Central Intelligence Agency. **Armenian Personal Names.** Washington, D.C., 1965. v.1, 50p.

(1225)
Varjabedian, Hermine D. **The Great 4: Mesrob, Komidas, Antranik, Toramanian**/by Hermine Varjabedian. Beirut, 1969. 62p.

(1226)
Villa-Hoogasian, Susie. **One Hundred Armenian Tales and Their Folkloristic Relevance**/by Susie Villa—Hoogasian. Detroit, 1966. (reprinted 1982), 602p.

(1227)
The Whole Armenian Catalogue/edited by Alicia Mamourian. N.Y.: Armenian Students Association, 1974. 174p.

(1228)
World Who's Who of Armenians/edited by Anne Avakian Bishop. Los Angeles. First edition 1977-

(1229)
Yacoubian, Adour H. **English Armenian & Armenian English Dictionary Romanized**/by Adour H. Yacoubian. Brooklyn, N.Y.: P. Shalom Pub. 176p.

INDEXES

Organization Names & Subject Index

Directors & Officers Index

Bibliography Index

Organization Names and Subject Index

*The numbers are referred to access numbers, unless specified.

A.A.A.A. (2)
A.A.A.A. (29) (113)
A.A.C.A. (8)
A.A.C.C.A. (91-A)
A.A.F.F. (23)
A.A.I.C. ALUMNI ASSOCIATION (1)
A.A.I.C. ALUMNI-MONITOR (317)
A.A.M.A. (112)
A.A.M.D.A. (116)
A.C.E.C. (31) (60)
A.C.H.C. (44)
A.C.O.M. (40)
A.C.Y.O.A. (43) (351)
A.E.C. (45)
A.F.F. (11)
A.G.A.U. BULLETIN (345)
A.G.A.U. (83)
A.G.B.U. (41-64-312-314-315-326-437-569-585)
A.G.B.U. ALEX MANOOGIAN SCHOOL (465)
A.G.B.U. ALEX MANOOGIAN SCHOOL — LIBRARY (448) (525)
A.G.B.U. ARARAT PRESS (595)
A.G.B.U. ARMENIAN ELEMENTARY SCHOOL (463)
A.G.B.U. BOOKSTORE (596)
A.G.B.U. DAY SCHOOL (467)
A.G.B.U. SAINT PETER SCHOOL (450)
A.H.R.A. (103)
A.N.A. (48) (115)
A.N.C. WESTERN REGION (70)
A.N.C.H.A. (55)
A.N.E.C. (47) (114)
A.N.E.C. SIAMANTO ACADEMY (543)
A.P.S. (107)
A.R.A. (32) (62)
A.R.S. ARMENIAN DAY SCHOOL (466)
A.R.S. MARZABED SCHOOL (510)
A.R.S. ZAVARIAN SCHOOL NO. 1 (493)
A.R.S. ZAVARIAN SCHOOL NO. 2 (494)
A.S.A. (50)
A.S.L.A. (14)
A.W.W.A. (96)
A.Y.F. (591)
ABACA (104)
ABACA NEWSLETTER (318)
ABRIL BOOKSTORE (307) (586)
ALDERMAN LIBRARY UNIVERSITY OF VIRGINIA (559)
ALEX AND MARIE MANOOGIAN FOUNDATION (518)
ALL SAINTS' ARMENIAN APOSTOLIC CHURCH (118)
ALL SAINTS' ARMENIAN APOSTOLIC CHURCH — SUNDAY SCHOOL (257)

ARMENIAN APOST. CHURCH OF SANTA CLARA VALLEY SATURDAY-SCHOOL (472)
ARMENIAN APOST. CHURCH OF SANTA CLARA VALLEY SUNDAY-SCHOOL (239)
ARMENIAN APOSTOLIC CHURCHES EASTERN DIOCESE SEE PAGE 47
ARMENIAN APOSTOLIC CHURCHES EASTERN PRELACY SEE PAGE 41
ARMENIAN APOSTOLIC CHURCHES WESTERN DIOCESE SEE PAGE 54
ARMENIAN APOSTOLIC CHURCHES WESTERN PRELACY SEE PAGE 45
ARMENIAN ARCHITECTURAL ARCHIVES (348) (438)
ARMENIAN ART SOCIETY OF AMERICA (8)
ARMENIAN ARTISTS ASSOCIATION OF AMERICA (29) (113)
ARMENIAN ARTISTS ASSOCIATION OF AMERICA — NEWSLETTER (336)
ARMENIAN ARTS (BIBLIOGRAPHIES) SEE PAGE 240
ARMENIAN ASSEMBLY JOURNAL (332)
ARMENIAN ASSEMBLY OF AMERICA INC. (24) (25) (73)
ARMENIAN ASSEMBLY OF AMERICA INC. — LOS ANGELES (68)
ARMENIAN BIBLE COLLEGE (228) (327) (660)
ARMENIAN BOOK CLEARINGHOUSE (593)
ARMENIAN BROTHERHOOD BIBLE CHURCH (208)
ARMENIAN BROTHERHOOD BIBLE CHURCH SUNDAY SCHOOL (240)
ARMENIAN BUSINESS ALLIANCE OF CALIFORNIA (104) (318)
ARMENIAN BUSINESS DEVELOPMENT AND TRAINING CENTER (105)
ARMENIAN CATHOLIC CHURCH QUEEN OF MARTYRS (234)
ARMENIAN CATHOLIC COMMUNITY (30) (87)
ARMENIAN CATHOLIC SISTERS' ACADEMY (471)
ARMENIAN CHURCH OF MARICOPA COUNTY (191)
ARMENIAN CHURCH OF NORTHERN WESTCHESTER (171)
ARMENIAN CHURCH OF SEATTLE (207)
ARMENIAN CHURCH OF SOUTH FLORIDA (152)
ARMENIAN CHURCH OF THE DESERT (144)
ARMENIAN CHURCH OF THE HOLY ASCENSION (148) (381)
ARMENIAN CHURCH OF THE NAZARENE (209) (363)
ARMENIAN CHURCH OF THE NAZARENE SATURDAY SCHOOL (473)
ARMENIAN CHURCH OF THE NAZARENE SUNDAY SCHOOL (241)
ARMENIAN CHURCH OF WESTCHESTER (172)
ARMENIAN CHURCH OF WESTERN QUEENS (173)
ARMENIAN CLUB OF HUNTER COLLEGE (44)
ARMENIAN COMMUNITY SCHOOL OF FRESNO (451)
ARMENIAN CONGREG. CHURCH OF CHICAGO (223) (385)
ARMENIAN CONGREG. CHURCH OF GREATER DETROIT (227)
ARMENIAN CONGREG. CHURCH OF GREATER DETROIT SATURDAY-SCHOOL (271)
ARMENIAN CONGREG. CHURCH OF GREATER DETROIT SUNDAY SCHOOL (495)
ARMENIAN CONGREG. CHURCH OF GREATER DETROIT — BULLETIN (396)
ARMENIAN COOKERY (BIBLIOGRAPHIES) SEE PAGE 247
ARMENIAN CULTURAL AND EDUCATIONAL CENTER (31) (60)
ARMENIAN CULTURAL ASSOCIATION HAMAZKAYIN — LOS ANGELES (9)
ARMENIAN CULTURAL ASSOCIATION HAMAZKAYIN — NEW YORK (51) (353)
ARMENIAN CULTURAL ASSOCIATION HAMAZKAYIN — SAN FRANCISCO (644)
ARMENIAN CULTURAL ASSOCIATION OF AMERICA (31-A)
ARMENIAN CULTURAL ASSOCIATION OF NEW JERSEY (498)
ARMENIAN CULTURAL FOUNDATION (10)
ARMENIAN CULTURAL FOUNDATION LIBRARY (564)
ARMENIAN CULTURAL HOUR (646)
ARMENIAN CULTURAL ORGANIZATION OF MINNESOTA — NEWSLETTER (344)
ARMENIAN CULTURAL ORGANIZATION OF MINNESOTA (40) (344)

ARMENIAN CULTURAL RADIO PROGRAM (639)
ARMENIAN DEMOCRATIC LIBERAL ORGANIZATION (69) (74) (304)
ARMENIAN DEMOCRATIC LIBERAL ORGANIZATION EASTERN DISTRICT (302)
ARMENIAN DEMOCRATIC LIBERAL ORGANIZATION — WESTERN DISTRICT (299)
ARMENIAN DIOCESAN BOOKSTORE (624) (596-A)
ARMENIAN DIRECTORY YELLOW PAGES (320)
ARMENIAN EDUCATIONAL COUNCIL INC (45) (342) (438)
ARMENIAN EDUCATIONAL FOUNDATION INC (513)
ARMENIAN EUPHRATES EVANGELICAL CHURCH (233)
ARMENIAN EUPHRATES EVANGELICAL CHURCH SUNDAY-SCHOOL (284)
ARMENIAN EUPHRATES EVANGELICAL CHURCH — NEWSLETTER (419)
ARMENIAN EVANGELICAL BRETHERN CHURCH LOS ANGELES (212) (242) (474)
ARMENIAN EVANGELICAL BRETHERN CHURCH PASADENA (210)
ARMENIAN EVANGELICAL CHURCH OF HOLLYWOOD (213)
ARMENIAN EVANGELICAL CHURCH OF NEW YORK (230)
ARMENIAN EVANGELICAL CHURCH OF NEW YORK — BULLETIN (405)
ARMENIAN EVANGELICAL CHURCH OF THE MARTYRS (224)
ARMENIAN EVANGELICAL CHURCH OF THE MARTYRS SUNDAY SCHOOL (262)
ARMENIAN EVANGELICAL CHURCHES SEE PAGE 58
ARMENIAN EVANGELICAL SCHOOL OF CALIFORNIA (454)
ARMENIAN EVANGELICAL SOCIAL SERVICE (56)
ARMENIAN EVANGELICAL UNION OF NORTH AMERICA (86)
ARMENIAN FILM FOUNDATION (11)
ARMENIAN GEN. ATHLETIC UNION (83) (685)
ARMENIAN GEN. BENEV. UNION (31-B) 41-(60-A) 64-312-314-315-437-569-686)
ARMENIAN GEN. BENEVOLENT UNION LOS ANGELES (12-57-603)
ARMENIAN GOSPEL HOUR INC (640)
ARMENIAN HISTORICAL RESEARCH ASSOCIATION INC. (103)
ARMENIAN HISTORICAL RESEARCH ASSOCIATION — NEWSLETTER (359) (442)
ARMENIAN HISTORY & CULTURAL (BIBLIOGRAPHIES) SEE PAGE 219
ARMENIAN HORIZON (321) (426)
ARMENIAN INDEPENDENT BROADCASTING OF BOSTON (647)
ARMENIAN LANGUAGE (BIBLIOGRAPHIES) SEE PAGE 229
ARMENIAN LANGUAGE LAB AND RESOURCE CENTER (45-A)
ARMENIAN LIBRARY AND MUSEUM OF AMERICA (377) (433) (565)
ARMENIAN LIBRARY AND MUSEUM OF AMERICA — NEWSLETTER (337) (433)
ARMENIAN LITERARY SOCIETY INC. (46) (352) (440) (611)
ARMENIAN LITERATURE (BIBLIOGRAPHIES) SEE PAGE 232
ARMENIAN MARTYRS' CONGREGATIONAL CHURCH (232)
ARMENIAN MASSACRES (BIBLIOGRAPHIES) SEE PAGE 213
ARMENIAN MEKHITARIST FATHERS SCHOOL (452) (612-A)
ARMENIAN MEMORIAL CONGREGATIONAL CHURCH (225) (389)
ARMENIAN MEMORIAL CONGREGATIONAL CHURCH — BULLETIN (389)
ARMENIAN MEMORIAL CONGREGATIONAL CHURCH — SUNDAY-SCHOOL (263)
ARMENIAN MESROBIAN ELEMENTARY AND HIGH SCHOOL (445) (453)
ARMENIAN MIRROR SPECTATOR (302) (609)
ARMENIAN MISSIONARY ASSOCIATION OF AMERICA (88-346-570-610-687)
ARMENIAN MUSICAL STUDIES PROGRAM (534)
ARMENIAN MUSICAL STUDIES PROGRAM — NEWSLETTER (322) (427)
ARMENIAN NATIONAL ARCHIVES (566)
ARMENIAN NATIONAL COMMITTEE — EASTERN REGION (75)
ARMENIAN NATIONAL COMMITTEE — WESTERN REGION (70) (323)
ARMENIAN NATIONAL COMMITTEE — WESTERN REGION — BULLETIN (323)

ARMENIAN NATIONAL EDUCATION COMMITTEE (47) (114)
ARMENIAN NETWORK OF AMERICA INC. (48) (115)
ARMENIAN NUMISMATIC JOURNAL (324) (428)
ARMENIAN NUMISMATIC SOCIETY (13) (106) (324) (428)
ARMENIAN OBSERVER (291) (605)
ARMENIAN PENTECOSTAL CHURCH (215)
ARMENIAN PRELACY BOOKSTORE (596-B) (625)
ARMENIAN PRESBYTERIAN CHURCH (229) (402)
ARMENIAN PROFESSIONAL SOCIETY (107) (662)
ARMENIAN PROFESSIONAL SOCIETY OF THE BAY AREA (107) (108) (661)
ARMENIAN PROGRESSIVE LEAGUE OF AMERICA (49)
ARMENIAN RADIO HOUR (RHODE ISLAND) (654)
ARMENIAN RADIO HOUR (SAN FRANCISCO) (641)
ARMENIAN RADIO HOUR OF GREATER LOS ANGELES (642)
ARMENIAN RADIO HOUR OF METROPOLITAN DETROIT (649)
ARMENIAN RADIO HOUR OF NEW JERSEY (651)
ARMENIAN RADIO HOUR OF PHILADELPHIA (653)
ARMENIAN REFERENCE BOOKS CO. (587)
ARMENIAN RELIEF SOC. OF N. AMERICA (47-61-114-268-338-466-680)
ARMENIAN RELIEF SOCIETY — LOS ANGELES (587)
ARMENIAN RELIGION (BIBLIOGRAPHIES) SEE PAGE 244
ARMENIAN RELIGIOUS EDUCATION COUNCIL (91)
ARMENIAN RENAISSANCE ASSOCIATION INC. (32) (62) (335) (681)
ARMENIAN REPORTER (306)
ARMENIAN REPORTER BOOKSTORE (612)
ARMENIAN REVIEW (311) (434)
ARMENIAN REVOLUTIONARY FEDERATION OF AMERICA (70) (76) (305)
ARMENIAN RIGHTS COUNCIL OF AMERICA (77)
ARMENIAN RIGHTS COUNCIL OF AMERICA LOS ANGELES (71-A)
ARMENIAN ROMAN CATHOLIC CHURCHES SEE PAGE 62
ARMENIAN RUGS SOCIETY (27) (111) (334)
ARMENIAN RUGS SOCIETY NEWSLETTER (334)
ARMENIAN SCHOOL OF LONGWOOD (482)
ARMENIAN SISTERS ACADEMY (464)
ARMENIAN SOCIETY OF LOS ANGELES (14) (475) (561)
ARMENIAN STUDENTS' ASSOCIATION OF AMERICA INC. (50) (693)
ARMENIAN STUDENTS' ASSOCIATION OF AMERICA — NEWSLETTER (349)
ARMENIAN STUDIES & RESEARCH CENTERS SEE PAGE 147
ARMENIAN STUDIES & RESEARCH PERIODICALS SEE PAGE 113
ARMENIAN STUDIES AT COLUMBIA UNIVERSITY — NEWSLETTER (350) (439)
ARMENIAN STUDIES PROGRAM A.A.I.C. (526)
ARMENIAN STUDIES PROGRAM C.S.U. FRESNO (527)
ARMENIAN STUDIES PROGRAMS SEE PAGE 147
ARMENIAN TELETIME (635)
ARMENIAN THEOLOGICAL STUDIES PROGRAM (289)
ARMENIAN WEEKLY (303) (608)
ARMENIAN WELFARE ASSOCIATION INC. (98)
ARMENIAN WOMEN'S WELFARE ASSOCIATION INC. (96)
ARMENIAN YOUTH FEDERATION OF AMERICA (33) (591)
ARMENIANS IN AMERICA (BIBLIOGRAPHIES) SEE PAGE 254
ARMENIANS IN FOREIGN COUNTRIES (BIBLIOGRAPHIES) SEE PAGE 253
ARMENOLOGICAL STUDIES RESEARCH AND EXHIBITS (99) (562) (627)
ARMENOLOGY (ARMENIAN STUDIES PROGRAMS) SEE PAGE 147

HOLY CROSS ARMENIAN APOSTOLIC CHURCH — UNION CITY (167)
HOLY CROSS ARMENIAN CATHOLIC CHURCH (87) (235)
HOLY CROSS ARMENIAN CHURCH — LAWRENCE (160)
HOLY CROSS ARMENIAN CHURCH — NEW YORK (174) (415)
HOLY MARTYR'S ARMENIAN APOSTOLIC CHURCH — BAYSIDE (175) (410)
HOLY MARTYR'S ARMENIAN DAY SCHOOL (469)
HOLY MARTYRS ARMENIAN APOSTOLIC CHURCH — ENCINE (143) (364)
HOLY MARTYRS ELEMENTARY AND FERRAHIAN HIGH SCHOOL (455)
HOLY RESURRECTION ARMENIAN APOSTOLIC CHURCH (188)
HOLY RESURRECTION ARMENIAN CHURCH (149)
HOLY SHOGHAGAT ARMENIAN CHURCH (154)
HOLY TRINITY ARMENIAN APOSTOLIC CHURCH OF GREATER BOSTON (161) (390)
HOLY TRINITY ARMENIAN APOSTOLIC CHURCH — CHELTENHAM (183)
HOLY TRINITY ARMENIAN APOSTOLIC CHURCH — FRESNO (144) (379)
HOLY TRINITY ARMENIAN APOSTOLIC CHURCH — SATURDAY-SCHOOL — WORCESTER (487)
HOLY TRINITY ARMENIAN APOSTOLIC CHURCH — SUNDAY-SCHOOL — FRESNO (245)
HOLY TRINITY ARMENIAN APOSTOLIC CHURCH — SUNDAY-SCHOOL — WORCESTER (265)
HOLY TRINITY ARMENIAN APOSTOLIC CHURCH — WORCESTER (122)
HOME FOR THE ARMENIAN AGED (97) (347)
HOMENMEN ARMENIAN ATHLETIC ASSOCIATION (80)
HOMENTMEN ARMENIAN GENERAL ATHLETIC UNION EASTERN U.S.A. (82-A)
HOMENTMEN ARMENIAN GENERAL ATHLETIC UNION WESTERN U.S.A. (81)
HOOSHARAR (315)
HOOSHARAR (363)
HOOSHARAR MIOUTUNE (314)
HOVID (364)
HOVNANIAN ARMENIAN SCHOOL (449) (468)
HOWARD KARAGHEUSIAN COMMEMORATIVE CORPORATION (66)
HRAIR'S MUSIC CENTER (652)
HROMGLA (365) (428-A)
HUNCHAKIAN SOCIAL DEMOCRATIC PARTY OF WESTERN U.S.A. (79)
HYE LIGHT (637)
HYE SHARZHOOM (328) (429)
HYE TAVLOO ASSOCIATION (37)
HYEDOUN (347)
ILLUMINATOR (397)
IMMANUEL (366)
IMMANUEL ARMENIAN CONGREGATIONAL CHURCH (219) (366)
IMMIGRATION HISTORY RESEARCH CENTER (555) (632)
INSTITUTIONS OR ORGANIZATIONS SEE PAGE 3
INTER-DOCUMENTATION CO. (348) (438)
JOHN M. AZARIAN MEMORIAL ARMENIAN YOUTH SCHOLARSHIP FUND (689)
JOURNAL OF THE SOCIETY FOR ARMENIAN STUDIES (329) (429-A)
JOURNALS & MAGAZINES SEE PAGE 82
K. ARAKELIAN FOUNDATION SCHOLARSHIP (664)
KACH NAZAR (294)
KAREKEN DER AVEDISIAN MEMORIAL ENDOWMENT FUND (675)
KASPAR HOVANNISIAN MEMORIAL SCHOLARSHIP (676)
KAZANJIAN FOUNDATION (515)
KEGHARD (351)

MIOUTIUN (343)
MOTHER CHURCH (369)
MOUNT ARARAT NEWS (399)
MOURAD ARMENIAN SCHOOL (509)
N.W.A.F. (54)
NAREG (410)
NAREG (424)
NAREG ARMENIAN SATURDAY-SCHOOL (500)
NAREG ARMENIAN SUNDAY-SCHOOL (275)
NAREKATSI PROGRAM OF ARMENIAN STUDIES (522)
NATIONAL ASSOCIATION FOR ARMENIAN STUDIES AND RESEARCH (100-593)
NATIONAL ASSOCIATION FOR ARMENIAN STUDIES AND RESEARCH — LIBRARY (567)
NAVASART (308) (431)
NAVASART FOUNDATION (607)
NESHAN ZOVICK SCHOLARSHIP (673)
NEW AGE PUBLISHERS (601)
NEW YORK ARMENIAN HOME FOR THE AGED (98) (354)
NEW YORK ARMENIAN HOME FOR THE AGED — NEWSLETTER (354)
NEW YORK PUBLIC LIBRARY (579)
NEWSLETTER — CHURCH SEE PAGE 96
NEWSLETTER — ORGANIZATION SEE PAGE 85
NEWSLETTER — SCHOOL SEE PAGE 119
NEWSPAPERS & PERIODICALS SEE PAGE 79
NEWSPAPERS (DAILY WEEKLY MONTHLY) SEE PAGE 79
NOAH WILSON ARMENIAN FOUNDATION (54)
NON-PRINT MEDIA (RADIO & T.V.) SEE PAGE 189
NOR ARABKIR DEGHEGADOU (340)
NOR GYANK (298)
NOR OR (299)
NOR OR PUBLISHERS ASSOCIATION (299)
NOR SEBASTIA (355)
NOR SEROOND (300)
NORCAL ARMENIAN HOME (95)
NURSING HOMES & HOSPITALS SEE PAGE 29
ONE-DAY OR SATURDAY-SCHOOLS SEE PAGE 128
OOSANOGH (445)
ORANGE COUNTY ARMENIAN APOSTOLIC CHURCH (141)
ORGANIZATION & RESEARCH LIBRARIES SEE PAGE 162
ORGANIZATION BULLETINS AND NEWSLETTERS SEE PAGE 85
ORGANIZATIONS SEE PAGE 3
OSHAGAN (370)
OUR VOICE (446)
OUTREACH (411)
OUTRIGHT GRANTS AND LOANS (693)
PAGOUMIAN BOOKSTORE (626)
PAN SEBASTIA REHABILITATION UNION (67) (355)
PAP OUKHTI (357)
PARI LOOR (371)
PAROS (301)
PAROS (416)
PAROS (421)
PASADENA CITY COLLEGE (532)

SAINT GREGORY ARM. APOST. CHURCH — PASADENA SUNDAY-SCHOOL (247)
SAINT GREGORY ARM. APOST. CHURCH — SAN FRANCISCO (146) (368)
SAINT GREGORY ARM. APOST. CHURCH — SAN FRANCISCO SATURDAY-SCHOOL (477)
SAINT GREGORY ARMENIAN SCHOOL (495)
SAINT GREGORY CHURCH BOOKSTORE (618)
SAINT GREGORY OF NAREG ARMENIAN CHURCH (182) (416)
SAINT GREGORY THE ILL. ARM. APOSTOLIC CHURCH (119) (386)
SAINT GREGORY THE ILL. ARM. APOSTOLIC CHURCH — HAVERHILL (392)
SAINT GREGORY THE ILL. ARM. APOSTOLIC CHURCH — NEWSLETTER (386)
SAINT GREGORY THE ILL. ARM. APOSTOLIC CHURCH — PHILADELPHIA (137) (282)
SAINT GREGORY THE ILL. ARM. APOSTOLIC CHURCH — SUNDAY-SCHOOL (259)
SAINT GREGORY THE ILL. ARM. CHURCH — BINGHAMTON (176) (414)
SAINT GREGORY THE ILL. ARM. CHURCH — BINGHAMTON SUNDAY-SCHOOL (279)
SAINT GREGORY THE ILL. ARM. CHURCH — CHICAGO (156)
SAINT GREGORY THE ILL CHURCH — NEW YORK (177)
SAINT HAGOP ARMENIAN APOSTOLIC CHURCH OF NIAGARA FALLS (131)
SAINT HAGOP'S ARMENIAN APOSTOLIC CHURCH (139) (424)
SAINT HAGOP'S ARMENIAN APOSTOLIC CHURCH — SUNDAY-SCHOOL (286)
SAINT ILLUMINATOR'S ARMENIAN APOSTOLIC CATHEDRAL (132) (409)
SAINT ILLUMINATOR'S ARMENIAN APOSTOLIC CATHEDRAL — SUNDAY-SCHOOL (280)
SAINT ILLUMINATOR'S ARMENIAN DAY SCHOOL (470)
SAINT ILLUMINATOR'S SATURDAY-SCHOOL (504)
SAINT JAMES ARMENIAN APOSTOLIC CHURCH — LOS ANGELES (196) (370)
SAINT JAMES ARMENIAN APOSTOLIC CHURCH — RICHMOND (187)
SAINT JAMES ARMENIAN APOSTOLIC CHURCH — SACRAMENTO (197)
SAINT JAMES ARMENIAN APOSTOLIC CHURCH — WATERTOWN (163-393-488)
SAINT JAMES ARMENIAN APOSTOLIC CHURCH — WATERTOWN SUNDAY-SCHOOL (269)
SAINT JAMES ARMENIAN CHURCH (157)
SAINT JAMES ARMENIAN CHURCH (172)
SAINT JOHN ARMENIAN APOSTOLIC CHURCH — SAN DIEGO (199) (380)
SAINT JOHN ARMENIAN APOSTOLIC CHURCH — SAN DIEGO — SUNDAY-SCHOOL (248)
SAINT JOHN ARMENIAN APOSTOLIC CHURCH — SAN FRANCISCO (200)
SAINT JOHN ARMENIAN CATHEDRAL (198)
SAINT JOHN ARMENIAN CHURCH (189) (423)
SAINT JOHN THE BAPTIST ARM. APOST. CHURCH (256)
SAINT JOHN THE BAPTIST ARM. APOST. CHURCH — MIAMI (153)
SAINT JOHN THE BAPTIST ARM. APOST. CHURCH — MIAMI SUNDAY-SCHOOL (256)
SAINT JOHN THE BAPTIST ARM. APOST. CHURCH — SYRACUSE (133)
SAINT JOHN THE DIVINE ARMENIAN APOSTOLIC CHURCH (394)
SAINT JOHN'S ARMENIAN APOSTOLIC CHURCH (166)
SAINT KEVORK ARM. APOST. CHURCH (186-422)
SAINT KEVORK ARM. APOST. CHURCH BOOKSTORE (626-A)
SAINT KEVORK ARM. APOST. CHURCH BULLETIN (422)
SAINT KEVORK ARM. APOST. CHURCH SATURDAY SCHOOL (509-A)
SAINT KEVORK ARM. APOST. CHURCH SUNDAY SCHOOL (285-A)
SAINT LEON ARMENIAN APOSTOLIC CHURCH (168) (403)
SAINT LEON ARMENIAN APOSTOLIC CHURCH — SUNDAY-SCHOOL (276)
SAINT LEON ARMENIAN APOSTOLIC CHURCH — WED. DAY-SCHOOL (501)
SAINT LEON BOOKSTORE (621)

VARAK (331)
VARAK (425)
VARTENIC (236) (398)
VOICE (379)
VOICE (380)
VOICE OF ARMENIANS RADIO (645)
VOSGEDAR PUBLISHING CO. (602)
W.A.A.A. (82)
WALTERS ART GALLERY — BALTIMORE (629)
WATERTOWN FREE PUBLIC LIBRARY (577)
WAYNE STATE UNIVERSITY (541) (684)
WAYNE STATE UNIVERSITY FOLKLORE ARCHIVE (554) (631)
WESTERN ARMENIAN ATHLETIC ASSOCIATION (82)
WESTERN DIOCESE (85) (140) (365) (428-A)
WESTERN PRELACY (84) (192) (369)
WILLIAM SAROYAN COLLECTION (573)
WORLD COUNCIL OF CHURCHES IN GENEVA (55)
YALE UNIVERSITY LIBRARY (551)
YELLOW PAGES — ARMENIAN BUSINESS DIRECTORY (320)
ZAVARIAN SCHOOL NO. 1 (493)
ZAVARIAN SCHOOL NO. 2 (494)
ZORYAN INSTITUTE (102) (342) (436) (683)
ZORYAN INSTITUTE BULLETIN (342) (436)
ZORYAN INSTITUTE LIBRARY (568)
ZUARTNOTZ (415)

Directors and Officers

*The numbers are referred to access numbers, not page numbers.

ABAJIAN, HELEN (93)
ABALIAN, ROUBEN (526)
ABDALIAN, TATEOS (189)
ABDO, ADRINE (651)
ABDO, VARTAN (499) (651)
ABRAHAM, G. ABRAHAM (521)
ABRAHAMIAN, HURANS (521)
AGBABIAN, MIHRAN (24) (73)
AGINIAN, ANITA (50)
AGOPIAN, NUBAR (450)
AIJIAN, RICHARD (516)
AINTABLIAN, ROSTOM (477)
AIVAZIAN, GIA (326) (550)
AJEMIAN, PETER (685)
AKGULIAN, KARI (425)
AKIAN, MICHAEL (234)
ALAHAYDOIAN, ZABEL (458)
ALAJAJI, HABIB (209)
ALEMIAN, PETER (37)
ALEXANIAN, HOYIG (384)
ALTOUNIAN, SHAHE (202-251-378)
AMBARIANTZ, ZABELLE (42)
AMIRIAN, ALICE (48) (115)

AMIRIAN, THOMAS JR. (50)
AMIRIAN, VAHE (47) (114)
AMIRKHAN, JIM (21)
ANDEKIAN, SAHAG (117-382-480)
ANDERSON, JOSEPH R. (572)
ANDIKIAN, J. (8)
ANDREASSIAN, SARKIS (384)
ANSOORIAN, DIANE (93) (319)
ANTREASSIAN, ELLIE (463)
ANTRESSIAN, JACK (597)
APKARIAN, RICHARD (465)
APRAHAMIAN, E. (601)
ARABIAN, ALBERT (654)
ARAKELIAN, ARAM (512)
ARAKELIAN, DENIS (91)
ARAKELIAN, LEVON (199-380)
ARAKELIAN, LUKE (87) (235)
ARAKELIAN, VARTAN (143) (364)
ARAKELIAN, YERELZGIN (380)
ARARADIAN, BEDIG (18)
ARAZ, BERC (65)
AROYAN, ASHKEN (242) (474)
ARSLAN, SHAH (98)

DADOURIAN, HAIG (42)
DADOURIAN, SARA (469)
DAGHLIAN, ARSHAG (125)
DAGHLIAN, NAZAR (516)
DAGHLIAN, NAZAR Y. (103)
DAGHLIAN, NORA (268) (491)
DANELIAN, LOUISE (516)
DAQLEY, HAIQOUHI (96)
DARAKJIAN, BARKEV N. (223) (385)
DASHO, JOHN (29) (113)
DAVIDIAN, DAJAD A. (163) (269) (488)
DAVIDIAN, SUE (40)
DAVITIAN, ARMINA (93)
DE BENKO, EUGENE (553)
DE CERVANTES, ROSINE (93) (319)
DELSIZIAN, JOHN S. (50)
DEMERJIAN, ANNA (96)
DEMIRDJIAN, ALICE (174) (415)
DEMIRJIAN, ARMEN (463)
DEMPSEY, PATRICK J. (238)
DER ASSADOURIAN, VARTAN (149)
DER GARABEDIAN, BARNES SEDA (59)
DER KALOUSTIAN, MOUSHEGH (132-409)
DER MKSIAN, SEMPAD (118)
DER MUGRDECHIAN, BARLOW (21-321-426)
DER OHANESSIAN, PAUL (45)
DER STEPANIAN, SYLVA (45-A 502)
DER TOROSSIAN GOMIDAS (123) (489)
DER YEGHIAYAN, GARBIS (329-A 430-526-655)
DERDERIAN, GEORGE (28)
DERDERIAN, HELEN (39) (63)
DERDERIAN, MOUSHEGH (79)
DERDIARIAN, VAHAN (67)
DEVLETIAN, ASSADOUR (526)
DICKRANIAN, ARSHAG (513)
DJAHUKIAN, G.B. (356) (441)
DJAMBAZIAN, BERDJ (222)
DJIRDJIRIAN, ANNA (44)
DOGHRAMADJIAN, HOVHANNES (625)
DOGHRAMJI, PETER (103)
DONABEDIAN, KEVORK (303) (305)
DONOYAN, ARMEN (308) (431) (607)
DOUDOUKJIAN, SONA (622)
DULGARIAN, VARTAN (204) (362)
ELSTON, DOROTHEA K (517)
ELSTON, LLOYD (517)
EMERZIAN, LOUISE (94)
ENKABABIAN, ARMEN (50)
EQUMLIAN, LUCY (96)
ERANOSIAN, EDWARD (50)
ERICKSON, LILLIAN (2)
ERMARKARYAN, HACATUR (65)
ESKIJIAN, LUTHER (13) (106)
ESKIJIAN, MARTIN (22)
FARAJIAN, TAMAR (644)
FATTAL, LUCIE (326)
FEREDJIAN, BERJDOUHI (276)
FIDANIAN, ALEK (637) (645)
FIDANIAN, CHRISTINE (637) (645)

FILSTRUP, E. CHRISTIAN (579)
FORBES, WILLIAM A. (517)
FUNOUKIAN (21)
GAHVEJIAN, JACK H. (59)
GALIK, BARBARA A. (560)
GALLO, THOMAS C. (98)
GALSTIAN (446)
GARABEDIAN, HARBIG (282)
GARABEDIAN, JOE (94)
GARABEDIAN, RITA (259)
GARAPEDIAN, LEO (11)
GARSOIAN, NINA G. (524)
GASPARIAN, RUSSEL (654)
GAZAL, AVEDIS (65)
GDANIAN, GAREN (179) (408)
GEWENIAN, WARTAN (13)
GHANIMIAN, MAGGIE (1)
GHARIBIAN, JERAIR H. (647)
GHAZARIAN, SALPI H. (583)
GHAZARIAN, SARKIS (292)
GHAZARIAN, VARTKES (446-461-584)
GHAZIL, BERJOUHI (248)
GHOTANIAN, ALICE (14)
GIGIRIAN, YEGHISHE (395)
GIRAGOSSIANTZ, ROXANA (95)
GOFF, LINDA (573)
GOSTANIAN, ZAVEN (162)
GOURJIAN, VAHE (292)
GOWENIAN, WARTAN (106)
GREGOR, AUDREY (22)
GREGORIAN, A.T. (27) (111)
GREGORIAN, ARTHUR T. (27) (111)
GREGORIAN, KARL (558-A)
GREGORIAN, VARTKES (46)
GREPPIN, JOHN (356) (441)
GUEKGUEZIAN, BERNARD (218)
GUERIGUIAN, JOHN L. (28) (563)
GUEYIKIAN, KAROON (258)
GULBENKIAN, AYLIN (661)
GULIAN, HIRANT (65)
GUZELIAN, EVA (32) (62)
HABESHIAN, KHOREN (129) (386)
HACHADOURIAN, ROSE (42)
HADIGIAN, HARRY (638)
HAGOPIAN, ALICE (267)
HAGOPIAN, ARSEN (137) (508)
HAGOPIAN, HAGOP (457)
HAGOPIAN, MICHAEL V. (11)
HAGOPIAN, TORKOM (126)
HAIG, ALICE (454)
HAIRAPETIAN, ARMEN (18)
HAIRAPETIAN, SHAHEN (18) (325)
HAITAYAN, VERA (16)
HALAJIAN, JOHN (692)
HALEBLIAN, KRIKOR (221-250-289)
HALLAJIAN, CARNIG (167)
HALVAJIAN, ARTHUR (50)
HAMALIAN, BEDROS (250)
HAMALIAN, LEO (312) (437)

KEHETIAN, MITCHELL (39) (63)
KELEGIAN, ROY (469)
KELEGIAN, YEPREM (150)
KELEJIAN, ASOGHIK (134) (413)
KELLY, LIAM M. (576)
KEOSIAN, A. (8)
KERMOYAN, MICHAEL (23)
KESHISHIAN, JAMES M (27-111-334)
KESHISHIAN, OSHEEN (291) (526)
KEUHNELIAN, JOHN G. (687)
KEUSHGERIAN, RIMA (569)
KEUSSEYAN, KRIKOR (304)
KHACHADOURIAN, ADRIENE (279)
KHACHATOORIAN (445)
KHACHATURIAN, A.A. (356) (441)
KHACHATURIAN, SOOREN (561)
KHACHERIAN, LEVON (428-A)
KHANDJIAN, MELKON A (99-562-627)
KHATCHADOURIAN, ARDEM (460)
KHATCHADOURIAN, ARSHAG (196)
KHODARIAN, KRIKOR (296)
KILLIAN, ARPY (483)
KIRIAN, MIRJAN (686)
KIRKPATRICK, ELIZABETH (23)
KLUDJIAN, BILL (93)
KOCHAKIAN, GARABED D. (190)
KOCHIAN, ASHOD (141)
KOCHYAN, ICHRAN (39) (63)
KOHAYAN, KRIKOR GREG (643)
KOKOUZIAN, DIANA (257)
KONDRALIAN, TERENIG (153)
KOOBATIAN, MARY (55)
KOOBATIAN, RAY (55)
KOPP, RICHARD (274)
KOUROUYAN, VARTKES (460)
KOUYMJIAN, DICKRAN (328-429-527)
KOUYOUMJIAN, KEVORK (240)
KOUZONIAN (161) (390)
KOUZOUJIAN, CHARLES (42)
KRADJIAN, HRATCH (667)
KRIKORIAN, BEN (451)
KRIKORIAN, CHARLES (50)
KRIKORIAN, VAN (26) (110)
KRIKORYAN, ASHOD N. (65)
KROCHIAN, ARDA (1)
KUBLER, GREGORY W. (16)
KUMKUMIAN, CHARLES (28)
KUREDJIAN, RAFFI (21)
KYRKOSTAS, MARGARET C.T. (98)
LACHINIAN, ENOCH (31) (60)
LALAIAN, VAROUJAN (14)
LANGLOIS, JANET L. (554) (631)
LANMAN, TOM (323)

LAWTON, THOMAS (628)
LEWIS, LILIAN A. (59)
LIBARIDIAN, GERARD (102-311-434-544-683)
LORANTH, ALICE N. (580)
MAGARIAN, JAMES K. (43) (351)
MAGARIAN, KACHATUR (46-352-440-611)
MAGARIAN, ROBERT ARMEN (136)
MAGDESIAN, ANUSH (18)
MAHAKIAN, KARNIG (606)
MAHAKIAN, LOUISE (153)
MAHJOUBIAN, CHARLES N (54-103-359-442)
MAHONEY, RONALD J. (548)
MANOOGIAN, HAROUTIUN (493)
MANOOGIAN, HERMINE (494)
MANOOGIAN, SYLVA (574)
MANOOGIAN, TORKOM (43-89-91-A)
MANOUKIAN, NARBIK (21)
MANUELIAN, PAPKEN (142) (244) (476) (613)
MARASHLIAN, ANOUSH (507)
MARASHLIAN, LEVON (11) (529)
MARDIGIAN, EDWARD (73)
MARDIROSIAN, LUTVIG (513)
MARDIROSSIAN, ARMENAK (97)
MARDIROSSIAN, MENOUHI (55)
MARK, SIRPUHI (506)
MARKARIAN, HARRY (107)
MARKARIAN, HRAND (51)
MARKARIAN, ROSA (14)
MAROOTIAN, SEDA (107)
MASON, GEORGE (293)
MASSEREDJIAN—APELIAN, SETA (116)
MASTERSON, JUNE (521)
MATHESIAN, DIANE (50)
MATOSSIAN, JOSEPH (208)
MEGERDICHIAN, MIKE (345)
MEGUERDICHIAN, KHATCHIG (130) (133)
MEKHSIAN, SIPAN (369)
MELCONIAN, MELINE (105)
MELITENESTI, GEVORK (357)
MELKONIAN, HAGOP (141)
MELKONIAN, HAIGAZOUN (183)
MENAKIAN, HERMINE (501)
MENSOIAN, MICHAEL G. JR. (50)
MERIGIAN, LILLIE (109)
METJIAN PAREE (168)
MICKAELIAN, FRED (22)
MIKAELIAN, KATHERINE (260) (485)
MIKAELIAN, MATTHEW (139) (424)
MIKAELIAN, SARA (510)
MILLS, ANNE (22)
MINASIAN, EDWARD (95)
MINASIAN, JANE (26) (110)
MINASIAN, M. (8)

SCALES, EMMET T. (671) (672) (673)
SCHMITT, RUDIGER (356) (441)
SCHRAMM, JOHN C. (517)
SELIAN, VERKIN T. (96)
SEMERDJIAN, SHAHE (203-252-371-479)
SEMERJIAN, MESROB (164) (394)
SEMPADIAN, ARTOON (197)
SERABIAN, HRANT (144) (379)
SERKAIAN, NERSES (649)
SETIAN, NERSES (238)
SEVAG, HELEN (103)
SHAHINIAN, DEAN (28)
SHAHINIAN, SIROON P. (692)
SHATIKIAN, KHACHIK (513)
SHEKOOKIAN, SONA (504)
SHIRIKIAN, NAREG (142)
SHIRINIAN, VAHRICH (128-275-404-500-623)
SHIRVANIAN, ARIS (200)
SHIRVANIAN, HACOP (513)
SHNORHOKIAN, MANASSEH (224)
SHRIKIAN, GORUN (127) (397)
SHUSHAN, DONALD (112)
SIMONIAN, HRAND (513)
SIMONIAN, POPKIN (93)
SIMONIAN, SIMON (116)
SIROONIAN, GRACE (32) (62)
SIVAS, JOHN T. (670)
SOGHOMONIAN, GARO (39)
SOGHOMONIAN, VEGA (40)
SONENTS, PAPAZIAN TATUL (102)
SOOKIKIAN, HELEN (31) (60)
SOXMAN, BEA (249)
SPENJIAN, GARO (97)
STANLEY, MARIE (573)
STATHOPOULOS, MARO (384)
STEIN, JOSEPH H. JR. (516)
STEIN, JOYCE (24) (73)
STEPANIAN, MARGARET (270)
STOLARICK, MARK M. (572)
SUNY, GRIGOR RONALD (539)
TACHDJIAN, VAHAKEN (116)
TAJIRIAN, THELMA (674)
TASHJIAN, HRANT (224)
TASHJIAN, MESROB (138) (285) (420) (509)
TASHJIAN, MOUSHEGH (195-247-377-459-478)
TASHJIAN, RICHARD H. (29) (113)
TATARIAN, GABRIEL (116)
TATEVOSSIAN, VARTAN (198)
TATEWOSIAN, PEGGY (284)
TATHEVOSSIAN, AREK (40) (344)
TATHEVOSSIAN, HANRIETTE (40)
TATOULIAN, DATEV (206) (253)
TAYLOR, JAMES K. III (82)

TCHADERJIAN, FLORA (328-429)
TEGNAZIAN, LEAH (347)
TEJIRIAN, ELEANOR H. (350) (439)
TEMREKJIAN, KHOSROV (1)
TERTZAG, HERB (93)
TERZIAN, AVED (159)
TERZIAN, JOHN (29) (113)
TERZIAN, ONNIG (171)
TERZIAN, SETA (32) (62)
TEZEL, JIRAYR (65)
TEZEL, LOUISE H. (65)
THOMAS, LORRAINE (92) (93)
THOMASIAN, RUTH (630)
THOMSON, R.W. (523)
THOMSON, WILLIAM (678)
TIRATSOUYAN, KARABET (505)
TOLAJIAN, SOPHIE (96)
TOOMANYAN, HAIG H. (393)
TOOTIKIAN, VAHAN
(227-271-396-495-538)
TOPALIAN, KRIKOR (135)
TOROSIAN, VARSEN (168)
TOTOVIAN, VAUGHAN (43)
TOURYAN, VAHRAM (211)
TOVMASSIAN, EDWARD (219) (366)
TOVMASSIAN, RON (225) (263) (389)
TUMANJAN, G. (8)
UNCIANO, RICHARD (530)
UNLANDHERM, FRANK H. (556)
VANDERGRAFT, PAULINE (40)
VARTABEDIAN, TOM (491)
VARTIAN, ROSS (24) (73)
VARTOUKIAN, JOYCE (651)
VASSILIAN, HAMO (587)
VECOLI, RUDOLPH J. (555) (632)
VERTANESSIAN, SAHAG (121) (387)
VOSGANIAN, KRIKOR (67-355-407-415)
VOSGANIAN, MAMIGON (173)
WELC, CYNTHIA (585)
WHITTALL, LISA (633)
YACOUB, ANY (22)
YAGHSEGIAN, GEORGE (40)
YARDEMIAN, DAJAD (612-A)
YARDUMIAN, LAURA (102) (568)
YEGPARIAN, GAREN (470)
YERETZIAN, BARET (160)
YERETZIAN, HAROUTOUN (307) (588)
YOUSSEFIAN, MIKE (458)
ZAKARIAN, HRAIR (652)
ZAKIAN, ARAM (50)
ZAMROUTIAN, KRIKOR (162) (392)
ZARIFIAN, JOHN (233)
ZARZATIAN, JACK SR. (418)

Bibliography Index
Author, Title, Translator and Editor

*The numbers are referred to access numbers, not page numbers.

CATALOGUE OF EARLY ARMENIAN BOOKS (1180)
CATALOGUE OF MEDIEVAL ARMENIAN MANUSCRIPTS IN THE U.S.A. (1221)
CATALOGUE OF TWENTY THREE IMPORTANT ARMENIAN ILLUMINATED . . . (1181)
CHAILIAND, GERARD (785)
CHAKALIAN, MANOUK (709) (1094)
CHAKMAKJIAN, H. H. (1182)
CHAKMAKJIAN, HAGOP A. (1044)
CHALIAND, GERARD (710)
CHANASHIAN, MESROP (1005)
CHARAKIAN, E. B. (947)
CHARAKIAN, ELISHA (839)
CHARANIS, PETER (786)
CHARKIAN, ELISHA (741)
CHOLAKIAN, ROUBEN (746)
CHOMAKLOU THE HISTORY OF AN ARMENIAN VILLAGE (1102)
CHOOKASZIAN, ISABEL (928)
CHOPOURIAN, GIRAGOS H. (1045) (1046)
CHRISTIAN LITERATURE AND FINE ARTS OF THE ARMENIANS (1017)
CHUNKOOSH (737)
CILICIAN KINGDOM OF ARMENIA (787)
CIVILIZED (754)
CLASH OF SOULS (694) (1081)
CLASSIC ARMENIAN RECIPES . . . (1069)
CLASSICAL AND MIDDLE ARMENIAN BIRD NAMES (876)
CLASSICAL ARMENIAN CULTURE INFLUENCES AND CREATIVITY (790)
CLASSICAL ARMENIAN GRAMMAR (897)
CLASSICAL ARMENIAN NOMINAL SUFFIXES (877)
CLINE, W.B. (841)
COINAGE OF CILICIAN ARMENIA (1002)
COINAGE OF CILICIAN ARMENIA — REV. EDITION (1003)
COINAGE OF THE ARTAXIADS OF ARMENIA (1001)
COLOPHONS OF ARMENIAN MANUSCRIPTS (837) (1030)
COMPLETE ARMENIAN COOKBOOK . . . (1073)
COMPREHENSIVE DICTIONARY ARMENIAN ENGLISH (885) (1201)
COMPREHENSIVE DICTIONARY ENGLISH ARMENIAN (1182)
COMPREHENSIVE DICTIONARY ENGLISH ARMENIAN (887) (1202)
COMPREHENSIVE DICTIONARY OF IDIOMS ENGLISH ARMENIAN (886) (1203)
CONE, LAWRENCE (1007)
CONFERENCE ON MODERN ARMENIAN HISTORY (788)
CONFESSIONS OF KITCHOONIE (904)
CONSECRATION OF A CATHEDRAL (1039)
CONTEST AN ARMENIAN FOLKTALE (943)
CONTRIBUTIONS TO THE ARCHAEOLOGY OF ARMENIA (1008)
COON, C. S. (841)
COUNCIL OF CHALCEDON AND THE ARMENIAN CHURCH (1063)
COUNTRY CAT CITY CAT (951)
COX, CLAUDE E. (921)
CRETAN, GLADYS YESSAYAN (922) (923)
CRIME UNLIMITED (725)
CROSS AND THE CRESCENT (701)
CULTURAL PERSISTENCE AND SOCIO ECONOMIC MOBILITY . . . (1145)
CUP OF BITTERNESS AND OTHER STORIES (903)
CUSINE OF ARMENIA (1078)

FAVORITE ARMENIAN AND SYRIAN RECIPES OF ANNE GETSOIAN (1074)
FEDERAL WRITERS' PROJECT MASSACHUSETTS (1144)
FIELD, HENRY (1008)
FIFTY YEARS IN FRESNO THE LIFE STORY OF BELLA KANDARIAN (1103)
FINDING HOME (952)
FIRST GENOCIDE A PLAY IN FOUR ACTS (937)
FIRST GENOCIDE OF THE 20TH CENTURY (916)
FIRST GENOCIDE OF THE 20TH CENTURY THE STORY OF . . . (736)
FIRST HOLOCAUST (715)
FIRST INTERNATIONAL CONFERENCE ON ARMENIAN LINGUISTICS (880)
FLOAN, HOWARD R. (1099)
FLYNN, BARBARA (923)
FOR THE SAKE OF HONOR (843) (981)
FORBIDDEN DAYS OF RAMAZAN (964)
FORTESCUE, EDWARD FRANCIS K. (1050)
FRENCH INFLUENCE ON THE WESTERN ARMENIAN . . . (793-932-1015)
FRESNO ARMENIANS TO 1919 (1153)
FRIVOLD, LEIF (1051)
FROM IMMIGRANT TO EDUCATOR (1112)
FUNCTIONAL ARMENIAN LEVEL ONE (871)
GARAB, M. (990)
GARDENS OF SILIHDAR AND OTHER WRITINGS (992)
GARSOIAN, NINA (757-791-813-850-1049-1052-1187-1211)
GERARD, JAMES M. (1148)
GERMANY AND THE OTTOMAN EMPIRE (857)
GETSOIAN, ANN (1074)
GHUSAYN, FA'IZ (716)
GIBBONS, HERBERT ADAMS (717)
GIDNEY, JAMES BROCK (718) (794)
GIFT FROM THE BRIDE (922)
GINK, RUDOLPH KARLOY (1016)
GLOCKLER, HENRY W. (719)
GLOGOEVA, FAINNA (991)
GODEL, ROBERT (875)
GOEKJIAN, VALERIA (1017)
GOLDEN AGE IN THE FIFTH CENTURY AN INTRODUCTION TO . . . (915) (1043)
GOMBOS, KAROLY (1016)
GOMIDAS, VARTABED HIS LIFE AND WORK (1085)
GOOCH, G. P. (731)
GOSDEN, ERIC W. (740) (1113)
GRADED WEST ARMENIAN READER SELECTIONS FROM ARMENIAN . . . (873) (1187-A)
GRANIAN PUZANT (935) (1100)
GREAT 4 MESROB KOMIDAS ANTRANIK TORAMANIAN (1123)
GREATER BOSTON ARMENIAN DIRECTORY (1189)
GREBANIER, BERNARD (1005)
GREPPIN, JOHN A. (876) (877) (878) (880)
GRIGORIAN, MESROP K. (795) (1131)
GUEST FOR NOAH'S ARK (818)
GUIDE BOOK FOR THE INTERNATIONAL SYMPOSIUM ON THE . . . (1190)
GUIDE ON ARMENIAN IMMIGRANTS STUDIES AND INSTITUTIONS (1209)
GULBEKIAN, YEDVARD (796)
GULBENKIAN, EDWARD V. (1191)

ROSENBERG, HAROLD (1028)
ROSZKO, CASIMIR F. (897)
ROTTENBERG, DORIAN (930) (989)
RUGS OF ARMENIA THEIR HISTORY AND ART (1027)
RYCAUT, PAUL (1061)
SACRED WRATH THE SELECTED POEMS OF VAHAN TEKEYAN (988)
SAD DAYS OF LIGHT POEMS (913)
SAGA OF SASSOUN THE ARMENIAN FOLK EPIC (960)
SAGSOORIAN, PAUL (843) (972) (973) (981)
SAHAKIAN, R.G. (839)
SALMASLIAN, ARMENAG (1220)
SAMUELIAN, THOMAS J. (790)
SANJIAN, AVEDIS K. (836-837-996-1030-1111-1137-1221)
SARAFIAN, KEVORK A. (1112)
SARAFIAN, KEVORK AVEDIS (838)
SARIAN, JOHN M. (1031) (1221)
SARIAN, NERSES (740) (1113)
SARKISIAN ARSHAG (731) (814)
SARKISIAN, ERVAND KAZAROVICH (741) (839)
SARKISSIAN, KAREKIN (1062) (1063)
SARKISYANZ, EMANUEL (840)
SAROYAN, ARAM (1114)
SAROYAN, WILLIAM (968) (969) (970)
SARXIAN, WARDAN (1037)
SARYAN, SARKIS (971)
SASOWNTSI, DAVIT (972) (973) (974) (975)
SCENES FROM AN ARMENIAN CHILDHOOD (853) (1122)
SCENT SMILE AND SORROW SELECTED VERSE (947)
SCHLUMBERGER, GUSTAVE (820) (1214)
SELECTED NUMISMATIC STUDIES OF PAUL Z. BEDOUKIAN (1004)
SELECTED POEMS (935) (976)
SELECTED WORKS POETRY AND PROSE (948)
SELTZER, CARL COLEMAN (841)
SEROPIANS FIRST ARMENIAN SETTLERS IN FRESNO COUNTY (1095) (1143)
SETH, MESROVB (1138)
SETIAN-HUALL, RALPH (993)
SEVEN BITES FROM A RAISIN PROVERBES FROM THE ARMENIAN (1032)
SEVEN SONGS OF ARMENIA (928) (929)
SEVOUGIAN, NOVRITZA K. (842)
SEWAK, PAROWYR (976)
SHADOWS OF TIME (950)
SHAHNOUR, SHAHAN (977)
SHAHVERDIAN, A. (1115)
SHALIAN, ARTIN K. (925) (975)
SHARIAN, BEDROS M. (1116)
SHEOHMELIAN, OHANNES (979)
SHIPLEY, ALICE M. (980)
SHIRAGIAN ARSHAVIR (742) (1117)
SHIRINIAN, LORNE (910)
SHIRVANZADE (843) (981)
SHORT CLASSICAL ARMENIAN GRAMMAR (872)
SILVER, BRIAN D. (1139)
SIMON SAMSONIAN HIS WORLD THROUGH PAINTINGS (1029)

HELP WANTED

Armenian American Almanac is a package of hundreds of answered questionnaires sent to us by Armenian organizations in this country. To expand the second edition, we ask that you help us prepare a more comprehensive almanac in the future.

Please, complete the **Questionnaire Request and the appropriate forms** on the next three pages. Your response to these forms is vital. It will help us up-to-date the information on hand and serve you better in the future.

QUESTIONNAIRE REQUEST FORM
ARMENIAN AMERICAN ALMANAC

If you are interested to include your organization's information, free of charge in the second edition of the **Armenian American Almanac,** please fill out this form in order to receive the questionnaire(s) accordingly.

I—Type of organization (check as many as apply):

     1— Organization _____
     2— Church _____
     3— Newspaper/Periodical _____
     4— Day school _____
     5— Saturday school _____
     6— Sunday school _____
     7— Theological school _____
     8— Library _____
     9— Foundation _____
     10— Radio/T.V. _____
     11— Armenian Studies Program _____
     12— Special collection _____
     13— Private collection _____
     14— Scholarships, grants, etc. _____
     15— Bookstore, book selling serv. _____
     16— Biography _____
     17— Bibliography _____

II—Name of Organization: _____

_____

III—Address: _____
              Street

_____
     City   State   Zip Code

IV—Telephone: ( ) _____ ( ) _____

V—Contact person (Name & Title): _____

_____

Please, mail the form to:

ARMENIAN REFERENCE BOOKS CO.
P.O. BOX 7106
GLENDALE, CALIFORNIA 91205
(818) 507-1525

YOUR OPINION
ARMENIAN AMERICAN ALMANAC

Please, take a minute to give us your opinion about this book. It will help us to improve the scope of the next edition, and be of better service to you. Your cooperation is appreciated.

Please, answer the following questions:

1— Do you think there is a need for this publication?

Yes _____ No _____ Why? _____

_____

_____

2— How do you rate the contents of the book?

Poor _____ Fair _____ Good _____ Very good _____

3— Which section(s) do you find to be the most interesting?

_____

4— What subject(s) do you think should be added in the next edition?

1 _____ 2 _____ 3 _____ 4 _____

5— Is the book well organized? Yes _____ No _____

6— How do you rate the indexes?
Fair _____ Good _____ Very good _____

7— How did you hear about this book? _____

8— Comments and suggestions: _____

_____

_____

_____

If you wish, please write your name, address and phone number.

Name: _____

Address: _____
     Street   City   State   Zip

Telephone: (   ) _____ (   ) _____

Please, mail the questionnaire to:

ARMENIAN REFERENCE BOOKS CO.
P.O. BOX 7106
GLENDALE, CALIFORNIA 91205
(818) 507-1525

Correction or Addition Form
ARMENIAN AMERICAN ALMANAC

Page or access no. (s) _____

Name of Organization: _____

Please make the following correction _____ addition _____:

_____

_____

_____

_____

_____

Your name & title: _____

Address: _____

City _____ State_____ Zip code _____

Telephone: (   ) _____

_____   _____
          Signature   Date:

Please, mail the form to:

Armenian Reference Books Co.
P.O. Box 7106
Glendale, California 91205   **(818) 507-1525**

Order form
ARMENIAN AMERICAN ALMANAC

The most comprehensive encyclopedic directory ever published for Armenian communities in the U.S.A. with three indexes.
ISBN: 0-931539-14-5 6 x 9 softbound.

Order your copy today!!

Please, send me _____ copy(ies) of **ARMENIAN AMERICAN ALMANAC** @ $24.95 in U.S. currency per copy (California residents add 6.5% for sales tax or $1.62) and @ $29.95 outside of U.S.A. My check or money order is enclosed.

SEND PAYMENT WITH ORDER, WE PAY YOUR POSTAGE!!!

Please, don't send cash.

Make checks or money orders payable to Armenian Reference Books Co.

Total amount $ _____   P.O. Number _____

Date: _____ • Check/money order enclosed. _____
              • Please bill me. _____

Ship to (please print)

Name: _____

Institution/Organization: _____

Street address: _____

City _____ State _____ Zip code _____

Country: _____

Please clip and mail with check or money order to:

Armenian Reference Books Co.
P.O. Box 7106
Glendale, California 91205   **(818) 507-1525**

All orders from individuals must be accompanied by a check or money order. Institutions and libraries may enclose a purchase order. If you are using a purchase order, please send this order form, too.